IN TWELVE VOLL

POEMS

BY

OLIVER WENDELL HOLMES

AND

JAMES RUSSELL LOWELL

WITH FRONTISPIECE IN DUOGRAPH

NEW YORK

P. F. COLLIER & SON

MCMIII

II

The Biglow Papers

" *He stood a spell on one foot first, then stood a spell on the t'other.*"

— Am. A., Vol. XI.

THE AUTHOR TO THE PUBLISHERS.

I THANK you for the pains you have taken to bring together the poems now added to this collection; one of them having been accidentally omitted and the existence of the others forgotten. So many productions which bear the plain marks of immaturity and inexperience have been allowed to remain, because they were in the earlier editions, that a few occasional and careless stanzas may be added to their company without any apology. I have no doubt you are right in thinking that there is no harm in allowing a few crudities to keep their place among the rest; for, as you suggest, the readers of a book are of various ages and tastes, and what sounds altogether schoolboy-like to the author may be very author-like to the schoolboy. Some of the more questionable extravagances to be found in the earlier portion of the volume have, as I learn, pleased a good many young people ; let us call these, and all the others that we have outgrown, *Juvenile Poems*, but keep them, lest some of the smaller sort that were, or are, or are to be, should lament their absence. I thought of mentioning the date at which the several poems were written, which would explain some of their differences ; but the reader can judge them nearly enough, perhaps without this assistance.

v

To save a question that is sometimes put, it is proper to say that in naming two of the poems after two of the Muses, nothing more was intended than a suggestion of their general character and aim. In a former note of mine (which you printed as a kind of preface to the last edition), I made certain explanations which I thought might be needed; but as nobody seems to have misinterpreted anything, we will trust our book hereafter to itself, not doubting that whatever is good in it will redeem and justify the rest.

Boston, January 13, 1849.

CONTENTS.

Biographical Sketch.................................... xi
Poetry ; A Metrical Essay............................. 1
    Cambridge Churchyard............................ 12
    Old Ironsides.................................... 20

LYRICS.

The Last Reader....................................... 35
Our Yankee Girls...................................... 37
La Grisette... 39
An Evening Thought.................................... 41
A Souvenir.. 43
" Qui vive ! ".. 45
The Wasp and the Hornet............................... 47
From a Bachelor's Private Journal..................... 48
Stanzas... 50
The Philosopher to his Love........................... 51
L'inconnue.. 53
The Star and the Water Lily........................... 54
Illustration of a Picture............................. 56
The Dying Seneca...................................... 58
A Portrait.. 59
A Roman Aqueduct...................................... 60
The Last Prophecy of Cassandra........................ 62
To a Caged Lion....................................... 64
To my Companions...................................... 66
The Last Leaf... 68
To a Blank Sheet of Paper............................. 70

vii

To an Insect... 72
The Dilemma... 74
My Aunt... 76
The Toadstool.. 78
The Meeting of the Dryads............................. 80
The Mysterious Visitor................................. 83
The Spectre Pig.. 87
Lines by a Clerk... 92
Reflections of a Proud Pedestrian....................... 94
The Poet's Lot... 95
Daily Trials.. 97
Evening.—By a Tailor..................................... 99
The Dorchester Giant..................................... 101
To the Portrait of " A Gentleman " 104
To the Portrait of " A Lady "............................. 107
The Comet... 109
A Noontide Lyric.. 112
The Ballad of the Oysterman............................. 114
The Music-grinders... 116
The Treadmill Song....................................... 119
The September Gale.. 121
The Height of the Ridiculous............................. 124
The Hot Season.. 126

POEMS ADDED SINCE THE FIRST EDITION.

Departed Days... 131
The Steamboat.... 133
The Parting Word... 135
Song... 138
Lines.. 140
Verses for After-dinner................................... 143
Song... 147
The Only Daughter.. 149
Lexington.. 152
The Island Hunting Song.................................. 155
Questions and Answers.................................... 157

CONTENTS.

Song.. 158
Terpsichore.............. 161

———

Urania : A Rhymed Lesson............................. 170
The Pilgrim's Vision............... 199
A Modest Request.................................... 204
Nux Postcœnatica.................................... 213
On Lending a Punch-bowl............................ 219

BIOGRAPHICAL SKETCH.

One of the most marked characteristics of Oliver Wendell Holmes was his geniality, his comradeship. While he was in college he wrote, " I am acquainted with a great many different fellows who do not speak to each other. Still I find pleasant companions and a few good friends among these jarring elements." These words are suggestive of much of his character through life. He had unusual power in drawing men to him, and therefore to one another, and in eliciting from them, or else creating in them, an abundance of good humor. That remarkable constellation of literary stars which brightened Boston and Cambridge, and indeed the United States, during many decades of this present century, can hardly be said to have been held together by any one man; and yet, if one was more influential than the others in this, that one was unquestionably Holmes. Always witty and humorous, frequently pathetic, he had the power of fascination. He readily took men into his confidence, and they naturally gave him theirs in return. This trait comes out decidedly in his writing as well as in his personal converse. Such chatty papers as the series of The Breakfast Table, leave in the reader a sense of personal acquaintance and confidential fellowship with the author. His personal influence gave an additional charm to all who were favored with his acquaintance.

The facts of his life are few. He was born in Cambridge in 1809, the year made illustrious by the birth of Lincoln, Gladstone, Darwin, and Tennyson. Except for two trips to Europe, one in early life and the other in old age—if so buoyant a spirit could ever be called old—he spent his life almost within sight of the State House in Boston.

He was graduated from Harvard College in 1829. Several famous men were in his class. Indeed it was considered a notable class. But the classmate who is to-day the best known was S. F. Smith, author of *My country 'tis of thee.* Even while in college Holmes developed poetical abilities of no mean order, but it never seems to have occurred to him that he was fitted for a literary career. He was barely twenty-one years of age when he wrote "Old Ironsides." These lines were reprinted far and wide in the newspapers of the country. In Washington city they were printed on handbills and circulated through the streets. It is not too much to say that they stirred the nation. They quickly accomplished their object and the frigate Constitution was saved from destruction. The youthful author became instantly famous. And yet he did not suspect that he was suited to a literary career.

After graduation he studied law, but at the end of a year gave it up and turned his attention to medicine. This proved congenial to him. It roused his enthusiasm, and soon we find him in Paris studying with zeal and cherishing the very highest ambitions for excellence in his profession. Having successfully completed his studies he returned home thoroughly equipped for the practice of his profession.

He did not, however, leap into sudden fame, nor even into that measure of success to which his preparation entitled him. Indeed, he never had more than a moderate practice. When a young doctor playfully remarks, " Small *fevers* gratefully received," men will laugh at the joke, but the average citizen prefers a more solemn doctor for his own fever. Neither were Holmes's poems a drawing advertisement for the building up of a medical practice. The general public are sceptical to believe that a poet, full of humor and fairly bubbling over with boyish exuberance, is the best person to be entrusted with a case of critical illness. He seems to have understood the situation perfectly for he wrote

Don't you know that people won't employ
A man that wrongs his manliness by laughing like a boy?

In short, he seemed to be lacking on the business side of his vocation. Thus while his practice was never large it gave him a fair living.

But upon the scientific side of his profession he was brilliantly successful. From the first he took prizes for medical essays. In 1838 he was appointed lecturer on Anatomy at Dartmouth College, and nine years later he became Professor of Anatomy and Physiology in Harvard College. This position he held with great popularity for the long period of thirty-five years. President Eliot regarded his work as highly efficient, and declared that he did a great deal to make the Harvard Medical School what it has become.

During the middle period of his life Holmes was in the lecture field. At that time lecture courses before lyceums and other associations were common. Far and wide, especially in New England, there was a demand for literary men to speak from the rostrum. The lectures of that day were of a high order, those of Emerson, perhaps, being the standard. The compensation was small as compared with the present day. Still it was something, and the proceeds of a successful lecture tour would be welcome to a literary man in moderate circumstances. But the trials and exposures of these tours forced him out. The conveniences of travelling in those days were crude. The railway cars were uncomfortable, ill-heated, and ill-ventilated at best. The winter rides from the railway stations, the accommodations of the hotel, the bleakness, frequently, of the spare room of private hospitality, made the lecture tour anything but a jolly excursion. Holmes's tendency to asthma made it a serious matter to him, as it was a discomfort to every one. Though he was in great demand, and was always sure of a cordial welcome wherever he appeared, still this business of lecturing was hard work and poor pay. It was therefore soon abandoned. But the delivery of a course before the Lowell Institute was in every respect different. The hall was near his home, reached by an easy and pleasant walk. His subject was the British Poets. He spoke to crowded audiences composed of the most intelligent and cultured of Boston people, and the lectures were received with enthusiasm. Such lecturing was a pleasure and an honor.

The last incident, in a life not overcrowded with incidents, was a brief trip with his daughter, which he has recorded in " Our Hundred Days in Europe." He was at this time seventy-seven years of age, The most of the time was spent in England, and this visit was an ovation from start to finish. He was lionized by society in an almost incredible number of receptions, etc. He was sought out by men of letters. But chiefly, he was decorated by three of the four universities of Great Britain. Edinburgh and Cambridge conferred on him the degree of LL. D., and Oxford that of D. C. L.

He glided gently into the period of old age ; persisting in calling himself young,—" eighty years *young*." The delightful spirits of youth he retained through a long life. But the signs and incidents of age came in quick succession. In 1873 Agassiz died. In 1877 Motley died. In 1882 he laid down the duties of his lectureship at Harvard after having completed thirty-six annual courses. The college elected him professor *emeritus*. That same year both Longfellow and Emerson died. In 1884 his son Edward died. Three years later his wife died, after which his daughter came to live with him. But two years later, or in 1889, she died. The previous year his classmate, the Rev. James Freeman Clarke, who for more than sixty years had been his intimate—possibly his most intimate—friend, died. In 1891 Lowell died, Whittier in 1892, and Parkman in 1893. Thus was the author of "The Last Leaf" left almost alone, so far as concerned his early friends. Two years later he followed Whittier.

Just here we may quote a few sentences from a letter to the Rev. Phillips Brooks, in which, after expressing warm appreciation of his friend's sermon, he says : "My natural Sunday home is King's Chapel. In that church I have worshipped for half a century. . . . There, on the fifteenth of June, 1840, I was married, there my children were all christened, from that church the dear companion of so many blessed years was buried. In her seat I must sit, and through its door I hope to be carried to my last resting-place." This hope was realized two days after his death, which occurred October 7, 1894. Death came to him quickly and gently He was sitting in his chair talking to his son, when he died suddenly.

His day's work was long and somewhat voluminous. Among his books may be noted the following : The Autocrat, Professor, and Poet, at the Breakfast Table, followed, in the evening of his life, by a series entitled Over the Teacups; various medical essays; Elsie Venner, and The Guardian Angel;

2

lives of Motley and of Emerson; and poems pub-
lished from time to time, but now collected in one
volume.

In estimating the quality of the man and his
work, it must be confessed that he was provincial.
His loyalty was first of all to his college class, then
to his college, next to the city of Boston, after that
to New England, and finally to his country. He
iudeed belonged to the best of Boston—the " Brah-
min Caste," to borrow his own phrase—but he was
essentially Bostonese. He spent substantially all
his life in Boston or Cambridge. In early life he
had a summer home in Pittsfield, but that was given
up and in late years his summer home was at Bev-
erley Farms, only twenty miles from the city. He
rarely got much beyond walking distance from the
State House on Beacon Hill, and apparently he had
no desire to do so. He was not cosmopolitan. To
him Boston was always what he playfully called it,
—the Hub of the solar system.

It may also be said that his work seems to lack
the elements of permanency when compared with
that of writers of the first grade. His work is ex-
cellent of its kind, but it is not the kind that is in-
tended to endure. He was chiefly the philosopher,
the poet, the wit of the hour; and, while un-
rivalled in his place, one must not claim for him

a permanency which belongs to a different type of author.

His excellence was seen in three degrees,—chiefly in his conversation, next in some of his prose writings, and finally in his poetry. His title to eminence rests upon his personality. In conversation he was at his best. Wherever he sat was the head of the table. Dr. Johnson was probably more learned, Coleridge more profound, De Quincy more subtile and melodious ; but no one combined these qualities, adding the good fellowship of Holmes.

Next in brilliancy after his conversation came his prose, specifically, the Autocrat of the Breakfast Table, and for the very reason that this most nearly resembles his conversation. But as this sketch is intended to concern chiefly his poetry, we must turn, however reluctantly, from his prose to his poetry—and it is always a pleasure to turn to the poetry of this man.

One instantly observes the very large proportion of occasional poems, a larger proportion probably than can be found in any other author. For thirty-nine consecutive years he furnished the poem for the annual dinner of the class of 1829 of Harvard College. Then he had poems for various benefit dinners, for birthdays, and other occasions. It is high phrase to say that he was always equal to the occasion. He was always sure of a welcome, and his fund of wit never failed, while his felicity of adaptation and the delicacy of his treatment secured for him an audience much wider than is the usual fortune of the writers of even the best of occasional poems.

In some of his poems the prevailing trait is boyish exuberance, pure fun. An excellent example of this is The Height of the Ridiculous. Its jollity is irresistible either by old or by young. Almost equal to this is, How the Old Horse Won the Bet. Other poems combine humor and pathos so exquisitely and delicately that it is impossible to analyze them. His biographer, John T. Morse, Jr., says of the Last Leaf, that it is " a lyric in which drollery, passing nigh unto ridicule, yet stopping short of it, and sentiment becoming pathos, yet not too profound, are . . . exquisitely intermingled. [It makes] the smile and the tear dispute for mastery in a rivalry which is never quite decided." Not far from this in general effect, though widely different in form, is Bill and Joe. This has a rough-and-ready exterior, but its heart is full of fine and tender sentiment. It represents two old comrades, both crowned with honors in the world, spending an evening together, when memory brings them together as in boyhood and discloses a warmth of fellowship unknown to the world.

> To-day, old friend, remember still
> That I am Joe and you are Bill.

Another group of his poems is distinguished by intense earnestness. One of these is his youthful poem of Old Ironsides, ringing with a sentiment of patriotism which thrills the reader even to this day. Even superior to this is the Chambered Nautilus. In a preliminary note the author suggests that you find a figure of one of these shells and a section of it. The last will show you a series of enlarging compartments successively dwelt in by the animal that inhabits the shell, which is built in a widening spiral." The poem, which is comprised in forty-two lines, is a model of sentiment, fancy, and diction. The poet follows the successive building of the animal until he reaches the message which it sends to us:

> Build thee more stately mansions, O my soul,
> As the swift seasons roll !
> Leave thy low-vaulted past !
> Let each new temple, nobler than the last,
> Shut thee from heaven with a dome more vast.
> Till thou at length art free,
> Leaving thine outgrown shell by life's unresting sea !

Among his longer poems may be named the Phi Beta Kappa poem on Poetry, A Rhymed Lesson

(Urania), An After-Dinner Poem (Terpsichore), and Harvard College Anniversary. However meritorious these may be, they are not equal to some of his shorter poems. The Deacon's Masterpiece, or The Wonderful " One-Hoss Shay," a Logical Story, has long been deservedly popular. It is as droll as can be, and is at the same time a good description of logic, showing that when one part of the syllogism fails the whole structure tumbles to pieces. His Angel of Peace is sung by school children throughout the land.

Holmes would not be called a religious writer. From the first he was hostile to the creed then prevailing in the orthodox churches. His real position was simple enough had it been understood. He was, in a sense, a puritan of the puritans. That is, he had the same right to criticise the creed of Jonathan Edwards as Edwards had to criticise the ecclesiasticism of the Pope. The orthodox churches were then under the influence of the theology of Edwards, and they regarded these criticisms with abhorrence. Holmes was thus a thorn in the flesh of the orthodox ministers, and his wit, wisdom, and imperturbable good humor made him a formidable antagonist. But while he showed no mercy to creeds, he was sincerely devout in his Christian faith. Most of the hymn-books now in use in the orthodox churches contain two hymns of his composition, and hymns more tender, more in accordance with the spirit of Christian sympathy and worship it would be hard to find anywhere. These are, O Love Divine, and Lord of all Being.

It is dangerous to predict what will be the most enduring of Holmes': writings, but it seems as if they will include most, if not all, of the following: Puerperal Fever as a Private Pestilence. This is strictly medical, and it stirred up much antagonism at the time, but it has long been accepted as standard authority and is such to-day. Elsie Venner, which is a popular contribution to, or presentation of, the problems involved in heredity. The Last Leaf, which was one of the favorites with the author, as it has been a favorite with many readers, including Abraham Lincoln. The Chambered Nautilus, above described. The two hymns may be added to this list.

His biographer declares that "Dr. Holmes was more ambitious to be thought a poet than anything else." During most of his lifetime his prose overshadowed his poetry, and so his ambition was not then gratified. But it is the nature of poetry to outlast prose, and it is probable that his ultimate fame will spring chiefly from his best poems.

In 1889, sixty years after graduation from college,

and when he had passed the scriptural limit of four-score years, he read at the class dinner his last class poem, significantly entitled After the Curfew. The opening and closing stanzas are well worth quoting:

> The Play is over. While the light
>   Yet lingers in the darkening hall,
> I come to say a last Good-night
>   Before the final *Exeunt all.*

.   .   .   .   .   .

> So ends "The Boys!"—a lifelong play.
>   We too must hear the Prompter's call
> To fairer scenes and brighter day :
>   Farewell ! I let the curtain fall.

There was but one class meeting after this, namely, in the following year. Only three were present. This, therefore, practically closed the long series of meetings.

One fact which greatly favored Holmes was the length of his literary career. The first poem which attracted general attention was Old Ironsides, published in 1830. His first volume was published in 1836 and made his reputation. Consequently he held the public attention for not less than fifty-eight years, or, if we date from Old Ironsides, for sixty-four years. During this long period he frequently issued volumes, all of which were well received, and he never alienated the cordial welcome of the reading public. The climax of his reputation was reached with the Autocrat papers, which not only insured for himself a wide circle of loyal admirers, but floated the young Atlantic Monthly through the first difficult and perilous period of its existence. His literary activity continued to the very end, and for many years his readers were of a later generation than his own. None the less they did him honor. His mission, in large part, was to bring sunshine into life. His humor is healthy and it has brightened many an hour.

When Holmes went to Europe in 1886, Lowell wrote for him a farewell poem. It was Holmes's wish that the lines should be used as his *envoi*. We conclude this sketch with the final stanza.

Go, then, dear friend, by all good hopes attended ;
To Mother England go, our carrier dove,
Saying that this great race, from hers descended,
Sends in its Holmes an Easter-gift of love.

HENRY KETCHAM.

POETRY;

A METRICAL ESSAY.

Scenes of my youth![1] awake its slumbering fire!
Ye winds of Memory, sweep the silent lyre!
Ray of the past, if yet thou canst appear,
Break through the clouds of Fancy's waning year;
Chase from her breast the thin autumnal snow,
If leaf or blossom still is fresh below!

Long have I wandered ; the returning tide
Brought back an exile to his cradle's side;
And as my bark her time-worn flag unrolled,
To greet the land-breeze with its faded fold,
So, in remembrance of my boyhood's time,
I lift these ensigns of neglected rhyme ;—
O more than blest, that, all my wanderings through,
My anchor falls where first my pennons flew !

[1] *"Scenes of my youth."*
This poem was commenced a few months subsequently to
the author's return to his native village, after an absence of
nearly three years.

1

THE morning light, which rains its quivering
    beams
Wide o'er the plains, the summits, and the streams,
In one broad blaze expands its golden glow
On all that answers to its glance below;
Yet, changed on earth, each far reflected ray
Braids with fresh hues the shining brow of day;
Now, clothed in blushes by the painted flowers,
Tracks on their cheeks the rosy-fingered hours;
Now, lost in shades, whose dark entangled leaves
Drip at the noontide from their pendent eaves,
Fades into gloom, or gleams in light again
From every dew-drop on the jewelled plain.

We, like the leaf, the summit, or the wave,
Reflect the light our common nature gave,
But every sunbeam, falling from her throne,
Wears, on our hearts, some coloring of our own;
Chilled in the slave, and burning in the free,
Like the sealed cavern by the sparkling sea;
Lost, like the lightning in the sullen clod,
Or shedding radiance, like the smiles of God;
Pure, pale in Virtue, as the star above,
Or quivering roseate on the leaves of Love;
Glaring like noontide, where it glows upon
Ambition's sands,—the desert in the sun;
Or soft suffusing o'er the varied scene
Life's common coloring,—intellectual green.

Thus Heaven, repeating its material plan,
Arched over all the rainbow mind of man;
But he who, blind to universal laws,

Sees but effects, unconscious of their cause,—
Believes each image in itself is bright,
Not robed in drapery of reflected light,—
Is like the rustic who, amidst his toil,
Has found some crystal in his meagre soil,
And, lost in rapture, thinks for him alone
Earth worked her wonders on the sparkling stone,
Nor dreams that Nature, with as nice a line.
Carved countless angles through the boundless
    mine.

    Thus err the many who, entranced to find
Unwonted lustre in some clearer mind,
Believe that Genius sets the laws at nought
Which chain the pinions of our wildest thought;
Untaught to measure, with the eye of art,
The wandering fancy or the wayward heart;
Who match the little only with the less,
And gaze in rapture at its slight excess,
Proud of a pebble, as the brightest gem
Whose light might crown an emperor's diadem.

    And, most of all, the pure ethereal fire,
Which seems to radiate from the poet's lyre,
Is to the world a mystery and a charm,
An Ægis wielded on a mortal's arm,
While Reason turns her dazzled eye away,
And bows her sceptre to her subject's sway;
And thus the poet, clothed with godlike state,
Usurped his Maker's title—to create;
He, whose thoughts differing not in shape, but
    dress,

What others feel, more fitly can express,
Sits like the maniac on his fancied throne,
Peeps through the bars, and calls the world his
    own.

There breathes no being but has some pretence
To that fine instinct called poetic sense ;
The rudest savage roaming through the wild,
The simplest rustic, bending o'er his child,
The infant listening to the warbling bird,
The mother smiling at its half-formed word ;
The boy uncaged, who tracks the fields at large,
The girl, turned matron to her babe-like charge ;
The freeman, casting with unpurchased hand
The vote that shakes the turrets of the land ;
The slave, who, slumbering on his rusted chain,
Dreams of the palm trees on his burning plain ;
The hot-cheeked reveller, tossing down the wine,
To join the chorus pealing " Auld lang syne " ;
The gentle maid, whose azure eye grows dim,
While Heaven is listening to her evening hymn ;
The jewelled beauty, when her steps draw near
The circling dance and dazzling chandelier ;
E'en trembling age, when Spring's renewing air
Waves the thin ringlets of his silvered hair ;—
All, all are glowing with the inward flame,
Whose wider halo wreathes the poet's name,
While, unembalmed, the silent dreamer dies,
His memory passing with his smiles and sighs !

If glorious visions, born for all mankind,
The bright auroras of our twilight mind ;

If fancies, varying as the shapes that lie
Stained on the windows of the sunset sky ;
If hopes, that beckon with delusive gleams,
Till the eye dances in the void of dreams ;
If passions, following with the winds that urge
Earth's wildest wanderer to her farthest verge;—
If these on all some transient hours bestow
Of rapture tingling with its hectic glow,
Then all are poets ; and, if earth had rolled
Her myriad centuries, and her doom were told,
Each moaning billow of her shoreless wave
Would wail its requiem o'er a poet's grave !

If to embody in a breathing word
Tones that the spirit trembled when it heard ;
To fix the image all unveiled and warm,
And carve in language its ethereal form,
So pure, so perfect, that the lines express
No meagre shrinking, no unlaced excess ;
To feel that art, in living truth, has taught
Ourselves, reflected in the sculptured thought;—
If this alone bestow the right to claim
The deathless garland and the sacred name ;
Then none are poets, save the saints on high,
Whose harps can murmur all that words deny !

But though to none is granted to reveal,
In perfect semblance, all that each may feel,
As withered flowers recall forgotten love,
So, warmed to life, our faded passions move
In every line, where kindling fancy throws
The gleam of pleasures, or the shade of woes.

When, schooled by time, the stately queen of art
Had smoothed the pathways leading to the heart,
Assumed her measured tread, her solemn tone,
And round her courts the clouds of fable thrown,
The wreaths of heaven descended on her shrine,
And wondering earth proclaimed the Muse divine;
Yet, if her votaries had but dared profane
The mystic symbols of her sacred reign,
How had they smiled beneath the veil to find
What slender threads can chain the mighty mind!

Poets, like painters, their machinery claim,
And verse bestows the varnish and the frame;
Our grating English, whose Teutonic jar
Shakes the racked axle of Art's rattling car,
Fits like mosaic in the lines that gird
Fast in its place each many-angled word;
From Saxon lips Anacreon's numbers glide,
As once they melted on the Teian tide,
And, fresh transfused, the Iliad thrills again
From Albion's cliffs as o'er Achaia's plain!
The proud heroic, with its pulse-like beat,
Rings like the cymbals clashing as they meet;
The sweet Spenserian, gathering as it flows,
Sweeps gently onward to its dying close,
Where waves on waves in long succession pour,
Till the ninth billow melts along the shore;
The lonely spirit of the mournful lay,
Which lives immortal as the verse of Gray,
In sable plumage slowly drifts along,
On eagle pinion, through the air of song;

The glittering lyric bounds elastic by,
With flashing ringlets and exulting eye,
While every image, in her airy whirl,
Gleams like a diamond on a dancing girl! [1]

[1] A few lines, perhaps deficient in dignity, were introduced at this point, in delivering the poem, and are appended in this clandestine manner for the gratification of some of my audience.

How many a stanza, blushing like the rose,
Would turn to fustian if resolved to prose!
How many an epic, like a gilded crown,
If some cold critic dared to melt it down,
Roll in his crucible a shapeless mass,
A grain of gold-leaf to a pound of brass!
Shorn of their plumes, our moonstruck sonneteers
Would seem but jackdaws croaking to the spheres:
Our gay Lotharios, with their Byron curls,
Would pine like oysters cheated of their pearls!

Wo to the spectres of Parnassus' shade,
If truth should mingle in the masquerade.
Lo, as the songster's pale creations pass,
Off come at once the " Dearest " and " Alas! "
Crack go the lines and levers used to prop
Top-heavy thoughts, and down at once they drop.
Flowers weep for *hours; Love,* shrieking for his *dove,*
Finds not the solace that he seeks—above.
Fast in the mire, through which in happier time
He ambled dryshod on the stilts of rhyme,
The prostrate poet finds at length a tongue
To curse in prose the thankless stars he sung.

And though, perchance, the haughty muse it shames,
How deep the magic of harmonious names!
How sure the story of romance to please,
Whose rounded stanza ends with Heloise!
How rich and full our intonations ride

Born with mankind, with man's expanded range
And varying fates the poet's numbers change ;
Thus in his history may we hope to find
Some clearer epochs of the poet's mind,
As from the cradle of its birth we trace,
Slow wandering forth, the patriarchal race.

I.

When the green earth, beneath the zephyr's wing,
Wears on her breast the varnished buds of Spring ;
When the loosed current, as its folds uncoil,
Slides in the channels of the mellowed soil ;
When the young hyacinth returns to seek
The air and sunshine with her emerald beak ;

" On Torno's cliffs, or Pambamarca's side " !
But were her name some vulgar " proper noun,"
And Pambamarca changed to Belchertown,
She might be pilloried for her doubtful fame,
And no enthusiast would arise to blame ;
And he who outraged the poetic sense,
Might find a home at Belchertown's expense !

The harmless boys, scarce knowing right from wrong,
Who libel others and themselves in song,
When their first pothooks of poetic rage
Slant down the corners of an album's page,
(Where crippled couplets spread their sprawling charms,
As half taught swimmers move their legs and arms,)
Will talk of " Hesper on the brow of eve,"
And call their cousins "lovely Genevieve " ,—
While thus transformed, each dear deluded maid,
Pleased with herself in novel grace arrayed,
Smiles on the Paris who has come to crown
This new-born Helen in a gingham gown !

When the light snowdrops, starting from their
    cells,
Hang each pagoda with its silver bells ;
When the frail willow twines her trailing bow
With pallid leaves that sweep the soil below ;
When the broad elm, sole empress of the plain,
Whose circling shadow speaks a century's reign,
Wreathes in the clouds her regal diadem,—
A forest waving on a single stem ; —
Then mark the poet ; though to him unknown
The quaint-mouthed titles, such as scholars own,
See how his eye in ecstasy pursues
The steps of Nature tracked in radiant hues ;
Nay, in thyself, whate'er may be thy fate,
Pallid with toil, or surfeited with state,
Mark how thy fancies, with the vernal rose,
Awake, all sweetness, from their long repose ;
Then turn to ponder o'er the classic page,
Traced with the idyls of a greener age,
And learn the instinct which arose to warm
Art's earliest essay, and her simplest form.

    To themes like these her narrow path confined
The first-born impulse moving in the mind ;
In vales unshaken by the trumpet's sound,
Where peaceful Labor tills his fertile ground,
The silent changes of the rolling years,
Marked on the soil, or dialled on the spheres,
The crested forests and the colored flowers,
The dewy grottos and the blushing bowers,
These, and their guardians, who, with liquid names,

Strephons and Chloes, melt in mutual flames,
Woo the young Muses from their mountain shade,
To make Arcadias in the lonely glade.

Nor think they visit only with their smiles
The fabled valleys and Elysian isles ;
He who is wearied of his village plain
May roam the Edens of the world in vain.
'Tis not the star-crowned cliff, the cataract's flow,
The softer foliage, or the greener glow,
The lake of sapphire, or the spar-hung cave,
The brighter sunset, or the broader wave,
Can warm his heart whom every wind has blown
To every shore, forgetful of his own.

Home of our childhood ! how affection clings
And hovers round thee with her seraph wings !
Dearer thy hills, though clad in autumn brown,
Than fairest summits which the cedars crown !
Sweeter the fragrance of thy summer breeze
Than all Arabia breathes along the seas !
The stranger's gale wafts home the exile's sigh,
For the heart's temple is its own blue sky !

O happiest they, whose early love unchanged,
Hopes undissolved, and friendship unestranged,
Tired of their wanderings, still can deign to see
Love, hopes, and friendship, centring all in thee !

And thou, my village ! as again I tread
Amidst thy living, and above thy dead ;
Though some fair playmates guard with chaster
　　fears

Their cheeks, grown holy with the lapse of years;
Though with the dust some reverend locks may
    blend,
Where life's last mile-stone marks the journey's
    end;
On every bud the changing year recalls,
The brightening glance of morning memory falls,
Still following onward as the months unclose
The balmy lilac or the bridal rose;
And still shall follow, till they sink once more
Beneath the snow-drifts of the frozen shore,
As when my bark, long tossing in the gale,
Furled in her port her tempest-rended sail!

What shall I give thee? Can a simple lay,
Flung on thy bosom like a girl's bouquet,
Do more than deck thee for an idle hour,
Then fall unheeded, fading like the flower?
Yet, when I trod, with footsteps wild and free,
The crackling leaves beneath yon linden tree,
Panting from play, or dripping from the stream,
How bright the visions of my boyish dream!
Or, modest Charles, along thy broken edge,
Black with soft ooze and fringed with arrowy sedge,
As once I wandered in the morning sun,
With reeking sandal and superfluous gun;
How oft, as Fancy whispered in the gale,
Thou wast the Avon of her flattering tale!
Ye hills, whose foliage, fretted on the skies,
Prints shadowy arches on their evening dyes,
How should my song, with holiest charm, invest —

Each dark ravine and forest-lifting crest!
How clothe in beauty each familiar scene,
Till all was classic on my native green!

As the drained fountain, filled with autumn leaves,
The field swept naked of its garnered sheaves;
So wastes at noon the promise of our dawn,
The springs all choking, and the harvest gone.

Yet hear the lay of one whose natal star
Still seemed the brightest when it shone afar;
Whose cheek, grown pallid with ungracious toil,
Glows in the welcome of his parent soil;
And ask no garlands sought beyond the tide,
But take the leaflets gathered at your side.

———

Our ancient church! its lowly tower,
    Beneath the loftier spire,
Is shadowed when the sunset hour
    Clothes the tall shaft in fire;
It sinks beyond the distant eye,
    Long ere the glittering vane,
High wheeling in the western sky,
    Has faded o'er the plain.

Like Sentinel and Nun, they keep
    Their vigil on the green;
One seems to guard, and one to weep,
    The dead that lie between;
And both roll out, so full and near,
    Their music's mingling waves,

They shade the grass, whose pennoned spear
    Leans on the narrow graves.

The stranger parts the flaunting weeds,
    Whose seeds the winds have strown
So thick beneath the line he reads,
    They shade the sculptured stone;
The child unveils his clustered brow,
    And ponders for a while
The graven willow's pendent bough,
    Or rudest cherub's smile.

But what to them the dirge, the knell?
    These were the mourner's share;—
The sullen clang, whose heavy swell
    Throbbed through the beating air;—
The rattling cord,—the rolling stone,—
    The shelving sand that slid,
And, far beneath, with hollow tone,
    Rung on the coffin's lid.

The slumberer's mound grows fresh and green,
    Then slowly disappears;
The mosses creep, the gray stones lean,
    Earth hides his date and years;
But, long before the once-loved name
    Is sunk or worn away,
No lip the silent dust may claim,
    That pressed the breathing clay.

Go where the ancient pathway guides,
    See where our sires laid down

Their smiling babes, their cherished brides,
    The patriarchs of the town;
Hast thou a tear for buried love?
    A sigh for transient power?
All that a century left above,
    Go, read it in an hour!

The Indian's shaft, the Briton's ball,
    The sabre's thirsting edge,
The hot shell, shattering in its fall,
    The bayonet's rending wedge,—
Here scattered death; yet, seek the spot,
    No trace thine eye can see,
No altar,—and they need it not
    Who leave their children free!

Look where the turbid rain-drops stand
    In many a chiselled square,
The knightly crest, the shield, the brand
    Of honored names were there;—
Alas! for every tear is dried
    Those blazoned tablets knew,
Save when the icy marble's side
    Drips with the evening dew.

Or gaze upon yon pillared stone,[1]
    The empty urn of pride;

[1] "*Or gaze upon yon pillared stone.*"

The tomb of the VASSALL family is marked by a free-stone tablet, supported by five pillars, and bearing nothing but the sculptured reliefs of the Goblet and the Sun,—*Vas–Sol*—which designated a powerful family, now almost forgotten.

The exile referred to in the next stanza was a native of Honfleur in Normandy.

There stand the Goblet and the Sun,—
    What need of more beside?
Where lives the memory of the dead,
    Who made their tomb a toy?
Whose ashes press that nameless bed?
    Go, ask the village boy!

Lean o'er the slender western wall,
    Ye ever roaming girls;
The breath that bids the blossom fall
    May lift your floating curls,
To sweep the simple lines that tell
    An exile's date and doom;
And sigh, for where his daughters dwell,
    They wreathe the stranger's tomb.

And one amid these shades was born,
    Beneath this turf who lies,
Once beaming as the summer's morn,
    That closed her gentle eyes;—
If sinless angels love as we,
    Who stood thy grave beside,
Three seraph welcomes waited thee,
    The daughter, sister, bride!

I wandered to thy buried mound
    When earth was hid below
The level of the glaring ground,
    Choked to its gates with snow,
And when the summer's flowery waves
    The lake of verdure rolled,

As if a Sultan's white-robed slaves
　　Had scattered pearls and gold.

Nay, the soft pinions of the air,
　　That lift this trembling tone,
Its breath of love may almost bear,
　　To kiss thy funeral stone ;—
And, now thy smiles have passed away,
　　For all the joy they gave,
May sweetest dews and warmest ray
　　Lie on thine early grave !

When damps beneath, and storms above,
　　Have bowed these fragile towers,
Still o'er the graves yon locust-grove
　　Shall swing its Orient flowers ;—
And I would ask no mouldering bust,
　　If e'er this humble line,
Which breathed a sigh o'er other's dust,
　　Might call a tear on mine.

II.

But times were changed ; the torch of terror came,
To light the summits with the beacon's flame ;
The streams ran crimson, the tall mountain pines
Rose a new forest o'er embattled lines ;
The bloodless sickle lent the warrior's steel,
The harvest bowed beneath his chariot wheel ;

Where late the wood-dove sheltered her repose,
The raven waited for the conflict's close;
The cuirassed sentry walked his sleepless round
Where Daphne smiled or Amaryllis frowned;
Where timid minstrels sung their blushing charms,
Some wild Tyrtæus called aloud, " To arms!"

When Glory wakes, when fiery spirits leap,
Roused by her accents from their tranquil sleep,
The ray that flashes from the soldier's crest,
Lights, as it glances, in the poet's breast;—
Not in pale dreamers, whose fantastic lay
Toys with smooth trifles like a child at play,
But men, who act the passions they inspire,
Who wave the sabre as they sweep the lyre!

Ye mild enthusiasts, whose pacific frowns
Are lost like dew-drops caught in burning towns,
Pluck as ye will the radiant plumes of fame,
Break Cæsar's bust to make yourselves a name,
But, if your country bares the avenger's blade
For wrongs unpunished, or for debts unpaid,
When the roused nation bids her armies form,
And screams her eagle through the gathering
    storm;
When from your ports the bannered frigate rides,
Her black bows scowling to the crested tides,
Your hour has past; in vain your feeble cry,
As the babe's wailings to the thundering sky!

Scourge of mankind! with all the dread array,
That wraps in wrath thy desolating way,

As the wild tempest wakes the slumbering sea,
Thou only teachest all that man can be.
Alike thy tocsin has the power to charm
The toil-knit sinews of the rustic's arm,
Or swell the pulses in the poet's veins,
And bid the nations tremble at his strains.

 The city slept beneath the moonbeam's glance,
Her white walls gleaming through the vines of
  France,
And all was hushed, save where the footsteps fell,
On some high tower, of midnight sentinel.
But one still watched ; no self-encircled woes
Chased from his lids the angel of repose ;
He watched, he wept, for thoughts of bitter years
Bowed his dark lashes, wet with burning tears ;
His country's sufferings and her children's shame
Streamed o'er his memory like a forest's flame ;
Each treasured insult, each remembered wrong,
Rolled through his heart and kindled into song ;
His taper faded ; and the morning gales
Swept through the world the war-song of Mar-
  seilles !¹

 Now, while around the smiles of Peace expand,
And Plenty's wreaths festoon the laughing land ;
While France ships outward her reluctant ore,
And half our navy basks upon the shore ;

¹ "*Swept through the world the war song of Marseilles.*"
The music and words of the Marseilles Hymn were com·
posed in one night,

From ruder themes our meek-eyed Muses turn
To crown with roses their enamelled urn.

If e'er again return those awful days
Whose clouds were crimsoned with the beacon's
    blaze,
Whose grass was trampled by the soldier's heel,
Whose tides were reddened round the rushing keel,
God grant some lyre may wake a nobler strain,
To rend the silence of our tented plain !
When Gallia's flag its triple fold displays,
Her marshalled legions peal the Marseillaise ;
When round the German close the war clouds dim,
Far through their shadows floats his battle-hymn :
When, crowned with joy, the camps of England
    ring,
A thousand voices shout, " God save the King ! "
When victory follows with our eagle's glance,
Our nation's anthem is a country dance ! [1]

Some prouder muse, when comes the hour at
    last,
May shake our hill-sides with her bugle-blast ;
Not ours the task ; but since the lyric dress
Relieves the statelier with its sprightliness,
Hear an old song, which some, perchance, have seen
In stale gazette, or cobwebbed magazine.
There was an hour when patriots dared profane

---

[1] " *Our nation's anthem is a country dance !* "

The popular air of " Yankee Doodle," like the dagger of
Hudibras, serves a pacific as well as a martial purpose.

The mast that Britain strove to bow in vain ; [1]
And one who listened to the tale of shame,
Whose heart still answered to that sacred name,
Whose eye still followed o'er his country's tides
Thy glorious flag, our brave Old Ironsides!
From yon lone attic, on a summer's morn,
Thus mocked the spoilers with his school-boy scorn.

Ay, tear her tattered ensign down!
    Long has it waved on high,
And many an eye has danced to see
    That banner in the sky;
Beneath it rung the battle shout,
    And burst the cannon's roar;—
The meteor of the ocean air
    Shall sweep the clouds no more.

Her deck, once red with heroes' blood,
    Where knelt the vanquished foe,
When winds were hurrying o'er the flood,
    And waves were white below,
No more shall feel the victor's tread,
    Or know the conquered knee;—
The harpies of the shore shall pluck
    The eagle of the sea!

Oh, better that her shattered hulk
    Should sink beneath the wave ;

[1] " *The mast that Britain strove to bow in vain.*"

The lyric which follows was printed in the " Boston Daily Advertiser," at the time when it was proposed to break up the frigate Constitution as unfit for service.

Her thunders shook the mighty deep,
  And there should be her grave;
Nail to the mast her holy flag,
  Set every threadbare sail,
And give her to the god of storms,
  The lightning and the gale!

III.

When florid Peace resumed her golden reign,
And arts revived, and valley bloomed again;
While War still panted on his broken blade,
Once more the Muse her heavenly wing essayed.
Rude was the song; some ballad, stern and wild,
Lulled the light slumbers of the soldier's child;
Or young romancer with his threatening glance
And fearful fables of his bloodless lance,
Scared the soft fancy of the clinging girls,
Whose snowy fingers smoothed his raven curls.
But when long years the stately form had bent,
And faithless memory her illusions lent,
So vast the outlines of Tradition grew,
That History wondered at the shapes she drew,
And veiled at length their too ambitious hues
Beneath the pinions of the Epic Muse.

Far swept her wing; for stormier days had brought
With darker passions deeper tides of thought.
The camp's harsh tumult and the conflict's glow,
The thrill of triumph and the gasp of woe,
The tender parting and the glad return,

The festal banquet and the funeral urn,—
And all the drama which at once uprears
Its spectral shadows through the clash of spears,
From camp and field to echoing verse transferred,
Swelled the proud song that listening nations heard.

Why floats the amaranth in eternal bloom
O'er Ilium's turrets and Achilles' tomb?
Why lingers fancy, where the sunbeams smile
On Circe's gardens and Calypso's isle?
Why follows memory to the gate of Troy
Her plumed defender and his trembling boy?
Lo, the blind dreamer, kneeling on the sand,
To trace these records with his doubtful hand;
In fabled tones his own emotion flows,
And other lips repeat his silent woes;
In Hector's infant see the babes that shun
Those deathlike eyes, unconscious of the sun,
Or in his hero hear himself implore,
" Give me to see, and Ajax asks no more! "

Thus live undying through the lapse of time
The solemn legends of the warrior's clime;
Like Egypt's pyramid, or Pæstum's fane,
They stand the heralds of the voiceless plain;
Yet not like them, for Time, by slow degrees,
Saps the gray stone, and wears the chiselled frieze,
And Isis sleeps beneath her subject Nile,
And crumbled Neptune strews his Dorian pile;
But Art's fair fabric, strengthening as it rears
Its laurelled columns through the mist of years,
As the blue arches of the bending skies

Still gird the torrent, following as it flies,
Spreads, with the surges bearing on mankind,
Its starred pavilion o'er the tides of mind!

In vain the patriot asks some lofty lay
To dress in state our wars of yesterday.
The classic days, those mothers of romance,
That roused a nation for a woman's glance;
The age of mystery with its hoarded power,
That girt the tyrant in his storied tower,
Have past and faded like a dream of youth,
And riper eras ask for history's truth.

On other shores, above their mouldering towns,
In sullen pomp the tall cathedral frowns,
Pride in its aisles, and paupers at the door,
Which feeds the beggars whom it fleeced of yore.
Simple and frail, our lowly temples throw
Their slender shadows on the paths below;
Scarce steal the winds, that sweep his woodland
        tracks,
The larch's perfume from the settler's axe,
Ere, like a vision of the morning air,
His slight-framed steeple marks the house of prayer;
Its planks all reeking, and its paint undried,
Its rafters sprouting on the shady side,
It sheds the raindrops from its shingled eaves,
Ere its green brothers once have changed their leaves.

Yet Faith's pure hymn, beneath its shelter rude,
Breathes out as sweetly to the tangled wood,

As where the rays through blazing oriels pour
On marble shaft and tessellated floor;—
Heaven asks no surplice round the heart that feels,
And all is holy where devotion kneels.

Thus on the soil the patriot's knee should bend,
Which holds the dust once living to defend;
Where'er the hireling shrinks before the free,
Each pass becomes "a new Thermopylæ"!
Where'er the battles of the brave are won,
There every mountain "looks on Marathon"!

Our fathers live; they guard in glory still
The grass-grown bastions of the fortressed hill;
Still ring the echoes of the trampled gorge,
With *God and Freedom! England and Saint
    George!*
The royal cipher on the captured gun
Mocks the sharp night-dews and the blistering sun!
The red-cross banner shades its captor's bust,
Its folds still loaded with the conflict's dust;
The drum, suspended by its tattered marge,
Once rolled and rattled to the Hessian's charge;
The stars have floated from Britannia's mast,
The redcoat's trumpets blown the rebel's blast.

Point to the summits where the brave have bled,
Where every village claims its glorious dead;
Say, when their bosoms met the bayonet shock,
Their only corselet was the rustic frock;
Say, when they mustered to the gathering horn,
The titled chieftain curled his lip in scorn,

Yet, when their leader bade his lines advance,
No musket wavered in the lion's glance;
Say, when they fainted in the forced retreat,
They tracked the snow-drifts with their bleeding
    feet,
Yet still their banners, tossing in the blast,
Bore *Ever Ready*,[1] faithful to the last,
Through storm and battle, till they waved again
On Yorktown's hills and Saratoga's plain !

Then, if so fierce the insatiate patriot's flame,
Truth looks too pale, and history seems too tame,
Bid him await some new Columbiad's page,
To gild the tablets of an iron age,
And save his tears, which yet may fall upon
Some fabled field, some fancied Washington!

———

IV.

But once again, from their Æolian cave,
The winds of Genius wandered on the wave.
Tired of the scenes the timid pencil drew,
Sick of the notes the sounding clarion blew;
Sated with heroes who had worn so long
The shadowy plumage of historic song;
The new-born poet left the beaten course,
To track the passions to their living source.

Then rose the Drama;—and the world admired
Her varied page with deeper thought inspired;

[1] " *Bore* **Ever Ready**, *faithful to the last.*"
" *Semper peratus*,"—a motto of the revolutionary standards.

Bound to no clime, for Passion's throb is one
In Greenland's twilight or in India's sun;
Born for no age,—for all the thoughts that roll
In the dark vortex of the stormy soul,
Unchained in song, no freezing years can tame;
God gave them birth, and man is still the same.

So full on life her magic mirror shone,
Her sister Arts paid tribute to her throne;
One reared her temple, one her canvas warmed,
And Music thrilled, while Eloquence informed.
The weary rustic left his stinted task
For smiles and tears, the dagger and the mask;
The sage, turned scholar, half forgot his lore,
To be the woman he despised before;
O'er sense and thought she threw her golden chain,
And Time, the anarch, spares her deathless reign.

Thus lives Medea, in our tamer age,
As when her buskin pressed the Grecian stage;
Not in the cells where frigid learning delves
In Aldine folios mouldering on their shelves;
But breathing, burning in the glittering throng,
Whose thousand bravos roll untired along,
Circling and spreading through the gilded halls
From London's galleries to San Carlo's walls!

Thus shall he live whose more than mortal name
Mocks with its ray the pallid torch of Fame;
So proudly lifted, that it seems afar
No earthly Pharos, but a heavenly star;

Who, unconfined to Art's diurnal bound,
Girds her whole zodiac in his flaming round,
And leads the passions, like the orb that guides,
From pole to pole, the palpitating tides!

V.

Though round the Muse the robe of song is
    thrown,
Think not the poet lives in verse alone.
Long ere the chisel of the sculptor taught
The lifeless stone to mock the living thought;
Long ere the painter bade the canvas glow
With every line the forms of beauty know;
Long ere the Iris of the Muses threw
On every leaf its own celestial hue;
In fable's dress the breath of genius poured,
And warmed the shapes that later times adored.

Untaught by Science how to forge the keys,
That loose the gates of Nature's mysteries;
Unschooled by Faith, who, with her angel tread,
Leads through the labyrinth with a single thread,
His fancy, hovering round her guarded tower,
Rained through its bars like Danae's golden shower.

He spoke; the sea-nymph answered from her
    cave:
He called; the naiad left her mountain wave:
He dreamed of beauty; lo, amidst his dream,
Narcissus mirrored in the breathless stream;
And night's chaste empress, in her bridal play,

Laughed through the foliage where Endymion lay :
And ocean dimpled, as the languid swell
Kissed the red lip of Cytherea's shell :
Of power,—Bellona swept the crimson field,
And blue-eyed Pallas shook her Gorgon shield ;
O'er the hushed waves their mightier monarch drove,
And Ida trembled to the tread of Jove !

So every grace, that plastic language knows,
To nameless poets its perfection owes.
The rough-hewn words to simplest thoughts con-
　　fined,
Were cut and polished in their nicer mind ;
Caught on their edge, imagination's ray
Splits into rainbows, shooting far away ;—
From sense to soul, from soul to sense, it flies,
And through all nature links analogies ;
He who reads right will rarely look upon
A better poet than his lexicon !

There is a race, which cold, ungenial skies
Breed from decay, as fungous growths arise ;
Though dying fast, yet springing fast again,
Which still usurps an unsubstantial reign.
With frames too languid for the charms of sense,
And minds worn down with action too intense ;
Tired of a world whose joys they never knew,
Themselves deceived, yet thinking all untrue ;
Scarce men without, and less than girls within.
Sick of their life before its cares begin ;—
The dull disease, which drains their feeble hearts,
To life's decay some hectic thrills imparts,

And lends a force which, like the maniac's power,
Pays with blank years the frenzy of an hour.

And this is Genius! Say, does Heaven degrade
The manly frame, for health, for action made?
Break down the sinews, rack the brow with pains,
Blanch the bright cheek, and drain the purple veins,
To clothe the mind with more extended sway,
Thus faintly struggling in degenerate clay?

No! gentle maid, too ready to admire,
Though false its notes, the pale enthusiast's lyre;
If this be genius, though its bitter springs
Glowed like the morn beneath Aurora's wings,
Seek not the source whose sullen bosom feeds
But fruitless flowers, and dark, envenomed weeds

But, if so bright the dear illusion seems,
Thou wouldst be partner of thy poet's dreams,
And hang in rapture on his bloodless charms,
Or die, like Raphael, in his angel arms;
Go, and enjoy thy blessed lot,—to share
In Cowper's gloom, or Chatterton's despair!

Not such were they whom, wandering o'er the
    waves,
I looked to meet, but only found their graves;
If friendship's smile, the better part of fame,
Should lend my song the only wreath I claim,
Whose voice would greet me with a sweeter tone,
Whose living hand more kindly press my own,
Than theirs,—could Memory, as her silent tread

Prints the pale flowers that blossom o'er the dead,
Those breathless lips, now closed in peace, restore,
Or wake those pulses hushed to beat no more?

Thou calm, chaste scholar![1] I can see thee now,
The first young laurels on thy pallid brow,
O'er thy slight figure floating lightly down
In graceful folds the academic gown,
On thy curled lip the classic lines, that taught
How nice the mind that sculptured them with
    thought,
And triumph glistening in the clear blue eye,
Too bright to live,—but oh, too fair to die!

And thou, dear friend,[2] whom Science still de-
    plores,
And love still mourns, on ocean-severed shores,
Though the bleak forest twice has bowed with snow,
Since thou wast laid its budding leaves below,
Thine image mingles with my closing strain,
As when we wandered by the turbid Seine,
Both blest with hopes, which revelled, bright and
    free,
On all we longed, or all we dreamed to be;
To thee the amaranth and the cypress fell,—
And I was spared to breathe this last farewell!

But lived there one in unremembered days,
Or lives there still, who spurns the poet's bays?

[1] " *Thou calm, chaste scholar.* "
Charles Chauncy Emerson ; died May 9th, 1886.
[2] " *And thou, dear friend.* "
James Jackson, Jr., M. D. ; died March 29th, 1834.

Whose fingers, dewy from Castalia's springs,
Rest on the lore, yet scorn to touch the strings?
Who shakes the senate with the silver tone
The groves of Pindus might have sighed to own?
Have such e'er been? Remember Canning's name!
Do such still live? Let " Alaric's Dirge " proclaim!

Immortal Art! where'er the rounded sky
Bends o'er the cradle where thy children lie,
Their home is earth, their herald every tongue
Whose accents echo to the voice that sung.
One leap of Ocean scatters on the sand
The quarried bulwarks of the loosening land;
One thrill of earth dissolves a century's toil,
Strewed like the leaves that vanish in the soil;
One hill o'erflows, and cities sink below,
Their marbles splintering in the lava's glow;
But one sweet tone, scarce whispered to the air,
From shore to shore the blasts of ages bear;
One humble name, which oft, perchance, has borne
The tyrant's mockery and the courtier's scorn,
Towers o'er the dust of earth's forgotten graves,
As once, emerging through the waste of waves,
The rocky Titan, round whose shattered spear
Coiled the last whirlpool of the drowning sphere!

LYRICS.

LYRICS.

THE LAST READER.

I SOMETIMES sit beneath a tree,
    And read my own sweet songs;
Though naught they may to others be,
    Each humble line prolongs
A tone that might have passed away,
But for that scarce remembered lay.

I keep them like a lock or leaf,
    That some dear girl has given;
Frail record of an hour, as brief
    As sunset clouds in heaven,
But spreading purple twilight still
High over memory's shadowed hill.

They lie upon my pathway bleak,
    Those flowers that once ran wild,
As on a father's care-worn cheek
    The ringlets of his child;
The golden mingling with the gray,
And stealing half its snows away.

What care I though the dust is spread
    Around these yellow leaves,

Or o'er them his sarcastic thread
    Oblivion's insect weaves;
Though weeds are tangled on the stream,
It still reflects my morning's beam.

And therefore love I such as smile
    On these neglected songs,
Nor deem that flattery's needless wile
    My opening bosom wrongs;
For who would trample, at my side,
A few pale buds, my garden's pride?

It may be that my scanty ore
    Long years have washed away,
And where were golden sands before,
    Is naught but common clay;
Still something sparkles in the sun
For Memory to look back upon.

And when my name no more is heard,
    My lyre no more is known,
Still let me, like a winter's bird,
    In silence and alone,
Fold over them the weary wing
Once flashing through the dews of spring.

Yes, let my fancy fondly wrap
    My youth in its decline,
And riot in the rosy lap
    Of thoughts that once were mine,
And give the worm my little store
When the last reader reads no more!

OUR YANKEE GIRLS.

Let greener lands and bluer skies,
    If such the wide earth shows,
With fairer cheeks and brighter eyes,
    Match us the star and rose;
The winds that lift the Georgian's veil,
    Or wave Circassia's curls,
Waft to their shores the sultan's sail,—
    Who buys our Yankee girls?

The gay grisette, whose fingers touch
    Love's thousand chords so well;
The dark Italian, loving much,
    But more than *one* can tell;
And England's fair-haired, blue-eyed dame,
    Who binds her brow with pearls;—
Ye who have seen them, can they shame
    Our own sweet Yankee girls?

And what if court or castle vaunt
    Its children loftier born?—
Who heeds the silken tassel's flaunt
    Beside the golden corn?
They ask not for the dainty toil
    Of ribboned knights and earls,
The daughters of the virgin soil,
    Our free-born Yankee girls!

By every hill whose stately pines
　　Wave their dark arms above
The home where some fair being shines,
　　To warm the wilds with love,
From barest rock to bleakest shore
　　Where farthest sail unfurls,
That stars and stripes are streaming o'er,—
　　God bless our Yankee girls!

LA GRISETTE.

Ah Clemence ! when I saw thee last
    Trip down the Rue de Seine,
And turning, when thy form had past,
    I said, " We meet again,"—
I dreamed not in that idle glance
    Thy latest image came,
And only left to memory's trance
    A shadow and a name.

The few strange words my lips had taught
    Thy timid voice to speak,
Their gentler signs, which often brought
    Fresh roses to thy cheek,
The trailing of thy long loose hair
    Bent o'er my couch of pain,
All, all returned, more sweet, more fair ;
    O had we met again !

I walked where saint and virgin keep
    The vigil lights of heaven,
I knew that thou hadst woes to weep,
    And sins to be forgiven ;
I watched where Genevieve was laid,
    I knelt by Mary's shrine,
Beside me low, soft voices prayed ;
    Alas ! but where was thine ?

39

And when the morning sun was bright,
 When wind and wave were calm,
And flamed, in thousand-tinted light,
 The rose of Notre Dame,
I wandered through the haunts of men,
 From Boulevard to Quai.
Till, frowning o'er Saint Etienne,
 The Pantheon's shadow lay.

In vain, in vain; we meet no more,
 Nor dream what fates befall;
And long upon the stranger's shore
 My voice on thee may call,
When years have clothed the line in moss,
 That tells thy name and days,
And withered, on thy simple cross,
 The wreaths of Père-la-Chaise!

AN EVENING THOUGHT.

WRITTEN AT SEA.

I_F sometimes in the dark blue eye,
    Or in the deep red wine,
Or soothed by gentlest melody,
    Still warms this heart of mine,
Yet something colder in the blood,
    And calmer in the brain,
Have whispered that my youth's bright flood
    Ebbs, not to flow again.

If by Helvetia's azure lake,
    Or Arno's yellow stream,
Each star of memory could awake,
    As in my first young dream,
I know that when mine eye shall greet
    The hill-sides bleak and bare,
That gird my home, it will not meet
    My childhood's sunsets there.

Oh, when love's first, sweet, stolen kiss
    Burned on my boyish brow,
Was that young forehead worn as this?
    Was that flushed cheek as now?
Were that wild pulse and throbbing heart
    Like these, which vainly strive,

41

In thankless strains of soulless art,
    To dream themselves alive?

Alas! the morning dew is gone,
    Gone ere the full of day;
Life's iron fetter still is on,
    Its wreaths all torn away;
Happy if still some casual hour
    Can warm the fading shrine,
Too soon to chill beyond the power
    Of love, or song, or wine!

A SOUVENIR.

Yes, lady! I can ne'er forget,
That once in other years we met;
Thy memory may perchance recall
A festal eve, a rose-wreathed hall,
Its tapers' blaze, its mirrors' glance,
Its melting song, its ringing dance;—
Why, in thy dream of virgin joy,
Shouldst thou recall a pallid boy?

Thine eye had other forms to seek,
Why rest upon his bashful cheek?
With other tones thy heart was stirred,
Why waste on him a gentle word?
We parted, lady,—all night long
Thine ear to thrill with dance and song,—
And I—to weep that I was born
A thing thou scarce wouldst deign to scorn.

And, lady! now that years have past,
My bark has reached the shore at last;
The gales that filled her ocean wing
Have chilled and shrunk thy hasty spring,
And eye to eye, and brow to brow,
I stand before thy presence now;—
Thy lip is smoothed, thy voice is sweet,
Thy warm hand offered when we meet.

Nay, lady! 'tis not now for me
To droop the lid or bend the knee.
I seek thee,—oh, thou dost not shun;
I speak,—thou listenest like a nun;
I ask thy smile,—thy lip uncurls,
Too liberal of its flashing pearls;
Thy tears,—thy lashes sink again,—
My Hebe turns to Magdalen!

O changing youth! that evening hour
Look down on ours,—the bud—the flower;
Thine faded in its virgin soil,
And mine was nursed in tears and toil;
Thy leaves were withering, one by one,
While mine were opening to the sun;—
Which now can meet the cold and storm,
With freshest leaf and hardiest form?

Ay, lady! that once haughty glance
Still wanders through the glittering dance,
And asks in vain from others' pride,
The charity thine own denied;
And as thy fickle lips could learn
To smile and praise,—that used to spurn,
So the last offering on thy shrine
Shall be this flattering lay of mine!

"QUI VIVE!"

"Qui vive!"   The sentry's musket rings,
  The channelled bayonet gleams ;
High o'er him, like a raven's wings
The broad tricolored banner flings
Its shadow, rustling as it swings
  Pale in the moonlight beams ;
Pass on ! while steel-clad sentries keep
Their vigil o'er the monarch's sleep,
  Thy bare, unguarded breast
Asks not the unbroken, bristling zone
That girds yon sceptred trembler's throne ;—
  Pass on, and take thy rest !

" *Qui vive !* "   How oft the midnight air
  That startling cry has borne !
How oft the evening breeze has fanned
The banner of this haughty land,
O'er mountain snow and desert sand,
  Ere yet its folds were torn !
Through Jena's carnage flying red,
Or tossing o'er Marengo's dead,
  Or curling on the towers
Where Austria's eagle quivers yet,
And suns the ruffled plumage, wet
  With battle's crimson showers !

45

" *Qui vive !* "   And is the sentry's cry,—
    The sleepless soldier's hand,—
Are these,—the painted folds that fly
And lift their emblems, printed high,
On morning mist and sunset sky,—
    The guardians of a land?
No! If the patriot's pulses sleep,
How vain the watch that hirelings keep,—
    The idle flag that waves,
When Conquest, with his iron heel,
Treads down the standards and the steel
    That belt the soil of slaves!

THE WASP AND THE HORNET.

The two proud sisters of the sea,
  In glory and in doom !—
Well may the eternal waters be
  Their broad, unsculptured tomb !
The wind that rings along the wave,
  The clear, unshadowed sun,
Are torch and trumpet o'er the brave,
  Whose last green wreath is won !

No stranger-hand their banners furled,
  No victor's shout they heard ;
Unseen, above them ocean curled,
  Save by his own pale bird ;
The gnashing billows heaved and fell ;
  Wild shrieked the midnight gale ;
Far, far beneath the morning swell
  Were pennon, spar, and sail.

The land of Freedom ! Sea and shore
  Are guarded now, as when
Her ebbing waves to victory bore
  Fair barks and gallant men ;
Oh, many a ship of prouder name
  May wave her starry fold,
Nor trail, with deeper light of fame,
  The paths they swept of old !

47

FROM A BACHELOR'S PRIVATE JOURNAL.

Sweet Mary, I have never breathed
    The love it were in vain to name,
Though round my heart a serpent wreathed,
    I smiled, or strove to smile, the same.

Once more the pulse of Nature glows
    With faster throb and fresher fire,
While music round her pathway flows
    Like echoes from a hidden lyre.

And is there none with me to share
    The glories of the earth and sky?
The eagle through the pathless air
    Is followed by one burning eye.

Ah, no! the cradled flowers may wake,
    Again may flow the frozen sea,
From every cloud a star may break,—
    There comes no second Spring to me.

Go,—ere the painted toys of youth
    Are crushed beneath the tread of years;
Ere visions have been chilled to truth,
    And hopes are washed away in tears.

48

Go,—for I will not bid thee weep,—
    Too soon my sorrows will be thine,
And evening's troubled air shall sweep
    The incense from the broken shrine.

If Heaven can hear the dying tone
    Of chords that soon will cease to thrill,
The prayer that Heaven has heard alone,
    May bless thee when those chords are still!

STANZAS.

STRANGE ! that one lightly whispered tone
　　Is far, far sweeter unto me,
Than all the sounds that kiss the earth,
　　Or breathe along the sea;
But, lady, when thy voice I greet,
Not heavenly music seems so sweet.

I look upon the fair blue skies,
　　And naught but empty air I see;
But when I turn me to thine eyes,
　　It seemeth unto me
Ten thousand angels spread their wings
Within those little azure rings.

The lily hath the softest leaf
　　That ever western breeze hath fanned,
But thou shalt have the tender flower,
　　So I may take thy hand;
That little hand to me doth yield
More joy than all the broidered field.

O lady ! there be many things
　　That seem right fair, below, above;
But sure not one among them all
　　Is half so sweet as love ;—
Let us not pay our vows alone,
But join two altars both in one.
50

THE PHILOSOPHER TO HIS LOVE.

Dearest, a look is but a ray
Reflected in a certain way ;
A word, whatever tone it wear,
Is but a trembling wave of air ;
A touch, obedience to a clause
In nature's pure material laws.

The very flowers that bend and meet,
In sweetening others, grow more sweet ;
The clouds by day, the stars by night,
Inweave their floating locks of light ;
The rainbow, Heaven's own forehead's braid,
Is but the embrace of sun and shade.

How few that love us have we found !
How wide the world that girds them round !
Like mountain streams we meet and part,
Each living in the other's heart,
Our course unknown, our hope to be
Yet mingled in the distant sea.

But Ocean coils and heaves in vain,
Bound in the subtle moonbeam's chain ;
And love and hope do but obey
Some cold, capricious planet's ray,
Which lights and leads the tide it charms,
To Death's dark caves and icy arms.

Alas ! one narrow line is drawn,
That links our sunset with our dawn ;
In mist and shade life's morning rose,
And clouds are round it at its close ;
But ah ! no twilight beam ascends
To whisper where that evening ends.

Oh ! in the hour when I shall feel
Those shadows round my senses steal,
When gentle eyes are weeping o'er
The clay that feels their tears no more,
Then let thy spirit with me be,
Or some sweet angel, likest thee !

L'INCONNUE.

Is thy name Mary, maiden fair?
    Such should, methinks, its music be;
The sweetest name that mortals bear,
    Were best befitting thee;
And she, to whom it once was given,
Was half of earth and half of heaven.

I hear thy voice, I see thy smile,
    I look upon thy folded hair;
Ah! while we dream not they beguile,
    Our hearts are in the snare;
And she, who chains a wild bird's wing,
Must start not if her captive sing.

So, lady, take the leaf that falls,
    To all but thee unseen, unknown;
When evening shades thy silent walls,
    Then read it all alone;
In stillness read, in darkness seal,
Forget, despise, but not reveal!

THE STAR AND THE WATER-LILY.

THE sun stepped down from his golden throne,
 And lay in the silent sea,
And the Lily had folded her satin leaves,
 For a sleepy thing was she ;
What is the Lily dreaming of ?
 Why crisp the waters blue ?
See, see, she is lifting her varnished lid !
 Her white leaves are glistening through !

The Rose is cooling his burning cheek
 In the lap of the breathless tide ;—
The Lily hath sisters fresh and fair,
 That would lie by the Rose's side ;
He would love her better than all the rest,
 And he would be fond and true ;—
But the Lily unfolded her weary lids,
 And looked at the sky so blue.

Remember, remember, thou silly one,
 How fast will thy summer glide,
And wilt thou wither a virgin pale,
 Or flourish a blooming bride ?
"Oh, the Rose is old, and thorny, and cold,
 And he lives on earth," said she ;
" But the Star is fair and he lives in the air,
 And he shall my bridegroom be."

54

But what if the stormy cloud should come
    And ruffle the silver sea?
Would he turn his eye from the distant sky,
    To smile on a thing like thee?
Oh, no, fair Lily, he will not send
    One ray from his far-off throne;
The winds shall blow and the waves shall flow,
    And thou wilt be left alone.

There is not a leaf on the mountain top,
    Nor a drop of evening dew,
Nor a golden sand on the sparkling shore,
    Nor a pearl in the waters blue,
That he has not cheered with his fickle smile,
    And warmed with his faithless beam,—
And will he be true to a pallid flower,
    That floats on the quiet stream?

Alas for the Lily! she would not heed,
    But turned to the skies afar,
And bared her breast to the trembling ray
    That shot from the rising star;
The cloud came over the darkened sky,
    And over the waters wide:
She looked in vain through the beating rain,
    And sank in the stormy tide.

ILLUSTRATION OF A PICTURE.

' A SPANISH GIRL IN REVERY."

SHE twirled the string of golden beads,
    That round her neck was hung,—
My grandsire's gift; the good old man
    Loved girls when he was young;
And, bending lightly o'er the cord,
    And turning half away,
With something like a youthful sigh,
    Thus spoke the maiden gray :

" Well, one may trail her silken robe,
    And bind her locks with pearls,
And one may wreathe the woodland rose
    Among her floating curls;
And one may tread the dewy grass,
    And one the marble floor,
Nor half-hid bosom heave the less,
    Nor broidered corset more !

"Some years ago, a dark-eyed girl
    Was sitting in the shade,—
There's something brings her to my mind
    In that young dreaming maid,—
And in her hand she held a flower,
    A flower, whose speaking hue

Said, in the language of the heart,
    ' Believe the giver true.'

" And, as she looked upon its leaves,
    The maiden made a vow
To wear it when the bridal wreath
    Was woven for her brow;
She watched the flower, as, day by day,
    The leaflets curled and died;
But he who gave it never came
    To claim her for his bride.

" Oh, many a summer's morning glow
    Has lent the rose its ray,
And many a winter's drifting snow
    Has swept its bloom away;
But she has kept that faithless pledge
    To this, her winter hour,
And keeps it still, herself alone,
    And wasted like the flower."

Her pale lip quivered, and the light
    Gleamed in her moistening eyes;—
I asked her how she liked the tints
    In those Castilian skies?
" She thought them misty,—'twas perhaps
    Because she stood too near;"
She turned away, and as she turned,
    I saw her wipe a tear.

THE DYING SENECA.

He died not as the martyr dies
    Wrapped in his living shroud of flame;
He fell not as the warrior falls,
    Gasping upon the field of fame;
A gentler passage to the grave,
The murderer's softened fury gave.

Rome's slaughtered sons and blazing piles
    Had tracked the purple demon's path,
And yet another victim lived
    To fill the fiery scroll of wrath;
Could not imperial vengeance spare
His furrowed brow and silver hair?

The field was sown with noble blood,
    The harvest reaped in burning tears,
When, rolling up its crimson flood,
    Broke the long-gathering tide of years;
His diadem was rent away,
And beggars trampled on his clay.

None wept,—none pitied;—they who knelt
    At morning by the despot's throne,
At evening dashed the laurelled bust,
    And spurned the wreaths themselves had
      strewn;
The shout of triumph echoed wide,
The self-stung reptile writhed and died!
58

A PORTRAIT.

A STILL, sweet, placid, moonlight face,
    And slightly nonchalant,
Which seems to claim a middle place
    Between one's love and aunt,
Where childhood's star has left a ray
    In woman's sunniest sky,
As morning dew and blushing day
    On fruit and blossom lie.

And yet,—and yet I cannot love
    Those lovely lines on steel ;
They beam too much of heaven above,
    Earth's darker shades to feel ;
Perchance some early weeds of care
    Around my heart have grown,
And brows unfurrowed seem not fair,
    Because they mock my own.

Alas ! when Eden's gates were sealed,
    How oft some sheltered flower
Breathed o'er the wanderers of the field,
    Like their own bridal bower ;
Yet, saddened by its loveliness,
    And humbled by its pride,
Earth's fairest child they could not bless,—
    It mocked them when they sighed.

A ROMAN AQUEDUCT.

THE sun-browned girl, whose limbs recline
    When noon her languid hand has laid
Hot on the green flakes of the pine,
    Beneath its narrow disk of shade;

As, through the flickering noontide glare,
    She gazes on the rainbow chain
Of arches, lifting once in air,
    The rivers of the Roman's plain;—

Say, does her wandering eye recall
    The mountain-current's icy wave,—
Or for the dead one tear let fall,
    Whose founts are broken by their grave?

From stone to stone the ivy weaves
    Her braided tracery's winding veil,
And lacing stalks and tangled leaves
    Nod heavy in the drowsy gale.

And lightly floats the pendent vine,
    That swings beneath her slender bow,
Arch answering arch,—whose rounded line
    Seems mirrored in the wreath below.

How patient Nature smiles at Fame!
    The weeds, that strewed the victor's way,
Feed on his dust to shroud his name,
    Green where his proudest towers decay.

60

See, through that channel, empty now,
    The scanty rain its tribute pours,—
Which cooled the lip and laved the brow
    Of conquerors from a hundred shores.

Thus bending o'er the nation's bier,
    Whose wants the captive earth supplied,
The dew of Memory's passing tear
    Falls on the arches of her pride!

THE LAST PROPHECY OF CASSANDRA.

THE sun is fading in the skies
    And evening shades are gathering fast;
Fair city, ere that sun shall rise,
    Thy night hath come,—thy day is past!

Ye know not,—but the hour is nigh:
    Ye will not heed the warning breath;
No vision strikes your clouded eye,
    To break the sleep that wakes in death.

Go, age, and let thy withered cheek
    Be wet once more with freezing tears;
And bid thy trembling sorrow speak,
    In accents of departed years.

Go, child, and pour thy sinless prayer
    Before the everlasting throne;
And He who sits in glory there,
    May stoop to hear thy silver tone.

Go, warrior, in thy glittering steel,
    And bow thee at the altar's side;
And bid thy frowning gods reveal
    The doom their mystic counsels hide.

Go, maiden, in thy flowing veil,
    And bare thy brow, and bend thy knee;
When the last hopes of mercy fail,
    Thy God may yet remember thee.

Go, as thou didst in happier hours,
    And lay thine incense on the shrine;
And greener leaves, and fairer flowers,
    Around the sacred image twine.

I saw them rise,—the buried dead,—
    From marble tomb and grassy mound;
I heard the spirits' printless tread,
    And voices not of earthly sound.

I looked upon the quivering stream,
    And its cold wave was bright with flame;
And wild, as from a fearful dream,
    The wasted forms of battle came.

Ye will not hear—ye will not know,—
    Ye scorn the maniac's idle song;
Ye care not! but the voice of woe
    Shall thunder loud, and echo long.

Blood shall be in your marble halls,
    And spears shall glance, and fires shall glow;
Ruin shall sit upon your walls,
    But ye shall lie in death below.

Ay, none shall live to hear the storm
    Around their blackened pillars sweep;
To shudder at the reptile's form,
    Or scare the wild bird from her sleep.

TO A CAGED LION.

Poor conquered monarch! though that haughty
  glance
 Still speaks thy courage unsubdued by time,
And in the grandeur of thy sullen tread
 Lives the proud spirit of thy burning clime;—
Fettered by things that shudder at thy roar,
Torn from thy pathless wilds to pace this narrow
  floor!

Thou wast the victor, and all nature shrunk
 Before the thunders of thine awful wrath;
The steel-armed hunter viewed thee from afar,
 Fearless and trackless in thy lonely path!
The famished tiger closed his flaming eye,
And crouched and panted as thy step went by!

Thou art the vanquished, and insulting man
 Bars thy broad bosom as a sparrow's wing;
His nerveless arms thine iron sinews bind,
 And lead in chains the desert's fallen king;
Are these the beings that have dared to twine
Their feeble threads around those limbs of thine?

64

So must it be; the weaker, wiser race,
    That wields the tempest and that rides the sea,
Even in the stillness of thy solitude
    Must teach the lesson of its power to thee;
And thou, the terror of the trembling wild,
Must bow thy savage strength, the mockery of a
      child!

TO MY COMPANIONS.

MINE ancient Chair! thy wide-embracing arms
    Have clasped around me even from a boy;
Hadst thou a voice to speak of years gone by,
    Thine were a tale of sorrow and of joy,
Of fevered hopes and ill-foreboding fears,
And smile unseen, and unrecorded tears.

And thou, my Table! though unwearied Time
    Hath set his signet on thine altered brow,
Still can I see thee in thy spotless prime,
    And in my memory thou art living now;
Soon must thou slumber with forgotten things,
The peasant's ashes and the dust of kings.

Thou melancholy Mug! thy sober brown
    Hath something pensive in its evening hue,
Not like the things that please the tasteless clown,
    With gaudy streaks of orange and of blue;
And I must love thee, for thou art mine own,
Pressed by my lip, and pressed by mine alone.

My broken Mirror! faithless, yet beloved,
    Thou who canst smile, and smile alike on all,
Oft do I leave thee, oft again return,
    I scorn the siren, but obey the call;
I hate thy falsehood, while I fear thy truth,
But most I love thee, flattering friend of youth.

Primeval Carpet! every well-worn thread
    Has slowly parted with its virgin dye;
I saw thee fade beneath the ceaseless tread,
    Fainter and fainter in mine anxious eye;
So flies the color from the brightest flower,
And heaven's own rainbow lives but for an hour.

I love you all! there radiates from our own
    A soul that lives in every shape we see;
There is a voice, to other ears unknown,
    Like echoed music answering to its key.
The dungeoned captive hath a tale to tell,
Of every insect in his lonely cell;
And these poor frailties have a simple tone,
That breathes in accents sweet to me alone.

THE LAST LEAF.

I saw him once before,
As he passed by the door,
   And again
The pavement stones resound,
As he totters o'er the ground
   With his cane.

They say that in his prime,
Ere the pruning-knife of Time
   Cut him down,
Not a better man was found
By the Crier on his round
   Through the town.

But now he walks the streets,
And he looks at all he meets
   Sad and wan,
And he shakes his feeble head,
That it seems as if he said,
   " They are gone."

The mossy marble rest
On the lips that he has prest
   In their bloom,
And the names he loved to hear
Have been carved for many a year
   On the tomb.

My grandmamma has said,—
Poor old lady, she is dead
    Long ago,—
That he had a Roman nose,
And his cheek was like a rose
    In the snow.

But now his nose is thin,
And it rests upon his chin
    Like a staff,
And a crook is in his back,
And a melancholy crack
    In his laugh.

I know it is a sin
For me to sit and grin
    At him here ;
But the old three-cornered hat,
And the breeches, and all that,
    Are so queer !

And if I should live to be
The last leaf upon the tree
    In the spring,
Let them smile, as I do now,
At the old forsaken bough
    Where I cling.

TO A BLANK SHEET OF PAPER.

Wan-visaged thing! thy virgin leaf
    To me looks more than deadly pale,
Unknowing what may stain thee yet,—
    A poem or a tale.

Who can thy unborn meaning scan?
    Can Seer or Sibyl read thee now?
No,—seek to trace the fate of man
    Writ on his infant brow.

Love may light on thy snowy cheek,
    And shake his Eden-breathing plumes;
Then shalt thou tell how Lelia smiles,
    Or Angelina blooms.

Satire may lift his bearded lance,
    Forestalling Time's slow-moving scythe,
And, scattered on thy little field,
    Disjointed bards may writhe.

Perchance a vision of the night,
    Some grizzled spectre, gaunt and thin,
Or sheeted corpse, may stalk along,
    Or skeleton may grin!

If it should be in pensive hour
    Some sorrow-moving theme I try,
Ah, maiden, how thy tears will fall,
    For all I doom to die!

But if in merry mood I touch
    Thy leaves, then shall the sight of thee
Sow smiles as thick on rosy lips
    As ripples on the sea.

The Weekly press shall gladly stoop
    To bind thee up among its sheaves;
The Daily steal thy shining ore,
    To gild its leaden leaves.

Thou hast no tongue, yet thou canst speak,
    Till distant shores shall hear the sound;
Thou hast no life, yet thou canst breathe
    Fresh life on all around.

Thou art the arena of the wise,
    The noiseless battle-ground of fame;
The sky where halos may be wreathed
    Around the humblest name.

Take, then, this treasure to thy trust,
    To win some idle reader's smile,
Then fade and moulder in the dust,
    Or swell some bonfire's crackling pile

TO AN INSECT.

I LOVE to hear thine earnest voice,
    Wherever thou art hid,
Thou testy little dogmatist,
    Thou pretty Katydid!
Thou mindest me of gentlefolks,—
    Old gentlefolks are they,—
Thou say'st an undisputed thing
    In such a solemn way.

Thou art a female, Katydid!
    I know it by the trill
That quivers through thy piercing notes,
    So petulant and shrill,
I think there is a knot of you
    Beneath the hollow tree,—
A knot of spinster Katydids,—
    Do Katydids drink tea?

Oh, tell me where did Katy live,
    And what did Katy do?
And was she very fair and young,
    And yet so wicked, too?
Did Katy love a naughty man,
    Or kiss more cheeks than one?
I warrant Katy did no more
    Than many a Kate has done.

72

Dear me! I'll tell you all about
    My fuss with little Jane,
And Ann, with whom I used to walk
    So often down the lane,
And all that tore their locks of black,
    Or wet their eyes of blue,—
Pray tell me, sweetest Katydid,
    What did poor Katy do?

Oh, no! the living oak shall crash,
    That stood for ages still,
The rock shall rend its mossy base
    And thunder down the hill,
Before the little Katydid
    Shall add one word, to tell
The mystic story of the maid
    Whose name she knows so well.

Peace to the ever murmuring race!
    And when the latest one
Shall fold in death her feeble wings
    Beneath the autumn sun,
Then shall she raise her fainting voice
    And lift her drooping lid,
And then the child of future years
    Shall hear what Katy did.

THE DILEMMA.

Now, by the blessed Paphian queen,
Who heaves the breast of sweet sixteen:
By every name I cut on bark
Before my morning star grew dark ;
By Hymen's torch, by Cupid's dart,
By all that thrills the beating heart ;
The bright black eye, the melting blue,—
I cannot choose between the two.

I had a vision in my dreams ;—
I saw a row of twenty beams ;
From every beam a rope was hung,
In every rope a lover swung ;
I asked the hue of every eye,
That bade each luckless lover die ;
Ten shadowy lips said, heavenly blue,
And ten accused the darker hue.

I asked a matron, which she deemed
With fairest light of beauty beamed ;
She answered, some thought both were fair,—
Give her blue eyes and golden hair.
I might have liked her judgment well,
But, as she spoke, she rung the bell,
And all her girls, nor small nor few,
Came marching in,—their eyes were blue.

74

I asked a maiden; back she flung
The locks that round her forehead hung,
And turned her eye, a glorious one,
Bright as a diamond in the sun,
On me, until beneath its rays
I felt as if my hair would blaze;
She liked all eyes but eyes of green;
She looked at me; what could she mean?

Ah! many lids Love lurks between,
Nor heeds the coloring of his screen;
And when his random arrows fly,
The victim falls, but knows not why.
Gaze not upon his shield of jet,
The shaft upon the string is set;
Look not beneath his azure veil,
Though every limb were cased in mail.

Well, both might make a martyr break
The chain that bound him to the stake;
And both, with but a single ray,
Can melt our very hearts away;
And both, when balanced, hardly seem
To stir the scales, or rock the beam;
But that is dearest, all the while,
That wears for us the sweetest smile.

MY AUNT.

My aunt! my dear unmarried aunt!
　　Long years have o'er her flown;
Yet still she strains the aching clasp
　　That binds her virgin zone;
I know it hurts her,—though she looks
　　As cheerful as she can;
Her waist is ampler than her life,
　　For life is but a span.

My aunt! my poor deluded aunt!
　　Her hair is almost gray;
Why will she train that winter curl
　　In such a spring-like way?
How can she lay her glasses down,
　　And say she reads as well,
When, through a double convex lens,
　　She just makes out to spell?

Her father,—grandpapa! forgive
　　This erring lip its smiles,—
Vowed she should make the finest girl
　　Within a hundred miles;
He sent her to a stylish school;
　　'Twas in her thirteenth June;
And with her, as the rules required,
　　"Two towels and a spoon."

They braced my aunt against a board,
    To make her straight and tall;
They laced her up, they starved her down,
    To make her light and small;
They pinched her feet, they singed her hair,
    They screwed it up with pins;
Oh, never mortal suffered more
    In penance for her sins.

So, when my precious aunt was done,
    My grandsire brought her back;
(By daylight, lest some rabid youth
    Might follow on the track;)
" Ah!" said my grandsire, as he shook
    Some powder in his pan,
" What could this lovely creature do
    Against a desperate man!"

Alas! nor chariot, nor barouche,
    Nor bandit cavalcade,
Tore from the trembling father's arms
    His all-accomplished maid.
For her how happy had it been!
    And heaven had spared to me
To see one sad, ungathered rose
    On my ancestral tree.

THE TOADSTOOL.

THERE'S a thing that grows by the fainting flower,
And springs in the shade of the lady's bower;
The lily shrinks, and the rose turns pale,
When they feel its breath in the summer gale,
And the tulip curls its leaves in pride,
And the blue-eyed violet starts aside;
But the lily may flaunt, and the tulip stare,
For what does the honest toadstool care?

She does not glow in a painted vest,
And she never blooms on the maiden's breast;
But she comes, as the saintly sisters do,
In a modest suit of a Quaker hue.
And, when the stars in the evening skies
Are weeping dew from their gentle eyes,
The toad comes out from his hermit cell,
The tale of his faithful love to tell.
Oh, there is light in her lover's glance,
That flies to her heart like a silver lance;
His breeches are made of spotted skin,
His jacket is tight, and his pumps are thin;
In a cloudless night you may hear his song,
As its pensive melody floats along,
And, if you will look by the moonlight fair,
The trembling form of the toad is there.

78

And he twines his arms round her slender stem,
In the shade of her velvet diadem;
But she turns away in her maiden shame,
And will not breathe on the kindling flame;
He sings at her feet through the livelong night,
And creeps to his cave at the break of light;
And whenever he comes to the air above,
His throat is swelling with baffled love.

THE MEETING OF THE DRYADS.[1]

It was not many centuries since,
    When, gathered on the moonlit green,
Beneath the Tree of Liberty,
    A ring of weeping sprites were seen.

The freshman's lamp had long been dim,
    The voice of busy day was mute,
And tortured melody had ceased
    Her sufferings on the evening flute.

They met not as they once had met,
    To laugh o'er many a jocund tale;
But every pulse was beating low,
    And every cheek was cold and pale.

There rose a fair but faded one,
    Who oft had cheered them with her song;
She waved a mutilated arm,
    And silence held the listening throng.

"Sweet friends," the gentle nymph began,
    "From opening bud to withering leaf,
One common lot has bound us all,
    In every change of joy and grief.

[1] Written after a general pruning of the trees around Harvard College.

80

" While all around has felt decay,
    We rose in ever living prime,
With broader shade and fresher green,
    Beneath the crumbling step of Time.

" When often by our feet has past
    Some biped, nature's walking whim,
Say, have we trimmed one awkward shape,
    Or lopped away one crooked limb ?

" Go on, fair Science ; soon to thee
    Shall Nature yield her idle boast ;
Her vulgar fingers formed a tree,
    But thou hast trained it to a post.

" Go paint the birch's silver rind,
    And quilt the peach with softer down ;
Up with the willow's trailing threads,
    Off with the sunflower's radiant crown !

" Go, plant the lily on the shore,
    And set the rose among the waves,
And bid the tropic bud unbind
    Its silken zone in arctic caves ;

" Bring bellows for the panting winds,
    Hang up a lantern by the moon,
And give the nightingale a fife,
    And lend the eagle a balloon !

" I cannot smile,—the tide of scorn,
    That rolled through every bleeding vein,
Comes kindling fiercer as it flows
    Back to its burning source again.

" Again in every quivering leaf
    That moment's agony I feel,
When limbs, that spurned the northern blast,
    Shrunk from the sacrilegious steel.

" A curse upon the wretch who dared
    To crop us with his felon saw !
May every fruit his lip shall taste.
    Lie like a bullet in his maw.

" In ever julep that he drinks,
    May gout, and bile, and headache be ;
And when he strives to calm his pain,
    May colic mingle with his tea.

" May nightshade cluster round his path,
    And thistles shoot, and brambles cling ;
May blistering ivy scorch his veins,
    And dogwood burn, and nettles sting.

" On him may never shadow fall,
    When fever racks his throbbing brow,
And his last shilling buy a rope
    To hang him on my highest bough ! "

She spoke ;—the morning's herald beam
    Sprang from the bosom of the sea,
And every mangled sprite returned
    In sadness to her wounded tree.[1]

[1] A little poem, on a similar occasion, may be found in the
works of Swift, from which, perhaps, the idea was borrowed ;
although I was as much surprised as amused to meet with it
some time after writing the preceding lines.

THE MYSTERIOUS VISITOR.

There was a sound of hurrying feet,
  A tramp on echoing stairs,
There was a rush along the aisles,—
  It was the hour of prayers.

And on, like Ocean's midnight wave,
  The current rolled along,
When, suddenly, a stranger form
  Was seen amidst the throng.

He was a dark and swarthy man,
  That uninvited guest;
A faded coat of bottle green
  Was buttoned round his breast.

There was not one among them all
  Could say from whence he came;
Nor beardless boy, nor ancient man,
  Could tell that stranger's name.

All silent as the sheeted dead,
  In spite of sneer and frown,
Fast by a gray-haired senior's side
  He sat him boldly down.

83

There was a look of horror flashed
    From out the tutor's eyes;
When all around him rose to pray,
    The stranger did not rise!

A murmur broke along the crowd,
    The prayer was at an end;
With ringing heels and measured tread
    A hundred forms descend.

Through sounding aisles, o'er grating stair,
    The long procession poured,
Till all were gathered on the seats
    Around the Commons board.

That fearful stranger! down he sat,
    Unasked, yet undismayed;
And on his lip a rising smile
    Of scorn or pleasure played.

He took his hat and hung it up,
    With slow but earnest air;
He stripped his coat from off his back,
    And placed it on a chair.

Then from his nearest neighbor's side
    A knife and plate he drew;
And, reaching out his hand again,
    He took his teacup too.

How fled the sugar from the bowl!
    How sunk the azure cream!

They vanished like the shapes that float
    Upon a summer's dream.

A long, long draught,—an outstretched hand,
    And crackers, toast, and tea,
They faded from the stranger's touch
    Like dew upon the sea.

Then clouds were dark on many a brow,
    Fear sat upon their souls,
And, in a bitter agony,
    They clasped their buttered rolls.

A whisper trembled through the crowd,—
    Who could the stranger be?
And some were silent, for they thought
    A cannibal was he.

What if the creature should arise,
    For he was stout and tall,—
And swallow down a sophomore,
    Coat, crow's foot, cap, and all!

All suddenly the stranger rose;
    They sat in mute despair;
He took his hat from off the peg,
    His coat from off the chair.

Four freshmen fainted on the seat,
    Six swooned upon the floor;
Yet on the fearful being passed,
    And shut the chapel door.

There is full many a starving man,
    That walks in bottle green,
But never more that hungry one
    In Common's-hall was seen.

Yet often at the sunset hour,
    When tolls the evening bell,
The freshman lingers on the steps,
    That frightful tale to tell.

THE SPECTRE PIG.

A BALLAD.

It was the stalwart butcher man,
    That knit his swarthy brow,
And said the gentle Pig must die,
    And sealed it with a vow.

And oh! it was the gentle Pig
    Lay stretched upon the ground,
And ah! it was the cruel knife
    His little heart that found.

They took him then, those wicked men,
    They trailed him all along;
They put a stick between his lips,
    And through his heels a thong;

And round and round an oaken beam
    A hempen cord they flung,
And, like a mighty pendulum,
    All solemnly he swung!

Now say thy prayers, thou sinful man,
    And think what thou hast done,
And read thy catechism well,
    Thou bloody minded one;

For if his sprite should walk by night,
　　It better were for thee,
That thou wert mouldering in the ground,
　　Or bleaching in the sea.

It was the savage butcher then,
　　That made a mock of sin,
And swore a very wicked oath,
　　He did not care a pin.

It was the butcher's youngest son,—
　　His voice was broke with sighs,
And with his pocket handkerchief
　　He wiped his little eyes;

All young and ignorant was he,
　　But innocent and mild,
And, in his soft simplicity,
　　Out spoke the tender child;—

"O father, father, list to me;
　　The pig is deadly sick,
And men have hung him by his heels,
　　And fed him with a stick."

It was the bloody butcher then,
　　That laughed as he would die,
Yet did he soothe the sorrowing child,
　　And bid him not to cry;—

"O Nathan, Nathan, what's a Pig,
　　That thou shouldst weep and wail?
Come, bear thee like a butcher's child,
　　And thou shalt have his tail!"

It was the butcher's daughter then,
    So slender and so fair,
That sobbed as if her heart would break,
    And tore her yellow hair;

And thus she spoke in thrilling tone,—
    Fast fell the tear-drops big ;
" Ah ! woe is me! Alas! Alas!
    The Pig! The Pig! The Pig!"

Then did her wicked father's lips
    Make merry with her woe,
And call her many a naughty name,
    Because she whimpered so.

Ye need not weep, ye gentle ones,
    In vain your tears are shed,
Ye cannot wash his crimson hand,
    Ye cannot soothe the dead.

The bright sun folded on his breast
    His robes of rosy flame,
And softly over all the west
    The shades of evening came.

He slept, and troops of murdered Pigs
    Were busy with his dreams;
Loud rang their wild, unearthly shrieks,
    Wide yawned their mortal seams.

The clock struck twelve; the Dead hath heard;
    He opened both his eyes,
And sullenly he shook his tail
    To lash the feeding flies.

One quiver of the hempen cord,—
 One struggle and one bound,—
With stiffened limb and leaden eye,
 The Pig was on the ground !

And straight towards the sleeper's house
 His fearful way he wended ;
And hooting owl, and hovering bat,
 On midnight wing attended.

Back flew the bolt, up rose the latch,
 And open swung the door,
And little mincing feet were heard
 Pat, pat along the floor.

Two hoofs upon the sanded floor,
 And two upon the bed ;
And they are breathing side by side,
 The living and the dead !

" Now wake, now wake, thou butcher man !
 What makes thy cheek so pale?
Take hold ! take hold ! thou dost not fear
 To clasp a spectre's tail ? "

Untwisted every winding coil ;
 The shuddering wretch took hold,
All like an icicle it seemed,
 So tapering and so cold.

" Thou com'st with me, thou butcher man ! "
 He strives to loose his grasp,
But, faster than the clinging vine,
 Those twining spirals clasp.

And open, open swung the door,
 And, fleeter than the wind,
The shadowy spectre swept before,
 The butcher trailed behind.

Fast fled the darkness of the night,
 And morn rose faint and dim ;
They called full loud, they knocked full long,
 They did not waken him.

Straight, straight towards that oaken beam,
 A trampled pathway ran ;
A ghastly shape was swinging there,—
 It was the butcher man.

LINES BY A CLERK.

Oh! I did love her dearly,
    And gave her toys and rings,
And I thought she meant sincerely,
    When she took my pretty things;
But her heart has grown as icy
    As a fountain in the fall,
And her love, that was so spicy,
    It did not last at all.

I gave her once a locket,
    It was filled with my own hair,
And she put it in her pocket
    With very special care.
But a jeweller has got it,—
    He offered it to me,
And another that is not it
    Around her neck I see.

For my cooings and my billings
    I do not now complain,
But my dollars and my shillings
    Will never come again;
They were earned with toil and sorrow,
    But I never told her that,
And now I have to borrow,
    And want another hat.

92

Think, think, thou cruel Emma,
　　When thou shalt hear my woe,
And know my sad dilemma,
　　That thou hast made it so.
See, see my beaver rusty,
　　Look, look upon this hole,
This coat is dim and dusty ;
　　Oh, let it rend thy soul !

Before the gates of fashion
　　I daily bent my knee,
But I sought the shrine of passion,
　　And found my idol,—thee ;
Though never love intenser
　　Had bowed a soul before it,
Thine eye was on the censer,
　　And not the hand that bore it.

REFLECTIONS OF A PROUD PEDESTRIAN.

I saw the curl of his waving lash,
    And the glance of his knowing eye,
And I knew that he thought he was cutting a dash,
    As his steed went thundering by.

And he may ride in the rattling gig,
    Or flourish the Stanhope gay,
And dream that he looks exceeding big
    To the people that walk in the way ;

But he shall think, when the night is still,
    On the stable-boy's gathering numbers,
And the ghost of many a veteran bill
    Shall hover around his slumbers ;

The ghastly dun shall worry his sleep,
    And constables cluster around him,
And he shall creep from the wood-hole deep
    Where their spectre eyes have found him !

Ay ! gather your reins, and crack your thong,
    And bid your steed go faster ;
He does not know, as he scrambles along,
    That he has a fool for his master ;

And hurry away on your lonely ride,
    Nor deign from the mire to save me ;
I will paddle it stoutly at your side
    With the tandem that nature gave me !

THE POET'S LOT.

What is a poet's love?—
 To write a girl a sonnet,
To get a ring, or some such thing,
 And fustianize upon it.

What is a poet's fame?—
 Sad hints about his reason,
And sadder praise from garreteers,
 To be returned in season.

Where go the poet's lines?—
 Answer, ye evening tapers!
Ye auburn locks, ye golden curls,
 Speak from your folded papers!

Child of the ploughshare, smile;
 Boy of the counter, grieve not,
Though muses round thy trundle-bed
 Their broidered tissue weave not.

The poet's future holds
 No civic wreath above him;
Nor slated roof, or varnished chaise,
 Nor wife nor child to love him.

Maid of the village inn,
  Who workest woe on satin
(The grass in black, the graves in green,
  The epitaph in Latin),

Trust not to them who say,
  In stanzas, they adore thee;
Oh rather sleep in churchyard clay,
  With urns and cherubs o'er thee!

DAILY TRIALS.

BY A SENSITIVE MAN.

Oh there are times
When all this fret and tumult that we hear
Do seem more stale than to the sexton's ear
    His own dull chimes.

    Ding dong! ding dong!
The world is in a simmer like a sea
Over a pent volcano,—woe is me
    All the day long!

    From crib to shroud!
Nurse o'er our cradles screameth lullaby,
And friends in boots tramp round us as we die,
    Snuffling aloud.

    At morning's call
The small-voiced pug-dog welcomes in the sun,
And flea-bit mongrels, wakening one by one,
    Give answer all.

    When evening dim
Draws round us, then the lonely caterwaul
Tart solo, sour duet, and general squall,—
    These are our hymn.

Women, with tongues
Like polar needles, ever on the jar,—
Men, plugless word-spouts, whose deep fountains are
   Within their lungs.

Children, with drums
Strapped round them by the fond paternal ass,
Peripatetics with a blade of grass
   Between their thumbs.

Vagrants, whose arts
Have caged some devil in their mad machine,
Which grinding, squeaks, with husky groans be-
   tween,
   Come out by starts.

Cockneys that kill
Thin horses of a Sunday,—men, with clams,
Hoarse as young bisons roaring for their dams
   From hill to hill.

Soldiers, with guns
Making a nuisance of the blessed air,
Child-crying bellmen, children in despair
   Screeching for buns.

Storms, thunders, waves !
Howl, crash, and bellow till ye get your fill;
Ye sometimes rest ; men never can be still
   But in their graves.

EVENING.

BY A TAILOR.

DAY hath put on his jacket, and around
His burning bosom buttoned it with stars.
Here will I lay me on the velvet grass,
That is like padding to earth's meagre ribs,
And hold communion with the things about me.
Ah me! how lovely is the golden braid,
That binds the skirt of night's descending robe!
The thin leaves, quivering on their silken threads,
Do make a music like to rustling satin,
As the light breezes smooth their downy nap.

Ha! what is this that rises to my touch,
So like a cushion? Can it be a cabbage?
It is, it is that deeply injured flower,
Which boys do flout us with;—but yet I love thee,
Thou giant rose, wrapped in a green surtout.
Doubtless in Eden thou didst blush as bright
As these, thy puny brethren; and thy breath
Sweetened the fragrance of her spicy air;
But now thou seemest like a bankrupt beau,
Stripped of his gaudy hues and essences,
And growing portly in his sober garments.

Is that a swan that rides upon the water?
Oh! no, it is that other gentle bird,

99

Which is the patron of our noble calling.
I well remember, in my early years,
When these young hands first closed upon a goose;
I have a scar upon my thimble finger,
Which chronicles the hour of young ambition.
My father was a tailor, and his father,
And my sire's grandsire, all of them were tailors;
They had an ancient goose,—it was an heirloom
From some remoter tailor of our race.
It happened I did see it on a time
When none was near, and I did deal with it,
And it did burn me, oh, most fearfully!

It is a joy to straighten out one's limbs,
And leap elastic from the level counter,
Leaving the petty grievances of earth,
The breaking thread, the din of clashing shears,
And all the needles that do wound the spirit,
For such a pensive hour of soothing silence.
Kind Nature, shuffling in her loose undress,
Lays bare her shady bosom;—1 can feel
With all around me;—I can hail the flowers
That sprig earth's mantle,—and yon quiet bird,
That rides the stream, is to me as a brother,
The vulgar know not all the hidden pockets,
Where Nature stows away her loveliness.
But this unnatural posture of the legs
Cramps my extended calves, and I must go
Where 1 can coil them in their wonted fashion.

THE DORCHESTER GIANT.

There was a giant in time of old,
    A mighty one was he;
He had a wife, but she was a scold,
So he kept her shut in his mammoth fold;
    And he had children three.

It happened to be an election day,
    And the giants were choosing a king;
The people were not democrats then,
They did not talk of the rights of men,
    And all that sort of thing.

Then the giant took his children three
    And fastened them in the pen;
The children roared; quoth the giant, " Be still ! "
And Dorchester Heights and Milton Hill
    Rolled back the sound again.

Then he brought them a pudding stuffed with plums,
    As big as the State-House dome;
Quoth he, " There's something for you to eat;
So stop your mouths with your 'lection treat,
    And wait till your dad comes home."

101

So the giant pulled him a chestnut stout,
    And whittled the boughs away ;
The boys and their mother set up a shout,
Said he, " You're in, and you can't get out,
    Bellow as loud as you may."

Off he went, and he growled a tune
    As he strode the fields along;
'Tis said a buffalo fainted away,
And fell as cold as a lump of clay,
    When he heard the giant's song.

But whether the story's true or not,
    It is not for me to show ;
There's many a thing that's twice as queer
In somebody's lectures that we hear,
    And those are true, you know.

What are those lone ones doing now,
    The wife and the children sad ?
Oh! they are in a terrible rout,
Screaming, and throwing their pudding about,
    Acting as they were mad.

They flung it over to Roxbury hills,
    They flung it over the plain,
And all over Milton and Dorchester too
Great lumps of pudding the giants threw ;
    They tumbled as thick as rain.

*　　*　　*　　*　　*　　*

Giant and mammoth have passed away,
 For ages have floated by ;
The suet is hard as a marrow bone,
And every plum is turned to a stone,
 But there the puddings lie.

And if, some pleasant afternoon,
 You'll ask me out to ride,
The whole of the story I will tell,
 And you shall see where the puddings fell,
 And pay for the punch besides.

TO THE PORTRAIT OF "A GENTLEMAN."

It may be so,—perhaps thou hast
    A warm and loving heart;
I will not blame thee for thy face,
    Poor devil as thou art.

That thing, thou fondly deem'st a nose,
    Unsightly though it be,—
In spite of all the cold world's scorn,
    It may be much to thee.

Those eyes,—among thine elder friends
    Perhaps they pass for blue:—
No matter,—if a man can see,
    What more have eyes to do?

Thy mouth,—that fissure in thy face
    By something like a chin,—
May be a very useful place
    To put thy victual in.

I know thou hast a wife at home,
    I know thou hast a child,
By that subdued, domestic smile
    Upon thy features mild.

That wife sits fearless by thy side,
That cherub on thy knee;
They do not shudder at thy looks,
They do not shrink from thee.

Above thy mantel is a hook,—
A portrait once was there;
It was thine only ornament,—
Alas! that hook is bare.

She begged thee not to let it go,
She begged thee all in vain;
She wept,—and breathed a trembling prayer
To meet it safe again.

It was a bitter sight to see
That picture torn away;
It was a solemn thought to think
What all her friends would say!

And often in her calmer hours,
And in her happy dreams,
Upon its long-deserted hook
The absent portrait seems.

Thy wretched infant turns his head
In melancholy wise,
And looks to meet the placid stare
Of those unbending eyes.

I never saw thee, lovely one,—
    Perchance I never may ;
It is not often that we cross
    Such people in our way ;

But if we meet in distant years,
    Or on some foreign shore,
Sure I can take my Bible oath,
    I've seen that face before.

TO THE PORTRAIT OF "A LADY."

WELL, Miss, I wonder where you live,
 I wonder what's your name,
I wonder how you came to be
 In such a stylish frame;
Perhaps you were a favorite child,
  Perhaps an only one;
Perhaps your friends were not aware
 You had your portrait done !

Yet you must be a harmless soul ;
 I cannot think that Sin
Would care to throw his loaded dice,
 With such a stake to win :
I cannot think you would provoke
 The poet's wicked pen,
Or make young women bite their lips,
 Or ruin fine young men.

Pray, did you ever hear, my love,
 Of boys that go about,
Who, for a very trifling sum
 Will snip one's picture out ?

107

I'm not averse to red and white,
But all things have their place,
I think a profile cut in black
Would suit your style of face!

I love sweet features; I will own
That I should like myself
To see my portrait on a wall,
Or bust upon a shelf;

But nature sometimes makes one up
Of such sad odds and ends,
It really might be quite as well
Hushed up among one's friends!

THE COMET.

THE Comet! He is on his way,
 And singing as he flies;
The whizzing planets shrink before
The spectre of the skies;
Ah! well may regal orbs burn blue,
And satellites turn pale,
Ten million cubic miles of head,
 Ten billion leagues of tail!

On, on by whistling spheres of light,
 He flashes and he flames;
He turns not to the left nor right,
 He asks them not their names;
One spurn from his demoniac heel,—
 Away, away they fly,
Where darkness might be bottled up
 And sold for " Tyrian dye."

And what would happen to the land,
 And how would look the sea,
If in the bearded devil's path
 Our earth should chance to be?
Full hot and high the sea would boil,
 Full red the forests gleam;
Methought I saw and heard it all
 In a dyspeptic dream!

I saw a tutor take his tube
　　The Comet's course to spy ;
I heard a scream, —the gathered rays
　　Had stewed the tutor's eye ;
I saw a fort,—the soldiers all
　　Were armed with goggles green ;
Pop cracked the guns ! whiz flew the balls !
　　Bang went the magazine !

I saw a poet dip a scroll
　　Each moment in a tub,
l read upon the warping back,
　　" The Dream of Beelzebub ";
He could not see his verses burn,
　　Although his brain was fried,
And ever and anon he bent
　　To wet them as they dried.

I saw the scalding pitch roll down
　　The crackling, sweating pines,
And streams of smoke, like water-spouts,
　　Burst through the rumbling mines;
I asked the firemen why they made
　　Such noise about the town ;
They answered not,—but all the while
　　The brakes went up and down.

I saw a roasting pullet sit
　　Upon a baking egg ;
I saw a cripple scorch his hand
　　Extinguishing his leg ;

I saw nine geese upon the wing
    Towards the frozen pole,
And every mother's gosling fell
    Crisped to a crackling coal.

I saw the ox that browsed the grass
    Writhe in the blistering rays,
The herbage in his shrinking jaws
    Was all a fiery blaze;
I saw huge fishes, boiled to rags,
    Bob through the bubbling brine;
And thoughts of supper crossed my soul;
    I had been rash at mine.

Strange sights! strange sounds! O fearful dream!
    Its memory haunts me still,
The steaming sea, the crimson glare,
    That wreathed each wooded hill;
Stranger! if through thy reeling brain,
    Such midnight visions sweep,
Spare, spare, oh, spare thine evening meal,
    And sweet shall be thy sleep!

A NOONTIDE LYRIC.

The dinner-bell, the dinner-bell
    Is ringing loud and clear;
Through hill and plain, through street and lane,
    It echoes far and near;
From curtained hall, and whitewashed stall,
    Wherever men can hide,
Like bursting waves from ocean caves,
    They float upon the tide.

I smell the smell of roasted meat!
    I hear the hissing fry!
The beggars know where they can go,
    But where, oh, where shall I?
At twelve o'clock men took my hand,
    At two they only stare,
And eye me with a fearful look,
    As if I were a bear!

The poet lays his laurels down
    And hastens to his greens;
The happy tailor quits his goose,
    To riot on his beans;
The weary cobbler snaps his thread,
    The printer leaves his pi;
His very devil hath a home,
    But what, oh, what have I?

112

Methinks 1 hear an angel voice,
    That softly seems to say :
" Pale stranger, all may yet be well,
    Then wipe thy tears away ;
Erect thy head, and cock thy hat,
    And follow me afar,
And thou shalt have a jolly meal
    And charge it at the bar."

I hear the voice ! I go ! 1 go !
    Prepare your meat and wine !
They little heed their future need,
    Who pay not when they dine.
Give me to-day the rosy bowl,
    Give me one golden dream,—
To-morrow kick away the stool,
    And dangle from the beam !

THE BALLAD OF THE OYSTERMAN.

Iᴛ was a tall young oysterman lived by the river-
    side,
His shop was just upon the bank, his boat was on
    the tide ;
The daughter of a fisherman, that was so straight
    and slim,
Lived over on the other bank, right opposite to
    him.

It was the pensive oysterman that saw a lovely
    maid,
Upon a moonlight evening, a sitting in the shade ;
He saw her wave her handkerchief, as much as if to
    say,
" I'm wide awake, young oysterman, and all the
    folks away."
Then up arose the oysterman, and to himself said
    he,
" I guess I'll leave the skiff at home, for fear that
    folks should see ;
I read it in the story-book, that, for to kiss his dear,
Leander swam the Hellespont,—and I will swim
    this here."

Tnd he has leaped into the waves, and crossed the
    shining stream,
114

And he has clambered up the bank, all in the moon-
    light gleam ;
Oh, there were kisses sweet as dew, and words as
    soft as rain,—
But they have heard her father's step, and in he
    leaps again !

Out spoke the ancient fisherman,—" Oh, what was
    that, my daughter ? "
" 'Twas nothing but a pebble, sir, I threw into the
    water ; "
" And what is that, pray tell me, love, that paddles
    off so fast ? "
" It's nothing but a porpoise, sir, that's been a
    swimming past."

Out spoke the ancient fisherman,—" Now bring me
    my harpoon!
I'll get into my fishing-boat, and fix the fellow
    soon ; "
Down fell that pretty innocent, as falls a snow-
    white lamb,
Her hair drooped round her pallid cheeks, like sea-
    weed on a clam.

Alas for those two loving ones ! she waked not from
    her swound,
And he was taken with the cramp, and in the
    waves was drowned ;
But Fate has metamorphosed them, in pity of their
    woe,
And now they keep an oyster-shop for mermaids
    down below.

THE MUSIC-GRINDERS.

THERE are three ways in which men take
    One's money from his purse,
And very hard it is to tell
    Which of the three is worse;
But all of them are bad enough
    To make a body curse.

You're riding out some pleasant day,
    And counting up your gains;
A fellow jumps from out a bush,
    And takes your horse's reins,
Another hints some words about
    A bullet in your brains.

It's hard to met such pressing friends
    In such a lonely spot;
It's very hard to lose your cash,
    But harder to be shot;
And so you take your wallet out,
    Though you would rather not.

Perhaps you're going out to dine,—
    Some filthy creature begs
You'll hear about the cannon-ball
    That carried off his pegs,
And says it is a dreadful thing
    For men to lose their legs.

116

He tells you of his starving wife,
    His children to be fed,
Poor little, lovely innocents,
    All clamorous for bread,—
And so you kindly help to put
    A bachelor to bed.

You're sitting on your window-seat
    Beneath a cloudless moon ;
You hear a sound, that seems to wear
    The semblance of a tune,
As if a broken fife should strive
    To drown a cracked bassoon.

And nearer, nearer still, the tide
    Of music seems to come,
There's something like a human voice,
    And something like a drum ;
You sit in speechless agony,
    Until your ear is numb.

Poor " home, sweet home," should seem to be
    A very dismal place ;
Your " auld acquaintance," all at once,
    Is altered in the face ;
Their discords sting through Burns and Moore,
    Like hedgehogs dressed in lace.

You think they are crusaders, sent
    From some infernal clime,
To pluck the eyes of Sentiment,
    And dock the tail of Rhyme,

To crack the voice of Melody,
　　And break the legs of Time.

But hark! the air again is still,
　　The music all is ground,
And silence, like a poultice, comes
　　To heal the blows of sound;
It cannot be,—it is,—it is,—
　　A hat is going round!

No! Pay the dentist when he leaves
　　A fracture in your jaw;
And pay the owner of the bear,
　　That stunned you with his paw,
And buy the lobster, that has had
　　Your knuckles in his claw;

But if you are a portly man,
　　Put on your fiercest frown,
And talk about a constable
　　To turn them out of town;
Then close your sentence with an oath,
　　And shut the window down!

And if you are a slender man,
　　Not big enough for that,
Or, if you cannot make a speech,
　　Because you are a flat,
Go very quietly and drop
　　A button in the hat!

THE TREADMILL SONG.

THE stars are rolling in the sky,
    The earth rolls on below,
And we can feel the rattling wheel
    Revolving as we go.
Then tread away, my gallant boys,
    And make the axle fly ;
Why should not wheels go round about,
    Like planets in the sky ?

Wake up, wake up, my duck-legged man,
    And stir your solid pegs !
Arouse, arouse, my gawky friend,
    And shake your spider legs ;
What though you're awkward at the trade,
    There's time enough to learn,—
So lean upon the rail, my lad,
    And take another turn.

They've built us up a noble wall,
    To keep the vulgar out ;
We've nothing in the world to do,
    But just to walk about ;
So faster, now, you middle men,
    And try to beat the ends,—
It's pleasant work to ramble round
    Among one's honest friends.

Here, tread upon the long man's toes,
    He shan't be lazy here,—
And punch the little fellow's ribs,
    And tweak that lubber's ear,—
He's lost them both,—don't pull his hair,
    Because he wears a scratch,
But poke him in the further eye,
    That isn't in the patch.

Hark ! fellows, there's the supper-bell,
    And so our work is done ;
It's pretty sport,—suppose we take
    A round or two for fun !
If ever they should turn me out,
    When I have better grown,
Now hang me, but I mean to have
    A treadmill of my own !

THE SEPTEMBER GALE.

I'M not a chicken ; I have seen
    Full many a chill September,
And though I was a youngster then,
    That gale I well remember ;
The day before, my kite-string snapped,
    And I, my kite pursuing,
The wind whisked off my palm-leaf hat ;—
    For me two storms were brewing !

It came as quarrels sometimes do,
    When married folks get clashing ;
There was a heavy sigh or two,
    Before the fire was flashing,—
A little stir among the clouds,
    Before they rent asunder,—
A little rocking of the trees,
    And then came on the thunder.

Lord ! how the ponds and rivers boiled,
    And how the shingles rattled !
And oaks were scattered on the ground
    As if the Titans battled ;
And all above was in a howl,
    And all below a clatter,—

The earth was like a frying-pan,
  Or some such hissing matter.

It chanced to be our washing-day,
  And all our things were drying:
The storm came roaring through the lines,
  And set them all a flying;
I saw the shirts and petticoats
  Go riding off like witches;
I lost, ah! bitterly I wept,—
  I lost my Sunday breeches!

I saw them straddling through the air,
  Alas! too late to win them;
I saw them chase the clouds as if
  The devil had been in them;
They were my darlings and my pride,
  My boyhood's only riches,—
" Farewell, farewell," I faintly cried,—
  "My breeches! O my breeches!"

That night I saw them in my dreams,
  How changed from what I knew them!
The dews had steeped their faded threads,
  The winds had whistled through them;
I saw the wide and ghastly rents
  Where demon claws had torn them;
A hole was in their amplest part,
  As if an imp had worn them.

I have had many happy years,
  And tailors kind and clever,

But those young pantaloons have gone
    Forever and forever !
And not till fate has cut the last
    Of all my earthly stitches,
This aching heart shall cease to mourn
    My loved, my long-lost breeches !

THE HEIGHT OF THE RIDICULOUS.

I WROTE some lines once on a time
    In wondrous merry mood,
And thought, as usual, men would say
    They were exceeding good.

They were so queer, so very queer,
    I laughed as I would die;
Albeit, in the general way,
    A sober man am I.

I called my servant, and he came;
    How kind it was of him,
To mind a slender man like me,
    He of the mighty limb!

"These to the printer," I exclaimed,
    And, in my humorous way,
I added (as a trifling jest),
    "There'll be the devil to pay."

He took the paper, and I watched,
    And saw him peep within;
At the first line he read, his face
    Was all upon the grin.

124

He read the next ; the grin grew broad,
    And shot from ear to ear ;
He read the third ; a chuckling noise
    I now began to hear.

The fourth ; he broke into a roar ;
    The fifth ; his waistband split ;
The sixth ; he burst five buttons off,
    And tumbled in a fit.

Ten days and nights, with sleepless eye,
    I watched that wretched man,
And since, I never dare to write
    As funny as I can.

THE HOT SEASON.

The folks, that on the first of May
    Wore winter-coats and hose,
Began to say, the first of June,
    "Good Lord! how hot it grows."
At last two Fahrenheits blew up,
    And killed two children small,
And one barometer shot dead
    A tutor with its ball!

Now all day long the locusts sang
    Among the leafless trees;
Three new hotels warped inside out,
    The pumps could only wheeze;
And ripe old wine, that twenty years
    Had cobwebbed o'er in vain,
Came spouting through the rotten corks,
    Like Jolys' best Champagne!

The Worcester locomotives did
    Their trip in half an hour;
The Lowell cars ran forty miles
    Before they checked the power;
Roll brimstone soon became a drug,
    And loco-focos fell;

All asked for ice, but everywhere
    Saltpetre was to sell.

Plump men of mornings ordered tights,
    But, ere the scorching noons,
Their candle-moulds had grown as loose
    As Cossack pantaloons!
The dogs ran mad,—men could not try
    If water they would choose;
A horse fell dead,—he only left
    Four red-hot, rusty shoes!

But soon the people could not bear
    The slightest hint of fire;
Allusions to caloric drew
    A flood of savage ire;
The leaves on heat were all torn out
    From every book at school,
And many blackguards kicked and caned,
    Because they said,—" Keep cool!"

The gas-light companies were mobbed,
    The bakers all were shot,
The penny press began to talk
    Of Lynching Poctor Nott;
And all about the warehouse steps
    Were angry men in droves,
Crashing and splintering through the doors
    To smash the patent stoves!

The abolition men and maids
    Were tanned to such a hue,

You scarce could tell them from their friends
    Unless their eyes were blue;
And, when I left, society
    Had burst its ancient guards,
And Brattle Street and Temple Place
    Were interchanging cards.

POEMS

ADDED SINCE THE FIRST EDITION.

DEPARTED DAYS.

Yes, dear departed, cherished days,
    Could Memory's hand restore
Your morning light, your evening rays,
    From Time's gray urn once more,—
Then might this restless heart be still,
    This straining eye might close,
And Hope her fainting pinions fold,
    While the fair phantoms rose.

But, like a child in ocean's arms,
    We strive against the stream,
Each moment farther from the shore
    Where life's young fountains gleam;—
Each moment fainter wave the fields,
    And wider rolls the sea;
The mist grows dark,—the sun goes down,-
    Day breaks,—and where are we?

THE STEAMBOAT.

SEE how yon flaming herald treads
　　The ridged and rolling waves,
As, crashing o'er their crested heads,
　　She bows her surly slaves!
With foam before and fire behind,
　　She rends the clinging sea,
That flies before the roaring wind,
　　Beneath her hissing lee.

The morning spray, like sea-born flowers,
　　With heaped and glistening bells
Falls round her fast, in ringing showers,
　　With every wave that swells;
And, burning o'er the midnight deep,
　　In lurid fringes thrown,
The living gems of ocean sweep
　　Along her flashing zone.

With clashing wheel, and lifting keel,
　　And smoking torch on high,
When winds are loud, and billows reel,
　　She thunders foaming by;
When seas are silent and serene,
　　With even beam she glides,

The sunshine glimmering through the green
    That skirts her gleaming sides.

Now, like a wild nymph, far apart
    She veils her shadowy form,
The beating of her restless heart
    Still sounding through the storm;
Now answers, like a courtly dame,
    The reddening surges o'er,
With flying scarf of spangled flame,
    The Pharos of the shore.

To-night yon pilot shall not sleep,
    Who trims his narrowed sail;
To-night yon frigate scarce shall keep
    Her broad breast to the gale;
And many a foresail, scooped and strained,
    Shall break from yard and stay,
Before this smoky wreath has stained
    The rising mist of day.

Hark! hark! I hear yon whistling shroud,
    I see yon quivering mast;
The black throat of the hunted cloud
    Is panting forth the blast!
An hour, and, whirled like winnowing chaff,
    The giant surge shall fling
His tresses o'er yon pennon staff,
    White as the sea-bird's wing!

Yet rest, ye wanderers of the deep ;
 Nor wind nor wave shall tire
Those fleshless arms, whose pulses leap
 With floods of living fire ;
Sleep on,—and, when the morning light
 Streams o'er the shining bay,
Oh, think of those for whom the night
 Shall never wake in day !

THE PARTING WORD.

I must leave thee, lady sweet!
Months shall waste before we meet;
Winds are fair, and sails are spread,
Anchors leave their ocean bed;
Ere this shining day grow dark,
Skies shall gird my shoreless bark;
Through thy tears, O lady mine,
Read thy lover's parting line.

When the first sad sun shall set,
Thou shalt tear thy locks of jet;
When the morning star shall rise
Thou shalt wake with weeping eyes;
When the second sun goes down,
Thou more tranquil shalt be grown,
Taught too well that wild despair
Dims thine eyes, and spoils thy hair.

All the first unquiet week
Thou shalt wear a smileless cheek;
In the first month's second half
Thou shalt once attempt to laugh;
Then in Pickwick thou shalt dip,
Slightly puckering round the lip,
Till at last, in sorrow's spite,
Samuel makes thee laugh outright.

135

While the first seven mornings last,
Round thy chamber bolted fast,
Many a youth shall fume and pout,
" Hang the girl, she's always out!"
While the second week goes round,
Vainly shall they ring and pound;
When the third week shall begin,
" Martha, let the creature in."

Now once more the flattering throng
Round thee flock with smile and song,
But thy lips, unweaned as yet,
Lisp, " Oh, how can I forget!"
Men and devils both contrive
Traps for catching girls alive;
Eve was duped, and Helen kissed,—
How, oh, how can you resist?

First be careful of your fan,
Trust it not to youth or man;
Love has filled a pirate's sail
Often with its perfumed gale.
Mind your kerchief most of all,
Fingers touch when kerchiefs fall;
Shorter ell than mercers clip,
Is the space from hand to lip.

Trust not such as talk in tropes,
Full of pistols, daggers, ropes;
All the hemp that Russia bears
Scarce would answer lovers' prayers;

Never thread was spun so fine,
Never spider stretched the line,
Would not hold the lovers true
That would really swing for you.

Fiercely some shall storm and swear,
Beating breasts in black despair;
Others murmur with a sigh,
You must melt or they will die;
Painted words on empty lies,
Grubs with wings like butterflies;
Let them die, and welcome, too;
Pray what better could they do?

Fare thee well, if years efface
From thy heart love's burning trace,
Keep, oh keep that hallowed seat
From the tread of vulgar feet;
If the blue lips of the sea
Wait with icy kiss for me,
Let not thine forget the vow,
Sealed how often, Love, as now!

SONG,

WRITTEN FOR THE DINNER GIVEN TO CHARLES DICKENS, BY THE YOUNG MEN OF BOSTON, FEBRUARY 1, 1842.

THE stars their early vigils keep,
    The silent hours are near
When drooping eyes forget to weep,—
    Yet still we linger here;
And what,—the passing churl may ask,—
    Can claim such wondrous power,
That Toil forgets his wonted task,
    And Love his promised hour?

The Irish harp no longer thrills,
    Or breathes a fainter tone;
The clarion blast from Scotland's hills
    Alas! no more is blown;
And Passion's burning lip bewails
    Her Harold's wasted fire,
Still lingering o'er the dust that veils
    The Lord of England's lyre.

But grieve not o'er its broken strings,
    Nor think its soul hath died,
While yet the lark at heaven's gate sings
    As once o'er Avon's side;

138

While gentle summer sheds her bloom,
 And dewy blossoms wave,
Alike o'er Juliet's storied tomb
 And Nelly's nameless grave.

Thou glorious island of the sea!
 Though wide the wasting flood
That parts our distant land from thee,
 We claim thy generous blood;
Nor o'er thy far horizon springs
 One hallowed star of fame,
But kindles, like an angel's wings,
 Our western skies in flame!

LINES

COME back to your mother, ye children, for shame,
Who have wandered like truants, for riches or
 fame !
With a smile on her face, and a sprig in her cap,
She calls you to feast from her bountiful lap.

Come out from your alleys, your courts, and your
 lanes,
And breathe, like young eagles, the air of our plains ;
Take a whiff from our fields, and your excellent wives
Will declare it's all nonsense insuring your lives.

Come you of the law, who can talk, if you please,
Till the man in the moon will allow it's a cheese,
And leave " the old lady, that never tells lies,"
To sleep with her handkerchief over her eyes.

Ye healers of men, for a moment decline
Your feats in the rhubarb and ipecac line ;
While you shut up your turnpike, your neighbors
 can go
The old roundabout road, to the regions below.
 140

You clerk, on whose ears are a couple of pens,
And whose head is an ant-hill of units and tens;
Though Plato denies you, we welcome you still
As a featherless biped, in spite of your quill.

Poor drudge of the city! how happy he feels,
With the burs on his legs, and the grass at his
    heels!
No *dodger* behind, his bandannas to share,
No constable grumbling, " You mustn't walk
    there!"

In yonder green meadow, to memory dear,
He slaps a mosquito and brushes a tear;
The dewdrops hang round him on blossoms and
    shoots,
He breathes but one sigh for his youth and his
    boots.

There stands the old schoolhouse, hard by the old
    church;
That tree at its side had the flavor of birch;
Oh, sweet were the days of his juvenile tricks,
Though the prarie of youth had so many " big
    licks."

By the side of yon river he weeps and he slumps,
The boots fill with water, as if they were pumps;
Till, sated with rapture, he steals to his bed,
With a glow in his heart and a cold in his head.

'Tis past,—he is dreaming,—I see him again ;
The ledger returns as by legerdemain ;
His neckcloth is damp with an easterly flaw,
And he holds in his fingers an omnibus straw.

He dreams the chill gust is a blossomy gale,
That the straw is a rose from his dear native vale ;
And murmurs, unconscious of space and of time,
" A 1. Extra-super. Ah, isn't it PRIME ! "

Oh, what are the prizes we perish to win
To the first little " shiner " we caught with a pin !
No soil upon earth is so dear to our eyes
As the soil we first stirred in terrestrial pies !

Then come from all parties, and parts, to our feast;
Though not at the " Astor," we'll give you at least
A bite at an apple, a seat on the grass,
And the best of old—water—at nothing a glass.

VERSES FOR AFTER-DINNER.

Φ. B. K. SOCIETY, 1844.

I was thinking last night, as I sat in the cars,
With the charmingest prospect of cinders and stars,
Next Thursday is—bless me!—how hard it will
     be,
If that cannibal president calls upon me!

There is nothing on earth that he will not devour,
From a tutor in seed to a freshman in flower;
No sage is too gray, and no youth is too green,
And you can't be too plump, though you're never
     too lean.

While others enlarge on the boiled and the roast,
He serves a raw clergyman up with a toast,
Or catches some doctor, quite tender and young,
And basely insists on a bit of his tongue.

Poor victim, prepared for his classical spit,
With a stuffing of praise, and a basting of wit,
You may twitch at your collar, and wrinkle your
     brow,
But you're up on your legs, and you're in for it
     now.

143

Oh, think of your friends,—they are waiting to
    hear
Those jokes that are thought so remarkably queer;
And all the Jack Horners of metrical buns
Are prying and fingering to pick out the puns.

Those thoughts which, like chickens, will always
    thrive best
When reared by the heat of the natural nest,
Will perish if hatched from their embryo dream
In the mist and the glow of convivial steam.

Oh pardon me, then, if I meekly retire,
With a very small flash of ethereal fire ;
No rubbing will kindle your Lucifer match,
If the *fiz* does not follow the primitive scratch.

Dear friends, who are listening so sweetly the while,
With your lips double reefed in a snug little
    smile,—
I leave you two fables, both drawn from the
    deep,—
The shells you can drop, but the pearls you may
    keep.

*   *   *   *   *   *

The fish called the FLOUNDER, perhaps you may know,
Has one side for use and another for show ;
One side for the public, a delicate brown,
And one that is white, which he always keeps
    down.

A very young flounder, the flattest of flats
(And they're none of them thicker than opera hats),
Was speaking more freely than charity taught
Of a friend and relation that just had been caught.

" My ! what an exposure ! just see what a sight !
I blush for my race,—he is showing his white !
Such spinning and wriggling,—why, what does he
    wish ?
How painfully small to respectable fish ! "

Then said an old SCULPIN,—" My freedom excuse,
But you're playing the cobbler with holes in your
    shoes ;
Your brown side is up,—but just wait till you're
    tried,
And you'll find that all flounders are white on one
    side."

     *   *   *   *   *   *

There's a slice near the PICKEREL's pectoral fins,
Where the *thorax* leaves off and the *venter* begins ;
Which his brother, survivor of fish-hooks and lines
Though fond of his family, never declines.

He loves his relations ; he feels they'll be missed ;
But that one little tit-bit he cannot resist ;
So your bait may be swallowed, no matter how
    fast,
For you catch your next fish with a piece of the
    last.

And thus, O survivor, whose merciless fate
Is to take the next hook with the president's bait,
You are lost while you snatch from the end of his
    line
The morsel he rent from this bosom of mine!

SONG.

FOR A TEMPERANCE DINNER TO WHICH LADIES WERE INVITED. (NEW YORK MERCANTILE LIBRARY ASSOCIATION, NOVEMBER, 1842.)

A HEALTH to dear woman! She bids us untwine,
From the cup it encircles, the fast-clinging vine;
But her cheek in its crystal with pleasure will glow,
And mirror its bloom in the bright wave below.

A health to sweet woman! Ahe days are no more
When she watched for her lord till the revel was o'er,
And smoothed the white pillow, and blushed when
    he came,
As she pressed her cold lips on his forehead of
    flame.
Alas for the loved one! too spotless and fair
The joys of his banquet to chasten and share;
Her eye lost its light that his goblet might shine,
And the rose of her cheek was dissolved in his
    wine.

Joy smiles in the fountain, health flows in the rills,
As their ribands of silver unwind from the hills;
They breathe not the mist of the bacchanal's
    dream,
But the lilies of innocence float on their stream.

147

Then a health and a welcome to woman once
    more!
She brings up a passport that laughs at our door ;
It is written on crimson,—its letters are pearls,—
It is countersigned *Nature.*——So, room for the
    Girls!

THE ONLY DAUGHTER.

(ILLUSTRATION OF A PICTURE.)

THEY bid me strike the idle strings,
   As if my summer days
Had shaken sunbeams from their wings,
   To warm my autumn lays ;
They bring to me their painted urn,
   As if it were not time
To lift my gauntlet and to spurn
   The lists of boyish rhyme;
And, were it not that I have still
   Some weakness in my heart
That clings around my stronger will
   And pleads for gentler art,
Perchance I had not turned away
   The thoughts grown tame with toil,
To cheat this lone and pallid ray,
   That wastes the midnight oil.

Alas! with every year I feel
   Some roses leave my brow ;
Too young for wisdom's tardy seal,
   Too old for garlands now ;
Yet, while the dewy breath of spring
   Steals o'er the tingling air,

And spreads and fans each emerald wing
　　The forest soon shall wear,
How bright the opening year would seem,
　　Had I one look like thine,
To meet me when the morning beam
　　Unseals these lids of mine!
Too long I bear this lonely lot,
　　That bids my heart run wild
To press the lips that love me not,
　　To clasp the stranger's child.

How oft beyond the dashing seas,
　　Amidst those royal bowers,
Where danced the lilacs in the breeze,
　　And swung the chestnut flowers,
I wandered like a wearied slave
　　Whose morning task is done,
To watch the little hands that gave
　　Their whiteness to the sun;
To revel in the bright young eyes,
　　Whose lustre sparkled through
The sable fringe of southern skies,
　　Or gleamed in Saxon blue!
How oft I heard another's name
　　Called in some truant's tone;
Sweet accents! which I longed to claim,
　　To learn and lisp my own!

Too soon the gentle hands, that pressed
　　The ringlets of the child,
Are folded on the faithful breast
　　Where first he breathed and smiled;

Too oft the clinging arms untwine,
 The melting lips forget,
And darkness veils the bridal shrine
 Where wreaths and torches met;
If Heaven but leaves a single thread
 Of Hope's dissolving chain,
Even when her parting plumes are spread,
 It bids them fold again;
The cradle rocks beside the tomb;
 The cheek now changed and chill,
Smiles on us in the morning bloom
 Of one that loves us still.

Sweet image! I have done thee wrong
 To claim this destined lay;
The leaf that asked an idle song
 Must bear my tears away.
Yet, in thy memory shouldst thou keep
 This else forgotten strain,
Till years have taught thine eyes to weep
 And flattery's voice is vain;
Oh, then, thou fledgling of the nest,
 Like the long-wandering dove,
Thy weary heart may faint for rest,
 As mine, on changeless love;
And, while these sculptured lines retrace
 The hours now dancing by,
This vision of thy girlish grace
 May cost thee, too, a sigh.

LEXINGTON.

Slowly the mist o'er the meadow was creeping,
  Bright on the dewy buds glistened the sun,
When from his couch, while his children were
    sleeping,
  Rose the bold rebel and shouldered his gun.
      Waving her golden veil
      Over the silent dale
Blithe looked the morning on cottage and spire;
      Hushed was his parting sigh,
      While from his noble eye
Flashed the last sparkle of liberty's fire.

On the smooth green where the fresh leaf is spring-
    ing
  Calmly the first-born of glory have met;
Hark! the death-volley around them is ringing!
  Look! with their life-blood the young grass is
    wet!
      Faint is the feeble breath,
      Murmuring low in death,
" Tell to our sons how their fathers have died;"
      Nerveless the iron hand,
      Raised for its native land,
Lies by the weapon that gleams at its side.

Over the hillsides the wild knell is tolling,
  From their far hamlets the yeomanry come

As through the storm-clouds the thunder-burst roll-
    ing
  Circles the beat of the mustering drum.
      Fast on the soldier's path
      Darken the waves of wrath,
Long have they gathered and loud shall they fall;
      Red glares the musket's flash,
      Sharp rings the rifle's crash,
Blazing and clanging from thicket and wall.

Gayly the plume of the horseman was dancir g,
  Never to shadow his cold brow again ;
Proudly at morning the war-steed was prancing,
  Reeking and panting he droops on the rein ;
      Pale is the lip of scorn,
      Voiceless the trumpet horn,
Torn is the silken-fringed red cross on high;
      Many a belted breast
      Low on the turf shall rest,
Ere the dark hunters the herd have past by.

Snow-girdled crags where the hoarse wind is raving,
  Rocks where the weary floods murmur and wail,
Wilds where the fern by the furrow is waving,
  Reeled with the echoes that rode on the gale ;
      Far as the tempest thrills
      Over the darkened hills,
Far as the sunshine streams over the plain,
      Roused by the tyrant band,
      Woke all the mighty land,
Girded for battle, from mountain to main.

Green be the graves where her martyrs are lying !
  Shroudless and tombless they sunk to their rest,—
While o'er their ashes the starry fold flying
  Wraps the proud eagle they roused from his
      nest.
         Borne on her northern pine,
         Long o'er the foaming brine
Spread her broad banner to storm and to sun ;
         Heaven keep her ever free,
         Wide as o'er land and sea
Floats the fair emblem her heroes have won.

THE ISLAND HUNTING SONG.

No more the summer floweret charms,
    The leaves will soon be sere,
And Autumn folds his jewelled arms
    Around the dying year;
So, ere the waning seasons claim
    Our leafless groves awhile,
With golden wine and glowing flame
    We'll crown our lonely isle.

Once more the merry voices sound
    Within the antlered hall,
And long and loud the baying hounds
    Return the hunter's call;
And through the woods, and o'er the hill,
    And far along the bay,
The driver's horn is sounding shrill,—
    Up, sportsmen, and away!

No bars of steel, or walls of stone,
    Our little empire bound,
But, circling with his azure zone,
    The sea runs foaming round;
The whitening wave, the purpled skies,
    The blue and lifted shore,
Braid with their dim and blending dyes
    Our wide horizon o'er.

And who will leave the grave debate
    That shakes the smoky town,
To rule amid our island-state,
    And wear our oak-leaf crown?
And who will be awhile content
    To hunt our woodland game,
And leave the vulgar pack that scent
    The reeking track of fame?

Ah, who that shares in toils like these
    Will sigh not to prolong
Our days beneath the broad-leaved trees,
    Our nights of mirth and song?
Then leave the dust of noisy streets,
    Ye outlaws of the wood,
And follow through his green retreats
    Your noble Robin Hood.

QUESTIONS AND ANSWERS.

Where, oh where are the visions of morning,
    Fresh as the dews of our prime?
Gone, like tenants that quit without warning,
    Down the back entry of time.

Where, oh where are life's lilies and roses,
    Nursed in the golden dawn's smile?
Dead as the bulrushes round little Moses,
    On the old banks of the Nile.

Where are the Marys, and Anns, and Elizas,
    Loving and lovely of yore?
Look in the columns of old *Advertisers,*—
    Married and dead by the score.

Where the gray colts and the ten-year-old fillies,
    Saturday's triumph and joy?
Gone like our friend πόδας ὠχυς Achilles,
    Homer's ferocious old boy.

Die-away dreams of ecstatic emotion,
    Hopes like young eagles at play,
Vows of unheard-of and endless devotion,
    How ye have faded away!

Yet, though the ebbing of Time's mighty river
    Leave our young blossoms to die,
Let him roll smooth in his current forever,
    Till the last pebble is dry.

157

A SONG,

WHEN the Puritans came over,
    Our hills and swamps to clear,
The woods were full of catamounts,
    And Indians red as deer,
With tomahawks and scalping-knives,
    That make folks' heads look queer ;—
Oh, the ship from England used to bring
    A hundred wigs a year !

The crows came cawing through the air
    To pluck the pilgrims' corn,
The bears came snuffing round the door
    Whene'er a babe was born,
The rattlesnakes were bigger round
    Than the butt of the old ram's horn
The deacon blew at meeting time
    On every " Sabbath " morn.

But soon they knocked the wigwams down,
    And pine-tree trunk and limb
Began to sprout among the leaves
    In shape of steeples slim ;

158

And out the little wharves were stretched
    Along the ocean's rim,
And up the little schoolhouse shot
    To keep the boys in trim.

And when, at length, the College rose,
    The sachem cocked his eye
At every tutor's meagre ribs
    Whose coat-tails whistled by ;
But, when the Greek and Hebrew words
    Came tumbling from their jaws,
The copper-colored children all
    Ran screaming to the squaws.

And who was on the Catalogue
    When college was begun ?
Two nephews of the President,
    And *the* Professor's son,
(They turned a little Indian by,
    As brown as any bun) ;
Lord ! how the seniors knocked about
    The freshman class of one !

They had not then the dainty things
    That commons now afford,
But *succotash* and *hominy*
    Were smoking on the board ;
They did not rattle round in gigs,
    Or dash in long-tail blues,
But always on Commencement Days
    The tutors blacked their shoes.

God bless the ancient Puritans!
   Their lot was hard enough;
But honest hearts make iron arms,
   And tender maids are tough;
So love and faith have formed and fed
   Our true-born Yankee stuff,
And keep the kernel in the shell
   The British found so rough!

TERPSICHORE.[1]

In narrowest girdle, O reluctant Muse,
In closest frock and Cinderella shoes,
Bound to the foot-lights for thy brief display,
One zephyr step, and then dissolve away !

———

Short is the space that gods and men can spare
To Song's twin brother when she is not there.
Let others water every lusty line,
As Homer's heroes did their purple wine;
Pierian revellers !   Known in strains like these
The native juice, the real honest squeeze,—
Strains that, diluted to the twentieth power,
In yon grave temple [2] might have filled an hour.

Small room for Fancy's many-chorded lyre,
For Wit's bright rockets with their trains of fire,
For Pathos, struggling vainly to surprise
The iron tutor's tear denying eyes,
For Mirth, whose finger with delusive wile

[1] Read at the Annual Dinner of the Φ. B. K. Society, at Cambridge, August 24, 1843.
[2] The Annual Poem is always delivered in the neighboring church.

Turns the grim key of many a rusty smile,
For Satire, emptying his corrosive flood
On hissing Folly's gas-exhaling brood,
The pun, the fun, the moral and the joke,
The hit, the thrust, the pugilistic poke,—
Small space for these, so pressed by niggard Time,
Like that false matron, known to nursery rhyme,—
Insidious Morey,—scarce her tale begun,
Ere listening infants weep the story done.

O had we room to rip the mighty bags
That Time, the harlequin, has stuffed with rags!
Grant us one moment to unloose the strings,
While the old gray-beard shuts his leather wings.
But what a heap of motley trash appears
Crammed in the bundles of successive years!
As the lost rustic on some festal day
Stares through the concourse in its vast array,—
Where in one cake a throng of faces runs,
All stuck together like a sheet of buns,—
And throws the bait of some unheeded name,
Or shoots a wink with most uncertain aim,
So roams my vision, wandering over all,
And strives to choose, but knows not where to fall.

Skins of flayed authors,—husks of dead reviews,—
The turn-coat's clothes,—the office-seeker's shoes,—
Scraps from cold feasts, where conversation runs
Through mouldy toasts to oxidated puns,
And grating songs a listening crowd endures,
Rasped from the throats of bellowing amateurs ;—

Sermons, whose writers played such dangerous tricks
Their own heresiarchs called them heretics
(Strange that one term such distant poles should
   link,
The Priestleyan's copper and the Puseyan's zinc) ;—
Poems that shuffle with superfluous legs
A blindfold minuet over addled eggs,
Where all the syllables that end in éd,
Like old dragoons, have cuts across the head ;—
Essays so dark Champollion might despair
To guess what mummy of a thought was there,
Where our poor English, striped with foreign phrase,
Looks like a Zebra in a parson's chaise ;—
Lectures that cut our dinners down to roots,
Or prove (by monkeys) men should stick to fruits ;
Delusive error,—as at trifling charge
Professor Gripes will certify at large ;—
Mesmeric pamphlets, which to facts appeal,
Each fact as slippery as a fresh-caught eel ;—
And figured heads, whose hieroglyphs invite
To wandering knaves that discount fools at sight ;—
Such things as these, with heaps of unpaid bills,
And candy puffs and homœopathic pills,
And ancient bell-crowns with contracted rim,
And bonnets hideous with expanded brim,
And coats whose memory turns the sartor pale,
Their sequels tapering like a lizard's tail ;—
How might we spread them to the smiling day,
And toss them, fluttering like the new-mown hay,
To laughter's light or sorrow's pitying shower,
Were these brief minutes lengthened to an hour.

The narrow moments fit like Sunday shoes,
How vast the heap, how quickly must we choose;
A few small scraps from out his mountain mass
We snatch in haste, and let the vagrant pass.

This shrunken CRUST that Cerberus could not bite,
Stamped (in one corner) " Pickwick copyright,"
Kneaded by youngsters, raised by flattery's yeast,
Was once a loaf, and helped to make a feast.
He for whose sake the glittering show appears
Has sown the world with laughter and with tears,
And they whose welcome wets the bumper's brim
Have wit and wisdom,—for they all quote him.
So, many a tongue the evening hour prolongs
With spangled speeches,—let alone the songs,—
Statesmen grow merry, lean attorneys laugh,
And weak teetotals warm to half and half,
And beardless Tullys, new to festive scenes,
Cut their first crop of youth's precocious greens,
And wits stand ready for impromptu claps,
With loaded barrels and percussion caps,
And Pathos, cantering through the minor keys,
Waves all her onions to the trembling breeze;
While the great yeasted views with silent glee
His scattered limbs in Yankee fricassee.

Sweet is the scene where genial friendship plays
The pleasing game of interchanging praise;
Self-love, grimalkin of the human heart,
Is ever pliant to the master's art;
Soothed with a word, she peacefully withdraws
And sheathes in velvet her obnoxious claws,

And thrills the hand that smooths her glossy fur
With the light tremor of her grateful purr.

But what sad music fills the quiet hall,
If on her back a feline rival fall;
And oh, what noises shake the tranquil house,
If old Self-interest cheats her of a mouse!

Thou, O my country, hast thy foolish ways,
Too apt to purr at every stranger's praise;
But, if the stranger touch thy modes or laws,
Off goes the velvet and out come the claws!
And thou, Illustrious! but too poorly paid
In toasts from Pickwick for thy great crusade,
Though, while the echoes labored with thy name,
The public trap denied thy little game,
Let other lips our jealous laws revile,—
The marble Talfourd or the rude Carlyle,—
But on thy lids, that Heaven forbids to close
Where'er the light of kindly nature glows,
Let not the dollars that a churl denies
Weigh like the shillings on a dead man's eyes!
Or, if thou wilt, be more discreetly blind,
Nor ask to see all wide extremes combined.

Not in our wastes the dainty blossoms smile,
That crowd the gardens of thy scanty isle.
There white-cheeked Luxury weaves a thousand
    charms;—
Here sun-browned Labor swings his naked arms.
Long are the furrows he must trace between
The ocean's azure and the prairie's green;

Full many a blank his destined realm displays,
Yet see the promise of his riper days:
Far through yon depths the panting engine moves,
His chariots ringing in their steel-shod grooves;
And Erie's naiad flings her diamond wave
O'er the wild sea-nymph in her distant cave!
While tasks like these employ his anxious hours,
What if his corn-fields are not edged with flowers?
Though bright as silver the meridian beams
Shine through the crystal of thine English streams,
Turbid and dark the mighty wave is whirled
That drains our Andes and divides a world!

But lo! a PARCHMENT! Surely it would seem
The sculptured impress speaks of power supreme;
Some grave design the solemn page must claim
That shows so broadly an emblazoned name:
A sovereign's promise! Look, the lines afford
All Honor gives when Caution asks his word;
There sacred Faith has laid her snow-white hands,
And awful Justice knit her iron bands;
Yet every leaf is stained with treachery's dye,
And every letter crusted with a lie.
Alas! no treason has degraded yet
The Arab's salt, the Indian's calumet;
A simple rite, that bears the wanderer's pledge,
Blunts the keen shaft and turns the dagger's edge;
While jockeying senates stop to sign and seal,
And freeborn statesmen legislate to steal.
Rise, Europe, tottering with thine Atlas load,
Turn thy proud eye to Freedom's blest abode,

And round her forehead, wreathed with heavenly
    flame,
Bind the dark garland of her daughter's shame!
Ye ocean clouds, that wrap the angry blast,
Coil her stained ensign round its haughty mast,
Or tear the fold that wears so foul a scar,
And drive a bolt through every blackened star!
Once more,—once only,—we must stop so soon,—
What have we here? A GERMAN-SILVER SPOON;
A cheap utensil, which we often see
Used by the dabblers in æsthetic tea;
Of slender fabric, somewhat light and thin,
Made of mixed metal, chiefly lead and tin;
The bowl is shallow, and the handle small
Marked in large letters with the name JEAN PAUL.
Small as it is, its powers are passing strange,
For all who use it show a wondrous change;
And first, a fact to make the barbers stare,
It beats Macassar for the growth of hair;
See those small youngsters whose expansive ears
Maternal kindness grazed with frequent shears;
Each bristling crop a dangling mass becomes,
And all the spoonies turn to Absaloms!

Nor this alone its magic power displays,
It alters strangely all their works and ways;
With uncouth words they tire their tender lungs,
The same bald phrases on their hundred tongues:
"Ever" "The Ages" in their page appear,
"Alway" the bedlamite is called a "Seer";

On every leaf the " earnest " sage may scan,
Portentous bore! their " many-sided " man,—
A weak eclectic, groping vague and dim,
Whose every angle is a half-starved whim,
Blind as a mole and curious as a lynx,
Who rides a beetle, which he calls a " Sphinx."
And oh what questions asked in club-foot rhyme
Of Earth the tongueless and the deaf-mute Time!
Here babbling " Insight " shouts in Nature's ears
His last conundrum on the orbs and spheres;
There Self-inspection sucks its little thumb,
With " Whence am I?" and " Wherefore did I
      come?"
Deluded infants! will they ever know
Some doubts must darken o'er the world below,
Though all the Platos of the nursery trail
Their " clouds of glory " at the go-cart's tail?
O might these couplets their attention claim,
That gain their author the Philistine's name;
(A stubborn race, that, spurning foreign law,
Was much belabored with an ass's jaw!)

Melodious Laura!   From the sad retreats
That hold thee, smothered with excess of sweets,
Shade of a shadow, spectre of a dream,
Glance thy wan eye across the Stygian stream!
The slip-shod dreamer treads thy fragrant halls,
The sophist's cobwebs hang thy roseate walls,
And o'er the crotchets of thy jingling tunes
The bard of mystery scrawls his crooked " runes."

Yes, thou art gone, with all the tuneful hordes
That candied thoughts in amber-colored words,
And in the precincts of thy late abodes
The clattering verse-wright hammers Orphic odes.
Thou, soft as zephyr, wast content to fly
On the gilt pinions of a balmy sigh;
He, vast as Phœbus on his burning wheels,
Would stride through ether at Orion's heels;
Thy emblem, Laura, was a perfume-jar,
And thine, young Orpheus, is a pewter star;
The balance trembles,—be its verdict told
When the new jargon slumbers with the old!

Cease, playful goddess! From thine airy bound
Drop like a feather softly to the ground;
This light bolero grows a ticklish dance,
And there is mischief in thy kindling glance.
To-morrow bids thee, with rebuking frown,
Change thy gauze tunic for a home-made gown,
Too blest by fortune, if the passing day
Adorn thy bosom with its frail bouquet,
But oh still happier if the next forgets
Thy daring steps and dangerous pirouettes!

URANIA:

A RHYMED LESSON.[1]

YES, dear Enchantress,—wandering far and long,
In realms unperfumed by the breath of song,
Where flowers ill-flavored shed their sweets around,
And bitterest roots invade the ungenial ground,
Whose gems are crystals from the Epsom mine,
Whose vineyards flow with antimonial wine,
Whose gates admit no mirthful feature in,
Save one gaunt mocker, the Sardonic grin,
Whose pangs are real, not the woes of rhyme
That blue-eyed misses warble out of time;—
Truant, not recreant to thy sacred claim,
Older by reckoning, but in heart the same,
Freed for a moment from the chains of toil,
I tread once more thy consecrated soil:
Here at thy feet my old allegiance own,
Thy subject still, and loyal to thy throne!

My dazzled glance explores the crowded hall;
Alas, how vain to hope the smiles of all!
I know my audience.   All the gay and young
Love the light antics of a playful tongue;

[1] This poem was delivered before the Boston Mercantile
Library Association, October 14, 1846.

170

And these, remembering some expansive line
My lips let loose among the nuts and wine,
Are all impatience till the opening pun
Proclaim the witty shamfight is begun.
Two fifths at least, if not the total half,
Have come infuriate for an earthquake laugh ;
I know full well what alderman has tied
His red bandanna tight about his side ;
I see the mother, who, aware that boys
Perform their laughter with superfluous noise,
Besides her kerchief, brought an extra one
To stop the explosions of her bursting son ;
I know a tailor, once a friend of mine,
Expects great doings in the button line ;—
For mirth's concussions rip the outward case,
And plant the stitches in a tenderer place.
I know my audience ;—these shall have their due ;
A smile awaits them ere my song is through !

I know myself.   Not servile for applause,
My Muse permits no deprecating clause ;
Modest or vain, she will not be denied
One bold confession, due to honest pride ;
And well she knows, the drooping veil of song
Shall save her boldness from the caviller's wrong.
Her sweeter voice the Heavenly Maid imparts
To tell the secrets of our aching hearts ;
For this, a suppliant, captive, prostrate, bound,
She kneels imploring at the feet of sound ;
For this, convulsed in thought's maternal pains,
She loads her arms with rhyme's resounding chains ;

Faint though the music of her fetters be,
It lends one charm ;—her lips are ever free!

Think not I come, in manhood's fiery noon,
To steal his laurels from the stage buffoon ;
His sword of lath the harlequin may wield ;
Behold the star upon my lifted shield !
Though the just critic pass my humble name,
And sweeter lips have drained the cup of fame,
While my gay stanza pleased the banquet's lords,
The soul within was tuned to deeper chords !
Say, shall my arms, in other conflicts taught
To swing aloft the ponderous mace of thought,
Lift, in obedience to a school-girl's law,
Mirth's tinsel wand or laughter's tickling straw ?
Say, shall I wound with satire's rankling spear
The pure, warm hearts that bid me welcome here?
No ! while I wander through the land of dreams
To strive with great and play with trifling themes,
Let some kind meaning fill the varied line ;
You have your judgment ; will you trust to mine ?

BETWEEN two breaths what crowded mysteries
    lie,—
The first short gasp, the last and long-drawn sigh!
Like phantoms painted on the magic slide,
Forth from the darkness of the past we glide,

As living shadows for a moment seen
In airy pageant on the eternal screen,

Traced by a ray from one unchanging flame,
Then seek the dust and stillness whence we came.

But whence and why, our trembling souls in-
quire,
Caught these dim visions their awakening fire?
Oh, who forgets when first the piercing thought
Through childhood's musings found its way un-
sought.
I AM ;—I LIVE. The mystery and the fear
When the dread question—WHAT HAS BROUGHT ME
HERE?
Burst through life's twilight, as before the sun
Roll the deep thunders of the morning gun!

Are angel faces, silent and serene,
Bent on the conflicts of this little scene,
Whose dreamlike efforts, whose unreal strife,
Are but the preludes to a larger life?

Or does life's summer see the end of all,
These leaves of being mouldering as they fall,
As the old poet vaguely used to deem,
As WESLEY questioned in his youthful dream?[1]
O could such mockery reach our souls indeed,
Give back the Pharaohs' or the Athenian's creed;
Better than this a heaven of man's device,—
The Indian's sports, the Moslem's paradise!

---

[1] Ογη περ φύλλων γενεή, τοιήδε καὶ ἀνδρῶν.

Iliad VI., 146.

Wesley quotes this line in his account of his early doubts
and perplexities. See Southey's *Life of Wesley*, vol. ii., p. 185.

Or is our being's only end and aim
To add new glories to our Maker's name,
As the poor insect, shrivelling in the blaze,
Lends a faint sparkle to its streaming rays?
Does earth send upwards to the Eternal's ear
The mingled discords of her jarring sphere
To swell his anthem, while Creation rings
With notes of anguish from its shattered strings?
Is it for this the immortal Artist means
These conscious, throbbing, agonized machines?

Dark is the soul whose sullen creed can bind
In chains like these the all-embracing Mind;
No! two-faced bigot, thou dost ill reprove
The sensual, selfish, yet benignant Jove,
And praise a tyrant throned in lonely pride,
Who loves himself, and cares for naught beside;
Who gave thee, summoned from primeval night,
A thousand laws, and not a single right,
A heart to feel and quivering nerves to thrill,
The sense of wrong, the death-defying will;
Who girt thy senses with this goodly frame,
Its earthly glories and its orbs of flame,
Not for thyself, unworthy of a thought,
Poor helpless victim of a life unsought,
But all for him, unchanging and supreme,
The heartless centre of thy frozen scheme!

Trust not the teacher with his lying scroll,
Who tears the charter of thy shuddering soul;
The God of love, who gave the breath that warms
All living dust in all its varied forms,

Asks not the tribute of a world like this
To fill the measure of his perfect bliss.
Though winged with life through all its radiant
 shores,
Creation flowed with unexhausted stores
Cherub and seraph had not yet enjoyed ;
For this he called thee from the quickening void !
Nor this alone ; a larger gift was thine,
A mightier purpose swelled his vast design ;
Thought,—conscience,—will,—to make them all
 thine own,
He rent a pillar from the eternal throne !

　Made in his image, thou must nobly dare
The thorny crown of sovereignty to share.
With eye uplifted it is thine to view,
From thine own centre, heaven's o'er-arching blue ;
So round thy heart a beaming circle lies
No fiend can blot, no hypocrite disguise ;
From all its orbs one cheering voice is heard,
Full to thine ear it bears the Father's word,
Now, as in Eden where his first-born trod :
" Seek thine own welfare, true to man and God ! "
　Think not too meanly of thy low estate ;
Thou hast a choice ; to choose is to create !
Remember whose the sacred lips that tell,
Angels approve thee when thy choice is well ;
Remember, One, a judge of righteous men,
Swore to spare Sodom if she held but ten !
Use well the freedom which thy Master gave,
(Think'st thou that Heaven can tolerate a slave ?)

And He who made thee to be just and true
Will bless thee, love thee,—ay, respect thee too!

Nature has placed thee on a changeful tide,
To breast its waves, but not without a guide;
Yet, as the needle will forget its aim,
Jarred by the fury of the electric flame,
As the true current it will falsely feel,
Warped from its axis by a freight of steel;
So will thy CONSCIENCE lose its balanced truth,
If passion's lightning fall upon thy youth ;
So the pure effluence quit its sacred hold,
Girt round too deeply with magnetic gold.

Go to yon tower, where busy science plies
Her vast antennæ, feeling through the skies;
That little vernier on whose slender lines
The midnight taper trembles as it shines,
A silent index, tracks the planets' march
In all their wanderings through the ethereal arch,
Tells through the mist where dazzled Mercury burns
And marks the spot where Uranus returns.
So, till by wrong or negligence effaced,
The living index which thy Maker traced
Repeats the line each starry Virtue draws
Through the wide circuit of creation's laws ;
Still tracks unchanged the everlasting ray
Where the dark shadows of temptation stray ;
But, once defaced, forgets the orbs of light,
And leaves thee wandering o'er the expanse of night!

" What is thy creed ? " a hundred lips inquire ;
"Thou seekest God beneath what Christian spire ?"
Nor ask they idly, for uncounted lies
Float upward on the smoke of sacrifice ;
When man's first incense rose above the plain,
Of earth's two altars one was built by Cain !

Uncursed by doubt, our earliest creed we take ;
We love the precepts for the teacher's sake ;
The simple lessons which the nursery taught
Fell soft and stainless on the buds of thought,
And the full blossom owes its fairest hue
To those sweet tear-drops of affection's dew.

Too oft the light that led our earlier hours
Fades with the perfume of our cradle flowers ;
The clear, cold question chills to frozen doubt ;
Tired of beliefs, we dread to live without ;
Oh, then, if reason waver at thy side,
Let humbler Memory be thy gentle guide ;
Go to thy birth-place, and, if faith was there,
Repeat thy father's creed, thy mother's prayer !

Faith loves to lean on Time's destroying arm,
And age, like distance, lends a double charm ;
In dim cathedrals, dark with vaulted gloom,
What holy awe invests the saintly tomb !
There pride will bow, and anxious care expand,
And creeping avarice come with open hand ;
The gay can weep, the impious can adore,
From morn's first glimmerings on the chancel floor
Till dying sunset sheds his crimson stains
Through the faint halos of the irised panes.

Yet there are graves, whose rudely shapen sod
Bears the fresh footprints where the sexton trod ;
Graves where the verdure has not dared to shoot,
Where the chance wild-flower has not fixed its root,
Whose slumbering tenants, dead without a name,
The eternal record shall at length proclaim
Pure as the holiest in the long array
Of hooded, mitred, or tiaraed clay !

Come, seek the air ; some pictures we may gain
Whose passing shadows shall not be in vain ;
Not from the scenes that crowd the stranger's soil,
Not from our own amidst the stir of toil,
But when the Sabbath brings its kind release,
And Care lies slumbering on the lap of Peace.

The air is hushed ; the street is holy ground ;
Hark! The sweet bells renew their welcome sound ;
As one by one awakes each silent tongue,
It tells the turret whence its voice is flung.[1]

The Chapel, last of sublunary things
That shocks our echoes with the name of Kings,

[1] The churches referred to in the lines which follow are—

1. " King's Chapel," the foundation of which was laid by Governor Shirley in 1749.

2. The church in Brattle Square, consecrated in 1773. The completion of this edifice, the design of which included a spire, was prevented by the troubles of the Revolution, and its plain square tower presents nothing more attractive than its massive simplicity. In the front of this tower is still seen, half embedded in the brick-work, a cannon-ball, which was thrown from the American fortification at Cambridge, during

Whose bell, just glistening from the font and forge,
Rolled its proud requiem for the second George,
Solemn and swelling, as of old it rang,
Flings to the wind its deep, sonorous clang ;—
The simpler pile, that, mindful of the hour
When Howe's artillery shook its half-built tower,
Wears on its bosom, as a bride might do,
The iron breastpin which the " Rebels " threw,
Wakes the sharp echoes with the quivering thrill
Of keen vibrations, tremulous and shrill ;—
Aloft, suspended in the morning's fire,
Crash the vast cymbals from the Southern spire ;—
The Giant, standing by the elm-clad green,
His white lance lifted o'er the silent scene,
Whirling in air his brazen goblet round,
Swings from its brim the swollen floods of sound ;—
While, sad with memories of the olden time,
The Northern Minstrel pours her tender chime,
Faint, single tones, that spell their ancient song,
But tears still follow as they breathe along.

Child of the soil, whom fortune sends to range
Where man and nature, faith and customs change,
Borne in thy memory, each familiar tone
Mourns on the winds that sigh in every zone.

the bombardment of the city, then occupied by the British
troops.

3. The " Old South," first occupied for public worship in
1730.

4. Park Street Church, built in 1809, the tall, white steeple
of which is the most conspicuous of all the Boston spires.

5. Christ Church, opened for public worship in 1723, and
containing a set of eight bells, the only chime in Boston.

When Ceylon sweeps thee with her perfumed breeze
Through the warm billows of the Indian seas;
When,—ship and shadow blended both in one,—
Flames o'er thy mast the equatorial sun,
From sparkling midnight to refulgent noon
Thy canvas swelling with the still monsoon;
When through thy shrouds the wild tornado sings,
And thy poor seabird folds her tattered wings,
Oft will delusion o'er thy senses steal,
And airy echoes ring the Sabbath peal!
Then, dim with grateful tears, in long array
Rise the fair town, the island-studded bay,
Home, with its smiling board, its cheering fire,
The half-choked welcome of the expecting sire,
The mother's kiss, and, still if aught remain,
Our whispering hearts shall aid the silent strain.—
    Ah, let the dreamer o'er the taffrail lean
To muse unheeded, and to weep unseen;
Fear not the tropic's dews, the evening's chills,
His heart lies warm among his triple hills !

    Turned from her path by this deceitful gleam,
My wayward fancy half forgets her theme;
See through the streets that slumbered in repose
The living current of devotion flows;
Its varied forms in one harmonious band,
Age leading childhood by its dimpled hand,
Want, in the robe whose faded edges fall
To tell of rags beneath the tartan shawl,
And wealth, in silks that, fluttering to appear,
Lift the deep borders of the proud cashmere.

See, but glance briefly, sorrow-worn and pale,
Those sunken cheeks beneath the widow's veil;
Alone she wanders where with *him* she trod,
No arm to stay her, but she leans on God.

While other doublets deviate here and there,
What secret handcuff binds that pretty pair?
Compactest couple! pressing side to side,—
Ah, the white bonnet that reveals the bride!
By the white neckcloth, with its straitened tie,
The sober hat, the Sabbath-speaking eye,
Severe and smileless, he that runs may read
The stern disciple of Geneva's creed;
Decent and slow, behold his solemn march;
Silent he enters through yon crowded arch.
A livelier bearing of the outward man,
The light-hued gloves, the undevout rattan,
Now smartly raised or half-profanely twirled,—
A bright, fresh twinkle from the week-day world,—
Tell their plain story;—yes, thine eyes behold
A cheerful Christian from the liberal fold.

Down the chill street that curves in gloomiest
    shade,
What marks betray yon solitary maid?
The cheek's red rose, that speaks of balmier air;
The Celtic blackness of her braided hair;[1]

[1] For the propriety of the term "*Celtic* blackness," see
Laurence's *Lectures* (Salem, 1828), pp. 452, 453. But the
ancient Celts appear to have been a xanthous, or fair-haired
race. See Pritchard's *Nat. Hist. of Man* (London, 1843), pp.
183, 193, 196.

The gilded missal in her kerchief tied ;
Poor Nora, exile from Killarney's side !

Sister in toil, though blanched by colder skies,
That left their azure in her downcast eyes,
See pallid Margaret, Labor's patient child,
Scarce weaned from home, the nursling of the wild
Where white Katahdin o'er the horizon shines,
And broad Penobscot dashes through the pines ;
Still, as she hastes, her careful fingers hold
The unfailing hymn-book in its cambric fold.
Six days at drudgery's heavy wheel she stands,
The seventh sweet morning folds her weary hands ;
Yes, child of suffering, thou may'st well be sure
He who ordained the Sabbath loves the poor !

This weekly picture faithful memory draws,
Nor claims the noisy tribute of applause ;
Faint is the glow such barren hopes can lend,
And frail the line that asks no loftier end.
Trust me, kind listener, I will yet beguile
Thy saddened features of the promised smile
This magic mantle thou must well divide,
It has its sable and its ermine side :
Yet, ere the lining of the robe appears,
Take thou in silence, what I give in tears.

Dear listening soul, this transitory scene
Of murmuring stillness, busily serene ;
This solemn pause, the breathing-space of man,
The halt of toil's exhausted caravan,
Comes sweet with music to thy wearied ear ;
Rise with its anthems to a holier sphere !

Deal meekly, gently, with the hopes that guide
The lowliest brother straying from thy side;
If right, they bid thee tremble for thine own,
If wrong, the verdict is for God alone!

What though the champions of thy faith esteem
The sprinkled fountain or baptismal stream;
Shall jealous passions in unseemly strife
Cross their dark weapons o'er the waves of life?

Let my free soul, expanding as it can,
Leave to his scheme the thoughtful Puritan;
But Calvin's dogma shall my lips deride?
In that stern faith my angel Mary died;—
Or ask if mercy's milder creed can save,
Sweet sister, risen from thy new-made grave?

True, the harsh founders of thy church reviled
That ancient faith, the trust of Erin's child;
Must thou be raking in the crumbled past
For racks and fagots in her teeth to cast?
See from the ashes of Helvetia's pile
The whitened skull of old Servetus smile!
Round her young heart thy "Romish Upas" threw
Its firm, deep fibres, strengthening as she grew;
Thy sneering voice may call them "Popish
     tricks,"—
Her Latin prayers, her dangling crucifix,—
But *De Profundis* blessed her father's grave;
That "idol" cross her dying mother gave!
What if some angel looks with equal eyes
On her and thee, the simple and the wise,

Writes each dark fault against thy brighter creed,
And drops a tear with every foolish bead !

Grieve, as thou must, o'er history's reeking page ;
Blush for the wrongs that stain thy happier age ;
Strive with the wanderer from the better path,
Bearing thy message meekly, not in wrath ;
Weep for the frail that err, the weak that fall,
Have thine own faith,—but hope and pray for all !

Faith ; Conscience ; Love.   A meaner task remains,
And humbler thoughts must creep in lowlier strains ;
Shalt thou be honest ?   Ask the wordly schools,
And all will tell thee knaves are busier fools :
Prudent ? Industrious ?   Let not modern pens
Instruct " Poor Richard's " fellow-citizens.
    Be firm ! one constant element in luck
Is genuine, solid, old Teutonic pluck ;
See yon tall shaft ; it felt the earthquake's thrill,
Clung to its base, and greets the sunrise still.

Stick to your aim ; the mongrel's hold will slip,
But only crowbars loose the bulldog's grip ;
Small as he looks, the jaw that never yields
Drags down the bellowing monarch of the fields !

Yet in opinions look not always back ;
Your wake is nothing, mind the coming track ;
Leave what you've done for what you have to do ;
Don't be " consistent," but be simply true.

Don't catch the fidgets; you have found your
    place
Just in the focus of a nervous race,
Fretful to change, and rabid to discuss,
Full of excitements, always in a fuss ;—
Think of the patriarchs ; then compare as men
These lean-cheeked maniacs of the tongue and pen !
Run, if you like, but try to keep your breath ;
Work like a man, but don't be worked to death ;
And with new notions,—let me change the rule,—
Don't strike the iron till it's slightly cool.

Choose well your *set ;* our feeble nature seeks
The aid of clubs, the countenance of cliques ;
And with this object settle first of all
Your weight of metal and your size of ball.
Track not the steps of such as hold you cheap,
Too mean to prize, though good enough to keep ;
The " real, genuine, no-mistake Tom Thumbs "
Are little people fed on great men's crumbs.
    Yet keep no followers of that hateful brood
That basely mingles with its wholesome food
The tumid reptile, which, the poet said,
Doth wear a precious jewel in his head.

If the wild filly, " Progress," thou would'st ride,
Have young companions ever at thy side ;
But, would'st thou stride the stanch old mare,
    " Success,"
Go with thine elders, though they please thee less.

Shun such as lounge through afternoons and eves,
And on thy dial write " Beware of thieves ! "
Felon of minutes, never taught to feel
The worth of treasures which thy fingers steal,
Pick my left pocket of its silver dime,
But spare the right,—it holds my golden time!

  Does praise delight thee? Choose some *ultra*
    side ;
A sure old recipe, and often tried ;
Be its apostle, congressman, or bard,
Spokesman, or jokesman, only drive it hard ;
But know the forfeit which thy choice abides,
For on two wheels the poor reformer rides,
One black with epithets the *anti* throws,
One white with flattery, painted by the *pros.*

  Though books on MANNERS are not out of print,
An honest tongue may drop a harmless hint.
  Stop not, unthinking, every friend you meet,
To spin your wordy fabric in the street ;
While you are emptying your colloquial pack,
The fiend *Lumbago* jumps upon his back.
  Nor cloud his features with the unwelcome tale
Of how he looks, if haply thin and pale ;
Health is a subject for his child, his wife,
And the rude office that insures his life.
  Look in his face, to meet thy neighbor's soul,
Not on his garments, to detect a hole ;
" How to observe," is what thy pages show,
Pride of thy sex, Miss Harriet Martineau !

Oh, what a precious book the one would be
That taught observers what they're *not* to see!

I tell in verse,—'twere better done in prose,—
One curious trick that everybody knows;
Once form this habit, and it's very strange
How long it sticks, how hard it is to change.
Two friendly people, both disposed to smile,
Who meet, like others, every little while,
Instead of passing with a pleasant bow,
And " How d'ye do? " or " How's your uncle now? "
Impelled by feelings in their nature kind,
But slightly weak, and somewhat undefined,
Rush at each other, make a sudden stand,
Begin to talk, expatiate, and expand;
Each looks quite radiant, seems extremely struck,
Their meeting so was such a piece of luck;
Each thinks the other thinks he's greatly pleased
To screw the vice in which they both are squeezed;
So there they talk, in dust, or mud, or snow,
Both bored to death, and both afraid to go!

Your hat once lifted, do not hang your fire,
Nor, like slow Ajax, fighting still, retire;
When your old castor on your crown you clap,
Go off; you've mounted your percussion cap!

Some words on LANGUAGE may be well applied,
And take them kindly, though they touch your
    pride;
Words leads to things; a scale is more precise,—
Coarse speech, bad grammar, swearing, drinking,
    vice.

Our cold Northeaster's icy fetter clips
The native freedom of the Saxon lips;
See the brown peasant of the plastic South,
How all his passions play about his mouth!
With us, the feature that transmits the soul,
A frozen, passive, palsied breathing-hole.
The crampy shackles of the ploughboy's walk
Tie the small muscles when he strives to talk;
Not all the pumice of the polished town
Can smooth this roughness of the barnyard down;
Rich, honored, titled, he betrays his race
By this one mark,—he's awkward in the face;—
Nature's rude impress, long before he knew
The sunny street that holds the sifted few.

It can't be helped, though, if we're taken young,
We gain some freedom of the lips and tongue;
But school and college often try in vain
To break the padlock of our boyhood's chain;
One stubborn word will prove this axiom true;—
No quondam rustic can enunciate *view.*
A few brief stanzas may be well employed
To speak of errors we can all avoid.

Learning condemns beyond the reach of hope
The careless lips that speak of sŏap for sōap;
Her edict exiles from her fair abode
The clownish voice that utters rŏad for rōad;
Less stern to him who calls his cōat a cŏat.
And steers his bōat, believing it a bŏat,
She pardoned one, our classic city's boast,
Who said at Cambridge, mŏst instead of mōst,

But knit her brows and stamped her angry foot
To hear a teacher call a rōot a rŏot.

Once more; speak clearly, if you speak at all;
Carve every word before you let it fall ;
Don't, like a lecturer or dramatic star,
Try over hard to roll the British R ;
Do put your accents in the proper spot ;
Don't,—let me beg you,—don't say " How ? " for
    " What ? "
And, when you stick on conversation's burs,
Don't strew your pathway with those dreadful *urs*.

From little matters let us pass to less,
And lightly touch the mysteries of DRESS;
The outward forms the inner man reveal,—
We guess the pulp before we cut the peel.

I leave the broadcloth,—coats and all the rest,—
The dangerous waistcoat, called by cockneys " vest,"
The things named " pants " in certain documents,
A word not made for gentlemen, but " gents " ;
One single precept might the whole condense:
Be sure your tailor is a man of sense ;
But add a little care, a decent pride,
And always err upon the sober side.

Three pairs of boots one pair of feet demands,
If polished daily by the owner's hands;
If the dark menial's visit save from this,
Have twice the number, for he'll sometimes miss.
One pair for critics of the nicer sex,
Close in the instep's clinging circumflex,

Long, narrow, light ; the Gallic boot of love,
A kind of cross between a boot and glove.
But, not to tread on everlasting thorns,
And sow in suffering what is reaped in corns,
Compact, but easy, strong, substantial, square,
Let native art compile the medium pair.
The third remains, and let your tasteful skill
Here show some relics of affection still ;
Let no stiff cowhide, reeking from the tan,
No rough caoutchouc, no deformed brogan,
Disgrace the tapering outline of your feet,
Though yellow torrents gurgle through the street ;
But the *patched* calfskin arm against the flood
In neat, light shoes, impervious to the mud.

Wear seemly gloves ; not black, nor yet too
        light,
And least of all the pair that once was white ;
Let the dead party where you told your loves
Bury in peace its dead bouquets and gloves ;
Shave like the goat, if so your fancy bids,
But be a parent,--don't neglect your kids.

Have a good hat ; the secret of your looks
Lives with the beaver in Canadian brooks ;
Virtue may flourish in an old cravat,
But man and nature scorn the shocking hat.
Does beauty slight you from her gay abodes ?
Like bright Apollo, you must take to *Rhoades*,
Mount the new castor,—ice itself will melt ;
Boots, gloves may fail ; the hat is always felt !

Be shy of breast-pins; plain, well-ironed white,
With small pearl buttons,—two of them in sight,—
Is always genuine, while your gems may pass,
Though real diamonds, for ignoble glass;
But spurn those paltry cis-Atlantic lies,
That round his breast the shabby rustic ties;
Breathe not the name, profaned to hallow things
The indignant laundress blushes when she brings!

Our freeborn race, averse to every check,
Has tossed the yoke of Europe from its *neck;*
From the green prairie to the sea-girt town,
The whole wide nation turns its collars down.

The stately neck is manhood's manliest part;
It takes the life-blood freshest from the heart;
With short, curled ringlets close around it spread,
How light and strong it lifts the Grecian head!
Thine, fair Erectheus of Minerva's wall;—
Or thine, young athlete of the Louver's hall,
Smooth as the pillar flashing in the sun
That filled the arena where thy wreaths were
    won,—
Firm as the band that clasps the antlered spoil
Strained in the winding anaconda's coil!

I spare the contrast; it were only kind
To be a little, nay, intensely blind:
Choose for yourself: I know it cuts your ear;
I know the points will sometimes interfere;
I know that often, like the filial John,
Whom sleep surprised with half his drapery on,

You show your features to the astonished town
With one side standing and the other down ;—
But, O my friend ! my favorite fellow-man !
If Nature made you on her modern plan,
Sooner than wander with your windpipe bare,—
The fruit of Eden ripening in the air,—
With that lean head-stalk, that protruding chin,
Wear standing collars, were they made of tin !
And have a neck-cloth,—by the throat of Jove !
Cut from the funnel of a rusty stove !

The long-drawn lesson narrows to its close,
Chill, slender, slow, the dwindled current flows ;
Tired of the ripples on its feeble springs,
Once more the Muse unfolds her upward wings.

Land of my birth, with this unhallowed tongue,
Thy hopes, thy dangers, I perchance had sung ;
But who shall sing, in brutal disregard
Of all the essentials of the " native bard ? "
Lake, sea, shore, prairie, forest, mountain, fall,
His eye omnivorous must devour them all ;
The tallest summits and the broadest tides
His foot must compass with its giant strides,
Where Ocean thunders, where Missouri rolls,
And tread at once the tropics and the poles ;
His food all forms of earth, fire, water, air,
His home all space, his birth-place everywhere.

Some grave compatriot, having seen perhaps
The pictured page that goes in Worcester's Maps,

And read in earnest what was said in jest,
" Who drives fat oxen "—please to add the rest,—
Sprung the odd notion that the poet's dreams
Grow in the ratio of his hills and streams;
And hence insisted that the aforesaid " bard "
Pink of the future—fancy's pattern-card,—
The babe of Nature in the " giant West,"
Must be of course her biggest and her best.

But, were it true that Nature's fostering sun
Saves all its daylight for that favorite one,
If for his forehead every wreath she means,
And we, poor children, must not touch the greens;
Since rocks and rivers cannot take the road
To seek the elected in his own abode,
Some voice must answer, for her precious heir,
One solemn question :—Who shall pay his fare?
  Oh, when at length the expected bard shall
    come,
Land of our pride, to strike thine echoes dumb
(And many a voice exclaims in prose and rhyme
It's getting late, and he's behind his time),
When all thy mountains clap their hands in joy,
And all thy cataracts thunder " That's the boy,"—
Say if with him the reign of song shall end,
And Heaven declare its final dividend ?

  Be calm, dear brother! whose impassioned strain
Comes from an alley watered by a drain:
The little Mincio, dribbling to the Po,
Beats all the epics of the Hoang Ho;
If loved in earnest by the tuneful maid,

Don't mind their nonsense,—never be afraid!
The nurse of poets feeds her winged brood
By common firesides, on familiar food;
In a low hamlet, by a narrow stream,
Where bovine rustics used to doze and dream,
She filled young William's fiery fancy full,
While old John Shakespeare talked of beeves and
    wool!

No Alpine needle, with its climbing spire,
Brings down for mortals the Promethean fire,
If careless Nature have forgot to frame
An altar worthy of the sacred flame.

Unblest by any save the goat-herd's lines,
Mont Blanc rose soaring through his " sea of pines ";
In vain the Arve and Arveiron dash,
No hymn salutes them but the Ranz des Vaches,
Till lazy Coleridge, by the morning's light,
Gazed for a moment on the fields of white,
And lo, the glaciers found at length a tongue,
Mont Blanc was vocal, and Chamouni sung!

Children of wealth or want, to each is given
One spot of green, and all the blue of heaven!
Enough, if these their outward shows impart;
The rest is thine,—the scenery of the heart.
If passion's hectic in thy stanzas glow
Thy heart's best life-blood ebbing as they flow,
If with thy verse thy strength and bloom distil,
Drained by the pulses of the fevered thrill;
If sound's sweet effluence polarize thy brain,

And thoughts turn crystals in thy fluid strain,—
Nor rolling ocean, nor the prairie's bloom,
Nor streaming cliffs, nor rayless cavern's gloom,
Need'st thou, young poet, to inform thy line;
Thy own broad signet stamps thy song divine!
    Let others gaze where silvery streams are rolled,
And chase the rainbow for its cup of gold;
To thee all landscapes were a heavenly dye,
Changed in the glance of thy prismatic eye;
Nature evoked thee in sublimer throes,
For thee her inmost Arethusa flows,—
The mighty mother's living depths are stirred,—
Thou art the starred Osiris of the herd!

    A few brief lines; they touch on solemn chords,
And hearts may leap to hear their honest words;
Yet, ere the jarring bugle-blast is blown,
The softer lyre shall breathe its soothing tone.
    New England! proudly may thy children claim
Their honored birthright by its humblest name!
Cold are thy skies, but, ever fresh and clear,
No rank malaria stains thine atmosphere;
No fungous weeds invade thy scanty soil,
Scarred by the ploughshares of unslumbering toil.
Long may the doctrines by thy sages taught,
Raised from the quarries where their sires have
      wrought,
Be like the granite of thy rock-ribbed land,—
As slow to rear, as obdurate to stand;
And as the ice, that leaves thy crystal mine,
Chills the fierce alcohol in the Creole's wine.

So may the doctrines of thy sober school
Keep the hot theories of thy neighbors cool!

If ever, trampling on her ancient path,
Cankered by treachery, or inflamed by wrath,
With smooth " Resolves," or with discordant cries,
The mad Briareus of disunion rise,
Chiefs of New England ! by your sires' renown,
Dash the red torches of the rebel down !
Flood his black hearth-stone till its flames expire,
Though your old Sachem fanned his council-fire !

But if at last,—her fading cycle run,—
The tongue must forfeit what the arm has won,
Then rise, wild Ocean ! roll thy surging shock
Full on old Plymouth's desecrated rock !
Scale the proud shaft degenerate hands have hewn,
Where bleeding Valor stained the flowers of June !
Sweep in one tide her spires and turrets down,
And howl her dirge above Monadnoc's crown !

List not the tale ; the Pilgrim's hallowed shore,
Though strewn with weeds, is granite at the core ;
Oh, rather trust that He who made her free
Will keep her true, as long as faith shall be!

Farewell! yet lingering through the destined
    hour,
Leave, sweet Enchantress, one memorial flower !

An Angel, floating o'er the waste of snow
That clad our western desert, long ago

(The same fair spirit who, unseen by day,
Shone as a star along the Mayflower's way),
Sent, the first herald of the Heavenly plan,
To choose on earth a resting-place for man,—
Tired with his flight along the unvaried field,
Turned to soar upwards, when his glance revealed
A calm, bright bay, enclosed·in rocky bounds,
And at its entrance stood three sister mounds.

The Angel spake: "This threefold hill shall be [1]
The home of Arts, the nurse of Liberty!
One stately summit from its shaft shall pour
Its deep-red blaze, along the darkened shore;
Emblem of thoughts that, kindling far and wide,
In danger's night shall be a nation's guide.
One swelling crest the citadel shall crown,
Its slanted bastions black with battle's frown,
And bid the sons that tread its scowling heights
Bare their strong arms for man and all his rights!

[1] The name first given by the English to Boston was TRI-MOUNTAIN. The three hills upon and around which the city is built are Beacon Hill, Fort Hill, and Copp's Hill.

In the early records of the colony, it is mentioned, under date of May 6, 1635, that " A BEACON is to be set on the Sentry hill, at Boston, to give notice to the country of any danger; to be guarded by one man stationed near, and fired as occasion may be." The last beacon was blown down in 1789.

The eastern side of Fort Hill was formerly " a ragged cliff, that seemed placed by nature in front of the entrance to the harbor for the purposes of defence, to which it was very soon applied, and from which it obtained its present name." Its summit is now a beautiful green enclosure.

Copp's Hill was used as a burial-ground from a very early

One silent steep along the northern wave
Shall hold the patriarch's and the hero's grave;
When fades the torch, when o'er the peaceful scene
The embattled fortress smiles in living green,
The cross of Faith, the anchor staff of Hope,
Shall stand eternal on its grassy slope;
There through all time shall faithful Memory tell:
" Here Virtue toiled, and Patriot Valor fell;
Thy free, proud fathers slumber at thy side,
Live as they lived, or perish as they died ! "

period. The part of it employed for this purpose slopes toward
the water upon the northern side. From its many interest-
ing records of the dead, I select the following, which may
serve to show what kind of dust it holds :—

"Here lies buried in a
Stone Grave 10 feet deep,
Capt DANIEL MALCOLM Mercht
who departed this Life
October 23d, 1769,
Aged 44 years,
a true son of Liberty,
a Friend to the Publick,
an Enemy to oppression,
and one of the foremost
in opposing the Revenue Acts
on America."

The gravestone from which I copied this inscription is
bruised and splintered by the bullets of the British soldiers.

THE PILGRIM'S VISION.

In the hour of twilight shadows
    The Puritan looked out ;
He thought of the " bloudy Salvages "
    That lurked all round about,
Of Wituwamet's pictured knife
    And Pecksuot's whooping shout ;
For the baby's limbs were feeble,
    Though his father's arms were stout.

His home was a freezing cabin
    Too bare for the hungry rat,
Its roof was thatched with ragged grass
    And bald enough of that ;
The hole that served for casement
    Was glazed with an ancient hat ;
And the ice was gently thawing
    From the log whereon he sat.

Along the dreary landscape
    His eyes went to and fro,
The trees all clad in icicles,
    The streams that did not flow ;
A sudden thought flashed o'er him,—
    A dream of long ago,—
He smote his leathern jerkin
    And murmured " Even so ! "

" Come hither, God-be-Glorified,
     And sit upon my knee,
Behold the dream unfolding,
     Whereof I spake to thee
By the winter's hearth in Leyden
     And on the stormy sea ;
True is the dream's beginning,—
     So may its ending be !

" I saw in the naked forest
     Our scattered remnant cast,
A screen of shivering branches
     Between them and the blast ;
The snow was falling round them,
     The dying fell as fast ;
I looked to see them perish,
     When lo, the vision passed.

" Again mine eyes were opened ;—
     The feeble had waxed strong,
The babes had grown to sturdy men,
     The remnant was a throng ;
By shadowed lake and winding stream
     And all the shores along,
The howling demons quaked to hear
     The Christian's godly song.

" They slept,—the village fathers,—
     By river, lake, and shore,
When far adown the steep of Time
     The vision rose once more ;

I saw along the winter snow
 A spectral column pour,
And high above their broken ranks
 A tattered flag they bore.

" Their Leader rode before them,
 Of bearing calm and high,
The light of Heaven's own kindling
 Throned in his awful eye ;
These were a Nation's champions
 Her dread appeal to try ;
God for the right ! I faltered,
 And lo, the train passed by.

" Once more ;—the strife is ended,
 The solemn issue tried,
The Lord of Hosts, His mighty arm
 Has helped our Israel's side ;
Gray stone and grassy hillock
 Tell where our martyrs died,
But peaceful smiles the harvest,
 And stainless flows the tide.

" A crash,—as when some swollen cloud
 Cracks o'er the tangled trees !
With side to side, and spar to spar,
 Whose smoking decks are these ?
I know Saint George's blood-red cross,
 Thou Mistress of the Seas,—
But what is she, whose streaming bars
 Roll out before the breeze ?

" Ah, well her iron ribs are knit,
    Whose thunders strive to quell
The bellowing throats, the blazing lips,
    That pealed the Armada's knell !
The mist was cleared,—a wreath of stars
    Rose o'er the crimsoned swell,
And, wavering from its haughty peak,
    The cross of England fell !

" O trembling Faith ! though dark the morn,
    A heavenly torch is thine ;
While feebler races melt away,
    And paler orbs decline,
Still shall the fiery pillar's ray
    Along thy pathway shine,
To light the chosen tribe that sought
    This Western Palestine !

" I see the living tide roll on ;
    It crowns with flaming towers
The icy capes of Labrador,
    The Spaniard's ' land of flowers ' !
It streams beyond the splintered ridge
    That parts the Northern showers;
From eastern rock to sunset wave
    The Continent is ours ! "

He ceased,—the grim old Puritan,—
    Then softly bent to cheer
The pilgrim-child, whose wasting face
    Was meekly turned to hear ;

And drew his toil-worn sleeve across,
    To brush the manly tear
From cheeks that never changed in woe,
    And never blanched in fear.

The weary pilgrim slumbers,
    His resting-place unknown ;
His hands were crossed, his lids were closed,
    The dust was o'er him strown ;
The drifting soil, the mouldering leaf,
    Along the sod were blown ;
His mound has melted into earth,
    His memory lives alone.

So let it live unfading,
    The memory of the dead,
Long as the pale anemone
    Springs where their tears were shed,
Or, raining in the summer's wind
    In flakes of burning red,
The wild rose sprinkles with its leaves
    The turf where once they bled !

Yea, when the frowning bulwarks
    That guard this holy strand
Have sunk beneath the trampling surge
    In beds of sparkling sand,
While in the waste of ocean
    One hoary rock shall stand
Be this its latest legend,—
    HERE WAS THE PILGRIM'S LAND !

A MODEST REQUEST.

COMPLIED WITH AFTER THE DINNER AT PRESIDENT
EVERETT'S INAUGURATION.

SCENE,—a back parlor in a certain square,
Or court, or lane,—in short no matter where;
Time,—early morning, dear to simple souls
Who love its sunshine, and its fresh-baked rolls;
Persons,—take pity on this telltale blush,
That, like the Æthiop, whispers " Hush, oh hush ! "

Delightful scene ! where smiling comfort broods,
Nor business frets, nor anxious care intrudes;
O si sic omnia ! were it ever so !
But what is stable in this world below !
Medio e fonte,—Virtue has her faults,—
The clearest fountains taste of Epsom salts;
We snatch the cup and lift to drain it dry,—
Its central dimple holds a drowning fly !

Strong is the pine by Maine's ambrosial streams,
But stronger augers pierce its thickest beams;
No iron gate, no spiked and panelled door,
Can keep out death, the postman, or the bore ;—
O for a world where peace and silence reign,
And blunted dulness terebrates in vain !
204

—The door bell jingles,—enter Richard Fox,
And takes this letter from his leathern box.

" Dear Sir,
            In writing on a former day,
One little matter I forgot to say ;
I now inform you in a single line,
On Thursday next our purpose is to *dine.*
The act of feeding, as you understand,
Is but a fraction of the work in hand ;
Its nobler half is that ethereal meat
The papers call ' the intellectual treat ' ;
Songs, speeches, toasts. around the festive board,
Drowned in the juice the College pumps afford ;
For only water flanks our knives and forks,
So, sink or float, we swim without the corks.
Yours is the art, by native genius taught,
To clothe in eloquence the naked thought ;
Yours is the skill its music to prolong
Through the sweet effluence of mellifluous song ;
Yours the quaint trick to cram the pithy line
That cracks so crisply over bubbling wine ;
And since success your various gifts attends,
We,—that is I and all your numerous friends,—
Expect from you,—your single self a host,—
A speech, a song, excuse me, *and* a toast ;
Nay, not to haggle on so small a claim,
A few of each, or several of the same.
(Signed)   Yours, *most truly,* —— "

            No ! my sight must fail,—
If that ain't Judas on the largest scale !

Well, this *is* modest; nothing else than that?
My coat? my boots? my pantaloons? my hat?
My stick? my gloves? as well as all my wits,
Learning and linen,—everything that fits!
Jack, said my lady, is it grog you'll try,
Or punch, or toddy, if perhaps you're dry?
Ah, said the sailor, though I can't refuse,
You know, my lady, 'tain't for me to choose;—
I'll take the grog to finish off my lunch,
And drink the toddy while you mix the punch.

————

The Speech.　(The speaker, rising to be seen,
Looks very red, because so very green.)
I rise—I rise—with unaffected fear,
(Louder!—speak louder!—who the deuce can hear?)
I rise—I said—with undisguised dismay—
—Such are my feelings as I rise, I say!
Quite unprepared to face this learned throng,
Already gorged with eloquence and song;
Around my view are ranged on either hand
The genius, wisdom, virtue of the land;
" Hands that the rod of empire might have swayed "
Close at my elbow stir their lemonade;
Would you like Homer learn to write and speak,
That bench is groaning with its weight of Greek;
Behold the naturalist that in his teens
Found six new species in a dish of greens;
And lo, the master in a statelier walk,
Whose annual ciphering takes a ton of chalk;

And there the linguist, that by common roots
Through all their nurseries tracks old Noah's
    shoots,—
How Shem's proud children reared the Assyrian piles,
While Ham's were scattered through the Sandwich
    Isles !

—Fired at the thought of all the present shows,
My kindling fancy down the future flows;
I see the glory of the coming days
O'er Time's horizon shoot its streaming rays ;
Near and more near the radiant morning draws
In living lustre (rapturous applause);
From east to west the blazing heralds run,
Loosed from the chariot of the ascending sun,
Through the long vista of uncounted years
In cloudless splendor (three tremendous cheers).
My eye prophetic, as the depths unfold,
Sees a new advent of the age of gold ;
While o'er the scene new generations press,
New heroes rise the coming time to bless,—
Not such as Homer's, who, we read in Pope,
Dined without forks and never heard of soap,—
Not such as May to Marlborough Chapel brings,
Lean, hungry, savage, anti-everythings,
Copies of Luther in the pasteboard style,—
But genuine articles,—the true Carlyle ;
While far on high the blazing orb shall shed
Its central light on Harvard's holy head,
And Learning's ensigns ever float unfurled
Here in the focus of the new-born world !

The speaker stops, and, trampling down the pause,
Roars through the hall the thunder of applause,
One stormy gust of long suspended Ahs!
One whirlwind chaos of insane hurrahs!

THE SONG.   But this demands a briefer line,—
A shorter muse and not the old long Nine;—
Long metre answers for a common song,
Though common metre does not answer long.

She came beneath the forest dome
     To seek its peaceful shade,
An exile from her ancient home,—
     A poor forsaken maid;
No banner, flaunting high above,
     No blazoned cross, she bore;
One holy book of light and love
     Was all her worldly store.

The dark brown shadows passed away,
     And wider spread the green,
And, where the savage used to stray,
     The rising mart was seen;
So, when the laden winds had brought
     Their showers of golden rain,
Her lap some precious gleanings caught,
     Like Ruth's amid the grain.

But wrath soon gathered uncontrolled
     Among the baser churls,
To see her ankles red with gold,
     Her forehead white with pearls;

" Who gave to thee the glittering bands
     That lace thine azure veins?
Who bade thee lift those snow-white hands
     We bound in gilded chains?"

These are the gems my children gave,
     The stately dame replied;
The wise, the gentle, and the brave,
     I nurtured at my side;
If envy still your bosom stings,
     Take back their rims of gold;
My sons will melt their wedding rings,
     And give a hundred-fold !

THE TOAST.—Oh, tell me, ye who thoughtless ask
Exhausted nature for a threefold task,
In wit and pathos if one share remains,
A safe investment for an ounce of brains?
Hard is the job to launch the desperate pun,
A pun-job dangerous as the Indian one.
Turned by the current of some stronger wit
Back from the object that you mean to hit,
Like the strange missile which the Australian
     throws,
Your verbal *boomerang* slaps you on the nose.
One vague inflection spoils the whole with doubt,
One trivial letter ruins all, left out;
A knot can choke a felon into clay,
A not will save him, spelt without the k;
The smallest word has some unguarded spot,
And danger lurks in i without a dot.

Thus great Achilles, who had shown his zeal
In healing wounds, died of a wounded heel;
Unhappy chief, who, when in childhood doused,
Had saved his bacon, had his feet been soused!
Accursed heel that killed a hero stout!
Oh, had your mother known that you were out,
Death had not entered at the trifling part
That still defies the small chirurgeon's art
With corns and bunions,—not the glorious John
Who wrote the book we all have pondered on,—
But other bunions, bound in fleecy hose,
To " Pilgrim's Progress " unrelenting foes!

A health, unmingled with the reveller's wine,
To him whose title is indeed divine;
Truth's sleepless watchman on her midnight tower,
Whose lamp burns brightest when the tempests
　　lower.
Oh, who can tell with what a leaden flight
Drag the long watches of his weary night;
While at his feet the hoarse and blinding gale
Strews the torn wreck and bursts the fragile sail,
When stars have faded, when the wave is dark,
When rocks and sands embrace the foundering
　　bark,
And still he pleads with unavailing cry,
Behold the light, O wanderer, look or die!

A health, fair Themis! Would the enchanted vine
Wreathed its green tendrils round this cup of
　　thine;

If Learning's radiance fill thy modern court,
Its glorious sunshine streams through Blackstone's
    port !
Lawyers are thirsty, and their clients too,
Witness at least, if memory serve me true,
Those old tribunals, famed for dusty suits,
Where men sought justice ere they brushed their
    boots ;—
And what can match, to solve a learned doubt,
The warmth within that comes from " cold with-
    out " ?

Health to the art whose glory is to give
The crowning boon that makes it life to live.
Ask not her home ;—the rock where Nature flings
Her arctic lichen, last of living things,
The gardens, fragrant with the Orient's balm,
From the low jasmine to the star-like palm,
Hail her as mistress o'er the distant waves,
And yield their tribute to her wandering slaves.
Wherever, moistening the ungrateful soil,
The tear of suffering tracks the path of toil,
There, in the anguish of his fevered hours,
Her gracious finger points to healing flowers ;
Where the lost felon steals away to die,
Her soft hand waves before his closing eye ;
Where hunted misery finds his darkest lair,
The midnight taper shows her kneeling there !

Virtue,—the guide that men and nations own ;
And Law, the bulwark that protects her throne

And HEALTH, — to all its happiest charm that
    lends;
These and their servants, man's untiring friends;
Pour the bright lymph that Heaven itself lets
    fall,—
In one fair bumper let us toast them all!

NUX POSTCŒNATICA.

I was sitting with my microscope, upon my parlor
  rug,
With a very heavy quartz and a very lively bug;
The true bug had been organized with only two
  antennæ,
But the humbug in the copperplate would have
  them twice as many.

And I thought, like Dr. Faustus, of the emptiness
  of art,
How we take a fragment for the whole, and call
  the whole a part,
When I heard a heavy footstep that was loud
  enough for two,
And a man of forty entered, exclaiming,—"How
  d'ye do?"

He was not a ghost, my visitor, but solid flesh and
  bone;
He wore a Palo Alto hat, his weight was twenty
  stone;
(It's odd how hats expand their brims as riper years
  invade,
As if when life had reached its noon, it wanted them
  for shade!)

I lost my focus,—dropped my book,—the bug, who
    was a flea,
At once exploded, and commenced experiments on
    me.
They have a certain heartiness that frequently ap-
    palls,—
Those mediæval gentlemen in semilunar smalls !

" My boy," he said—(colloquial ways,—the vast,
    broad-hatted man),
" Come dine with us on Thursday next,—you must,
    you know you can ;
We're going to have a roaring time, with lots of fun
    and noise,
Distinguished guests, et cetera, the JUDGE, and all
    the boys."

Not so,—I said,—my temporal bones are showing
    pretty clear
It's time to stop, just look and see that hair above
    this ear ;
My golden days are more than spent,—and, what is
    very strange,
If these are real silver hairs, I'm getting lots of
    change.

Besides—my prospects—don't you know that people
    won't employ
A man that wrongs his manliness by laughing like
    a boy ?

And suspect the azure blossom that unfolds upon a
  shoot,
As if wisdom's old potato could not flourish at its
  root!

It's a very fine reflection, when you're etching out
  a smile
On a copper plate of faces that would stretch at
  least a mile,
That, what with sneers from enemies, and cheapen-
  ing shrugs of friends,
It will cost you all the earnings that a month of
  labor lends!

It's a vastly pleasing prospect, when you're screw-
  ing out a laugh,
That your very next year's income is diminished by
  a half,
And a little boy trips barefoot that Pegasus may go,
And the baby's milk is watered that your Helicon
  may flow!

No;—the joke has been a good one,—but I'm get-
  ting fond of quiet,
And I don't like deviations from my customary
  diet;
So I think I will not go with you to hear the toasts
  and speeches,
But stick to old Montgomery Place, and have some
  pig and peaches.

The fat man answered :—Shut your mouth, and hear
the genuine creed ;
The true essentials of a feast are only fun and
feed ;
The force that wheels the planets round delights in
spinning tops,
And that young earthquake t'other day was great
at shaking props.

I tell you what, philosopher, if all the longest heads
That ever knocked their sinciputs in stretching on
their beds
Were round one great mahogany, I'd beat those
fine old folks
With twenty dishes, twenty fools, and twenty clever
jokes !

Why, if Columbus should be there, the company
would beg
He'd show that little trick of his of balancing the
egg !
Milton to Stilton would give in, and Solomon to
Salmon,
And Roger Bacon be a bore, and Francis Bacon
gammon !

And as for all the "patronage" of all the clowns
and boors
That squint their little narrow eyes at any freak of
yours,

Do leave them to your prosier friends,—such fel-
    lows ought to die
When rhubarb is so very scarce and ipecac so high !

And so I come,—like Lochinvar, to tread a single
    measure,
To purchase with a loaf of bread a sugar-plum of
    pleasure,
To enter for the cup of glass that's run for after
    dinner,
Which yields a single sparkling draught, then breaks
    and cuts the winner.

Ah, that's the way delusion comes,—a glass of old
    Madeira,
A pair of visual diaphragms revolved by Jane or
    Sarah,
And down go vows and promises without the slight-
    est question
If eating words won't compromise the organs of
    digestion !

And yet, among my native shades, beside my nurs-
    ing mother,
Where every stranger seems a friend, and every
    friend a brother,
I feel the old convivial glow (unaided) o'er me steal-
    ing,—
The warm, champagny, old-particular, brandy-
    punchy feeling.

We're all alike ;—Vesuvius flings the scoriæ from
 his fountain,
But down they come in volleying rain back to the
 burning mountain ;
We leave, like those volcanic stones, our precious
 Alma Mater,
But will keep dropping in again to see the dear old
 crater.

ON LENDING A PUNCH-BOWL.

THIS ancient silver bowl of mine,—it tells of good
    old times,
Of joyous days, and jolly nights, and merry Christ-
    mas chimes ;
They were a free and jovial race, but honest, brave,
    and true,
That dipped their ladle in the punch when this old
    bowl was new.

A Spanish galleon brought the bar,—so runs the
    ancient tale ;
'Twas hammered by an Antwerp smith, whose arm
    was like a flail ;
And now and then between the strokes, for fear his
    strength should fail,
He wiped his brow, and quaffed a cup of good old
    Flemish ale.

'Twas purchased by an English squire to please his
    loving dame,
Who saw the cherubs, and conceived a longing for
    the same ;
And oft, as on the ancient stock another twig was
    found,
'Twas filled with caudle spiced and hot, and handed
    smoking round.

But, changing hands, it reached at length a Puritan
    divine,
Who used to follow Timothy, and take a little wine,
But hated punch and prelacy ; and so it was, per-
    haps,
He went to Leyden, where he found conventicles and
    schnapps.

And then, of course, you know what's next,—it left
    the Dutchman's shore
With those that in the Mayflower came,—a hundred
    souls and more,—
Along with all the furniture, to fill their new
    abodes,—
To judge by what is still on hand, at least a hundred
    loads.

'Twas on a dreary winter's eve, the night was clos-
    ing dim,
When old Miles Standish took the bowl, and filled
    it to the brim ;
The little Captain stood and stirred the posset with
    his sword,
And all his sturdy men at arms were ranged about
    the board.

He poured the fiery Hollands in,—the man that
    never feared,—
He took a long and solemn draught, and wiped his
    yellow beard ;

And one by one the musketeers,—the men that
    fought and prayed,—
All drank as 'twere their mother's milk, and not a
    man afraid.

That night, affrighted from his nest, the screaming
    eagle flew,
He heard the Pequot's ringing whoop, the soldier's
    wild halloo ;
And there the sachem learned the rule he taught to
    kith and kin,
" Run from the white man when you find he smells
    of Hollands gin ! "

A hundred years, and fifty more, had spread their
    leaves and snows,
A thousand rubs had flattened down each little
    cherub's nose ;
When once again the bowl was filled, but not in
    mirth or joy,
'Twas mingled by a mother's hand to cheer her
    parting boy.

Drink, John, she said, 'twill do you good,—poor
    child, you'll never bear
This working in the dismal trench, out in the mid-
    night air ;
And if,—God bless me,—you were hurt, 'twould
    keep away the chill ;
So John *did* drink,—and well he wrought that
    night at Bunker's

I tell you, there was generous warmth in good old
    English cheer ;
I tell you, 'twas a pleasant thought to bring its
    symbol here.
'Tis but the fool that loves excess ;—hast thou a
    drunken soul ?
Thy bane is in thy shallow skull, not in my silver
    bowl !

I love the memory of the past,—its pressed yet
    fragrant flowers,—
The moss that clothes its broken walls,—the ivy on
    its towers,—
Nay, this poor bauble it bequeathed,—my eyes grow
    moist and dim,
To think of all the vanished joys that danced around
    its brim.

Then fill a fair and honest cup, and bear it straight
    to me ;
The goblet hallows all it holds, whate'er the liquid
    be ;
And may the cherubs on its face protect me from
    the sin,
That dooms one to those dreadful words,—" My
    dear, where *have* you been ? "

POEMS OF
JAMES RUSSELL LOWELL

JAMES RUSSELL LOWELL

JAMES RUSSELL LOWELL, the most distinguished member of a family honorably known in New England, was born on February 22, 1819, at Cambridge, Massachusetts. He graduated from Harvard twenty years later; then he studied law and was admitted to the bar; but soon he turned to literature. In 1844 he married Maria White, whose influence converted him to the anti-slavery cause; and on the outbreak of the Mexican War he protested against it in a series of satiric lyrics written in the homely and pungent Yankee dialect. This first series of the "Biglow Papers" was published in 1848; and in this same year he also issued both the "Vision of Sir Launfal" (his most important story in verse) and "A Fable for Critics" (a gallery of witty portraits of the chief figures in American literature).

In 1854 he delivered in Boston a series of lectures on the English poets which revealed him as the best equipped of American literary critics; and he was thereupon asked to succeed Longfellow at Harvard as the Professor of Modern Languages. When the "Atlantic Monthly" was founded, in 1857, he was its first editor; and in its pages he published the second series of "Biglow Papers," called forth by the Civil War, which resulted in the abolition of the slavery he abhorred. In the dozen years after the war he sent forth three volumes of prose essays and he wrote four patriotic odes, one in commemoration of the Harvard students who had fallen in battle, and three celebrating centenaries of the Revolution.

In 1877 he was sent as American minister to Spain and in 1880 he was transferred to Great Britain. While resident in London, he delivered various addresses, the most striking of which was on "Democracy;" and after his return home three years later he spoke on the "Independent in Politics," including this address in a volume of political essays published in 1888. In this year also appeared his final volume of poems, "Heartsease and Rue." He settled down again at Cambridge, at Elmwood, the house in which he had been born: and there he died at the age of seventy-two, on August 12, 1891.

Lowell's prose is at least as important as his poetry. He is easily the foremost of American literary critics, possessing abundantly all four of the qualifications which a critic of literature must needs have—insight, equipment, sympathy and disinterestedness. He had the insight of a poet and the equipment of a scholar: and he loved literature with unfaltering devotion. His essays on Dante, Spenser, Shakespeare, Milton, Dryden, Wordsworth and Keats are shrewd, suggestive and wise. They may lack the grace of careful structure, and they are often rather straggling and haphazard. But they contain the outpouring of a rich mind and they abound in pregnant phrases, unfailingly stimulating to the appreciative reader. His interest in life at large nourished his interest in mere literature; he was a man of the world as well as a man of letters; and his knowledge of men was as broad as his acquaintance with books.

Among the American poets, only Emerson surpasses him in intellectual power; and he is superior to both Longfellow and Whittier in range of imagination. But his serious poetry never won the wide popularity which was theirs, perhaps because he had not the unlearned directness of Whittier or the singing simplicity of Longfellow. His poetry suffers from two defects; he was prone to improvise and he was given to moralizing. He brooded over a theme and then he wrote at white heat, not having always perfected his plan before he began and rarely giving to his verse the final revision which perfection demands. The ore was rich, beyond all question; but Lowell was content often to leave the metal in an ingot when he might have struck it in a coin. The level to which he could attain was lofty, but he did not long sustain his flight at this altitude. His best was indisputably fine; but he did his best infrequently, because he was in a hurry to get out what he wished to express and because he begrudged the time needed to find the inevitable form and the irresistible phrase.

Artistically his humorous verse is finer than the average of his serious poetry. In the "Biglow Papers" especially the desire to send his point home, to make his stanzas sing themselves into the memory, forced him to take the trouble needed to find a fit form and to adjust the manner to the matter. Here his success is unquestionable; and there is nothing of its kind more perfect in the whole range of English poetry than the burning lines of "Jonathan to John" with the ingeniously varied refrain. Nor is there anything better than the "Courtin'," that Yankee idyl with its delicious commingling of playfulness and sentiment.

There is power in many of Lowell's graver poems— power and also charm, although marred now and again by a certain wilfulness and by a too obvious didacticism. Yet it may well be that Lowell, interesting as he is as a man, as a master of prose and as a poet, is destined to be remembered rather as the writer of the best American literary satire and as the author of the best political satires than as the bard who was able grandly to voice the ideals and aspirations of his people in a group of patriotic odes abounding in splendid and sonorous stanzas.

BRANDER MATTHEWS.

CONTENTS.

PAGE

BIOGRAPHICAL SKETCH.............................. vii

THE BIGLOW PAPERS.

No. I.—A letter from Mr. Ezekiel Biglow of Jaalam to
the Hon Joseph T. Buckingham, Editor of the Boston
Courier, inclosing a Poem of his Son, Mr. Hosea
Biglow..................................... 37

No. II.—A letter from Mr. Hosea Biglow to the Hon.
J. T. Buckingham, Editor of the Boston Courier,
covering a Letter from Mr. B. Sawin, Private in the
Massachusetts Regiment................... 46

No. III.—What Mr. Robinson thinks................... 60

No. IV.—Remarks of Increase D. O'Phace, Esquire, at
an Extrumpery Caucus in State Street, reported by
Mr. H. Biglow.... 73

No. 5.—The Debate in the Sennit. Sot to a Nusry Rhyme 87

No. VI.—The Pious Editor's Creed. 96

No. VII.—A Letter from a Candidate for the Presidency
in Answer to suttin Questions proposed by Mr.
Hosea Biglow, inclosed in a Note from Mr. Biglow
to S. H. Gay, Esq., Editor of the National Anti-
slavery Standard........................ 106

No. VIII.—A Second Letter from B. Sawin, Esq...... 118

No. IX.—A Third Letter from B. Sawin, Esq..... 136

A Fable for Critics....................... 153

The Vision of Sir Launfal......................... 227

BIOGRAPHICAL SKETCH.

THE genius of James Russell Lowell places him in the front rank of American poets. He is one of the few who are read and appreciated on both sides of the Atlantic. He made his mark in his earliest published volume, when he was but twenty-two years of age. From that time to the end of a long career he grew steadily in fame. Nor did his power wane, while his literary form showed an increasing perfection of polish.

He was born in Cambridge, Mass., Feb. 22, 1819. His father was the Rev. Charles Lowell, D.D., minister of the West Church (Unitarian) of Boston, a scholar of high standing and author of several devotional books. He was descended from Percival Lowell, who came from England in 1639 and settled in Newbury, Mass. The subject of this sketch showed throughout life a fine example of the Puritan conscience, joined with a rare tenderness of nature and winsomeness of character. While he never lacked the moral courage which dared to stand

> " in the right with two or three."

his nature and method were gentle and persuasive rather than severe or antagonizing.

He was more than a poet. He was symmetrically developed as a man of letters. To his admirers he was the ideal man of letters. As such his life was quiet, and his biography will record the growth and products of his mind rather than external events which were never romantic.

He was graduated from Harvard College in 1838. At that time he was class poet, but the reading of the poems was omitted from the exercises of Class Day owing to the unavoidable absence of the poet. This absence was caused by the fact that at just that time he happened to be under suspension from the college. His offence, however, was playful and in no wise serious, and his Alma Mater never ceased to do him honor in after years.

On leaving college Lowell entered a law office and after the usual preliminary studies was, in 1840, admitted to the bar. He was, however, by nature a man of letters and was unsuited to the peculiar exactions of the legal profession. One is therefore not surprised that there is no record of his practice of the law, but there was a tolerably steady stream of poems, essays and reviews flowing from his facile pen.

The first year of his nominal law practice records a volume of poems (1841) entitled "A Year's Life." In this were evidences that he was a true seer, a genuine poet. His friends recognized the promise of a brilliant career, and they were not mistaken.

Two years later he became editor of a magazine of which, however, only three numbers were issued. A year after that he issued another volume of poems.

In this year, 1844, he married Miss Maria White, of Watertown, Mass. She was a charming and accomplished woman, possessing literary talent of no mean order. To her translations from the German she added original poems of more than ordinary merit.

She died in 1853, and it was her death which elicited from Longfellow one of the sweetest and most beautiful of all poems on death. It is that entitled Two Angels.

'T was at thy door, O friend, and not at mine,
  The angel with the amaranthine wreath,
Pausing, descended, and, with voice divine,
  Whispered a word that had a sound like death.

Then fell upon the house a sudden gloom,
  A shadow on those features fair and thin,
And softly, from that hushed and darkened room,
  Two angels issued where but one went in.

In 1845 he published a volume of essays, "Conversations on Some of the Poets," and thus we see that he was permanently out of the current of the law and in that of literature.

In 1848 he published a volume that contained what have proved to be two of his most popular poems : namely, The Vision of Sir Launfal and The Biglow Papers.

In 1851–2 he made his first trip to Europe. Most of the time he spent in Italy, especially in Rome with his friend W. W. Story, the famous sculptor. In 1854–5 he delivered the Lowell Institute lectures on " British Poets."

The most important event occurred that year when he was appointed professor of Belles Lettres at Harvard to succeed his distinguished friend H. W. Longfellow. Before assuming the duties of the professorhip he spent another year in Europe, chiefly in Dresden.

In 1857 he married Miss Frances Dunlap of Portland, Maine.

When the Atlantic Monthly was established he was

its first regular editor, and continued in that work for about five years, or from 1857 to 1862. Relinquishing this he edited the North American Review, then a quarterly, for a period, of about ten years. In addition to his editorial work he contributed a large number of articles to this magazine,—thirty-four in all, not counting editorial notes, etc. During these fifteen years of editorship, while he had also the duties of professor, his general literary work did not lag, and he issued volumes both of poetry and of prose.

In 1872–4 he again travelled in Europe, receiving the unusual honors of the degrees of D. C. L. from the University of Oxford, and LL.D. from that of Cambridge, England.

In 1877 he was appointed Minister to Spain, and took up the duties of a post made illustrious by Irving. The lustre of the literary tradition suffered no diminution in his incumbency.

He was later (1880–5) minister to England, and it is not too much to say that in that difficult and exacting position he stands second to none of all who have ever served. His honest, sturdy, and outspoken democracy, his fineness of culture, his breadth of spirit, and his genial persuasiveness have had incalculable influence in promoting the friendliness between Americans and their British cousins. At this time he was honored by being appointed Lord Rector of St. Andrews University at St. Andrews, Scotland. But he soon resigned this position as being incompatible with his obligations as minister of the United States.

In his later years he published several volumes of essays and addresses, the latter being largely on patriotic or democratic subjects. The excellence of their

substance and the finish of their form entitle them to
a permanent place in literature. They are, however,
outside the scope of this sketch, which concerns Lowell
as a poet.

Lowell was one of a remarkable circle of literary
friends, such as has hardly existed before in all his-
tory, and certainly never in the United States. His
friendships included Longfellow, Emerson, R. H.
Dana, W. W. Story, Fields, Holmes, Whittier, Agas-
siz, E. E. Hale, and others of nearly equal prominence.
Such friendship greatly enriched his life, but it in no
wise quenched his originality nor weakened his vigor.

In looking over his poetical works for a critical esti-
mate, we find no one poem which towers up above
the rest, like Milton's Paradise Lost, Byron's Childe
Harold, or Wordsworth's Excursion. But there are
many shorter ones, each of which is sufficient to justify
the high reputation which he holds on both sides of
the Atlantic. In his first published volume, there is
one, entitled "Ode," which must have been written
when he was little more than a boy, which gave abun-
dant evidence of his high aspiration and of the earnest-
ness of his spirit. His admirers were justified in
predicting from this poem a brilliant future for the
author, and the result was not disappointing.

The Biglow Papers are a political satire upon the
Invasion by the United States of Mexico, the State of
the Slavery Question, etc. They are written in the
Yankee dialect verse by one Hosea Biglow, Birdofre-
dum Sawin, edited with an introduction, notes, glos-
sary, and copious index, by Homer Wilbur, A. M.,
pastor of the First Church in Jaalam, and (prospec-
tive) member of many literary, learned, and scientific

societies. These placed Lowell in the front rank of humorists. They were the first attempt to use the quaint New England dialect in verse, and they are probably the best imitations to be found either in poetry or in prose.

They were received with favor, and their keen satire, their quaint drollery, their irresistible good humor, have held them in popularity for a half century. Political opponents enjoyed them hardly less than political friends. The experiences of the Bay State recruit, with sly wit, set forth political questions and practices in a way to fill one with laughter. There is an undertone of seriousness, especially a hot hatred of slavery and all its concomitants, and indeed of all injustice. But the form is humorous, and they have been called an attempt to laugh down slavery. In the larger sense of the word, they are intensely patriotic. They are classic in their way, and are the only production in the English language worthy to stand by the side of Hudibras. It is this combination of fun that bubbles over and sturdy morality which places them on so high a plane both intellectual and ethical. They have held their place for fifty years and doubtless will hold it for many years to come.

A second series of these charming papers was called out by the Civil War of 1861–5. These had not the advantage of newness enjoyed by the first series, nevertheless they are worthy of their name and do not detract from the quality of the whole. If there is less rollicking fun in the second series, there is also more poetry. The Civil War was nearer to the poet than the Mexican War, and this fact could not other than influence his writing even of wit, humor, and satire.

Another masterly piece of humor is the Fable for Critics, which is no fable at all, but a rhymed review, or at least criticism, of some of the more prominent American writers. One after another they pass under his scrutiny and receive his criticism or characterization. It is not to be expected that this poem should have the balance of the regular review, but on the whole its criticisms are just. while his wit is as keen as a Damascus blade. It is to be noted that the poet does not spare himself, but raps his own knuckles quite as hard as any.

> There is Lowell, who's striving Parnassus to climb,
> With a whole bale of *isms* tied together with rhyme.
>
> .   .   .   .   .
> The top of the hill he will ne'er come nigh reaching
> Till he learns the distinction 'twixt singing and preaching.

The purpose and character of the Fable preclude the usual finish of form, so that it has been called clever doggerel. But along with its trenchant humor may be discovered a manly vigor, with occasional touches of the pathos which is rarely lacking in any of Lowell's poetry, either humorous or serious, and all joined by a good sense that bears the light of day.

In 1865 Harvard College had a memorial service for those of her sons who fell in the Civil War, and for this was written the Commemoration Ode, whose stately measures rise sometimes to sublime heights. Patriotism tinges much of his poetry. for love of country and of freedom was a passion with him, but in this poem it has a freer course than elsewhere. He touches the ideal manhood,—

God's plan
And measure of a stalwart man.

The concrete example of this manhood is Lincoln
"our Martyr-Chief." Then follows a characterization
of him unequalled certainly in poetry, leading up to
the climax,—

> The kindly-earnest, brave, foreseeing man,
> Sagacious, patient, dreading praise, not blame,
> New birth of our new soil, the first American.

The Present Crisis is probably the most quoted of
his poems. It was written in December, 1844, and
refers to one of the many crises of slavery. It displays
the author's noble loyalty to Truth and his withering
scorn of evasion or temporizing expedients. Later he
treated similar subjects with humorous form in the
Biglow papers ; but here he is serious in form as well
as earnest in thought. Lord Bacon raised the ques-
tion of "jesting Pilate." What is Truth ? Lowell
answers with a clarion ring :

> Truth forever on the scaffold, Wrong forever on the throne,—
> Yet that scaffold sways the future, and, behind the dim un-
> known,
> Standeth God within the shadow, keeping watch above His
> own.

History is to Lowell a divine revelation, and the crisis
of which he writes has the solemnity of the Judgment
Day.

> Once to every man and nation comes the moment to decide
> In the strife of Truth with Falsehood, for the good or evil
> side.

This leads us to speak of the religious characteristic
of the author's poetry. His poems are not religious in
the same sense as those of Cowper. Possibly they are

not evangelical. But they are religious in the finest sense of the word, holding to an unshaken belief in God's everlasting righteousness, with sweet confidence in His overruling providence, with a profound belief in the practical piety of considering the poor and unfortunate, and especially with broad sympathy for "seekers after God." His "Vision of Sir Launfal" is a universal favorite. It tells of the quest of the Holy Grail, or the cup which Our Lord blessed in the Last Supper. The way the knight treats the beggar on his issuing from the castle and the way he treats him upon his return from his wanderings present a striking contrast. Other poems which may be classed as distinctly religious are Parable (two by this name) Ambrose, Extreme Unction, and The Cathedral. The Death of a Friend's Child may be studied profitably by every preacher, and After the Burial should be mastered by every pastor for the purpose of entering into the experiences of others where one so easily misunderstands.

The Cathedral was originally entitled "A Day at Chartres." The reader can spend with profit and delight not merely one, but many, days in that poem. It opens with a discussion of first impressions, then describes the poet's overwhelming impressi n of the cathedral. Within he observes a solitary beldam listlessly counting her beads and has at first a scornful feeling towards her, which quickly gives place to sympathy. This leads to the discussion of the various Faiths that grope after God, and the teaching is that God is nearer than men realize. The ancient forms, bare to the refined descendant of the Puritans, have their uses.

> Be He nowhere else,
> God is in all that liberates and lifts,
> In all that humbles, sweetens, and consoles.

The cathedral was built with a sense of piety and consecration. Each person came bringing his "vote for God," for such were the stones built into that stately structure. From that work of conscience and devotion the " Western Goth " may learn that

>   nothing pays but God,
> Served whether on the smoke-shut battle-field,
> In work obscure done honestly, or vote
> For truth unpopular, or faith maintained
> To ruinous convictions, or good deeds
> Wrought for good's sake, mindless of heaven or hell.

The poem closes with witnessing to the universal presence of God, and leaves the reader in that frame of solemn awe as if he had shared the poet's own vision and experience in the aisles of that impressive cathedral.

One further poem ought to be mentioned for its delicacy of thought and perfectness of finish, and that is *Auf Wiedersehen.*

> Sweet piece of bashful maiden art !
>   The English words had seemed to fain,
> But these—they drew us heart to heart,
> Yet held us tenderly apart ;
>   She said, " *Auf Wiedersehen !* "

Gathering together the impressions of this poet, we find him fearless in moral courage, with unconquerable devotion to truth and scorn of temporizing expedients, with passionate love of freedom and hatred of slavery, with broad philanthropy and pervading piety. His satire is clever, his imagination vivid, his range of thought wide, his intellectual grasp firm, and his expression vigorous. The introductions to the two parts of The Vision of Sir Launfal are models of graceful and delicate fancy clothed in absolute beauty of expression.

Lowell's duties as minister to England came to an end in 1885. The later years of his life, however, were well filled with work. His residence was at Elmwood, Cambridge, where for many years he had been near neighbor to Longfellow. In 1885 he had buried in England his wife. The solitude of his latest years was broken by frequent visits to England where he had many friends, while his time was also occupied by lectures and addresses. He prepared his complete works for the press, so that the public now have them in the form which the author would wish. His friend, Prof. Charles Eliot Norton, has since published his life and letters, to which the reader is referred for a fuller knowledge of this rare man.

He died at Cambridge, August 12, 1891. He left an added dignity to American letters. He not only received the highest honors which his *alma mater*, Harvard, could give, but he was decorated by the universities of Glasgow, Edinburgh, and Bologna, in addition to Oxford and Cambridge above mentioned. To him may be applied the words which he wrote to a friend,—

> The birds are hushed, the poets gone
> Where no harsh critic's lash can reach,
> And still your wingèd brood sing on
> To all who love our English speech.

HENRY KETCHAM

MELIBŒUS-HIPPONAX.

THE

BIGLOW PAPERS

EDITED

WITH AN INTRODUCTION AND NOTES

BY

HOMER WILBUR, A. M.

PASTOR OF THE FIRST CHURCH IN JAALAM, AND (PROSPECTIVE) MEMBER OF
MANY LITERARY, LEARNED AND SCIENTIFIC SOCIETIES
(for which see page v)

The ploughman's whistle, or the trivial flute,
Finds more respect than great Apollo's lute.
Quarles's Emblems, B. II. E. 8.

Margaritas, munde porcine, calcâsti : en, siliquas accipe.
Jac. Car. Fil. ad Pub. Leg. § 1.

NOTE TO TITLE-PAGE.

IT will not have escaped the attentive eye, that I have, on the title-page, omitted those honorary appendages to the editorial name which not only add greatly to the value of every book, but whet and exacerbate the appetite of the reader. For not only does he surmise that an honorary membership of literary and scientific societies implies a certain amount of necessary distinction on the part of the recipient of such decorations, but he is willing to trust himself more entirely to an author who writes under the fearful responsibility of involving the reputation of such bodies as the *S. Archæol. Dahom.*, or the *Acad. Lit. et Scient. Kamtschat.* I cannot but think that the early editions of Shakspeare and Milton would have met with more rapid and general acceptance, but for the barrenness of their respective title-pages ; and I believe, that, even now, a publisher of the works of either of those justly distinguished men would find his account in procuring their admission to the membership of learned bodies on the Continent,—a proceeding no whit more incongruous than the reversal of the judgment against Socrates, when he was already more than twenty centuries beyond the reach of antidotes, and when his memory had acquired a deserved respectability. I conceive that it was a feeling of the importance of this precaution which induced Mr. Locke to style himself " Gent." on the title-page of his Essay, as who should say to his readers that they

could receive his metaphysics on the honor of a gentle-
man.

Nevertheless, finding, that, without descending to a
smaller size of type than would have been compatible
with the dignity of the several societies to be named, I
could not compress my intended list within the limits
of a single page, and thinking, moreover, that the act
would carry with it an air of decorous modesty, I have
chosen to take the reader aside, as it were, into my
private closet, and there not only exhibit to him the
diplomas which I already possess, but also to furnish
him with a prophetic vision of those which I may, with-
out undue presumption, hope for, as not beyond the
reach of human ambition and attainment. And I am
the rather induced to this from the fact, that my name
has been unaccountably dropped from the last triennial
catalogue of our beloved *Alma Mater*. Whether this is
to be attributed to the difficulty of Latinizing any of
those honorary adjuncts (with a complete list of which
I took care to furnish the proper persons nearly a year
beforehand), or whether it had its origin in any more
culpable motives, I forbear to consider in this place,
the matter being in course of painful investigation.
But, however this may be, I felt the omission the more
keenly, as I had, in expectation of the new catalogue,
enriched the library of the Jaalam Athenæum with the
old one then in my possession, by which means it has
come about that my children will be deprived of a
never-wearying winter-evening's amusement in looking
out the name of their parent in that distinguished roll.
Those harmless innocents had at least committed no——
but I forbear, having intrusted my reflections and
animadversions on this painful topic to the safe-keeping

of my private diary, intended for posthumous publication. I state this fact here, in order that certain nameless individuals, who are, perhaps, overmuch congratulating themselves upon my silence, may know that a rod is in pickle which the vigorous hand of a justly incensed posterity will apply to their memories.

The careful reader will note, that, in the list which I have prepared, I have included the names of several Cisatlantic societies to which a place is not commonly assigned in processions of this nature. I have ventured to do this, not only to encourage native ambition and genius, but also because I have never been able to perceive in what way distance (unless we suppose them at the end of a lever) could increase the weight of learned bodies. As far as I have been able to extend my researches among such stuffed specimens as occasionally reach America, I have discovered no generic difference between the antipodal *Fogrum Japonicum* and the *F. Americanum* sufficiently common in our own immediate neighborhood. Yet, with a becoming deference to the popular belief, that distinctions of this sort are enhanced in value by every additional mile they travel, I have intermixed the names of some tolerably distant literary and other associations with the rest.

I add here, also, an advertisement, which, that it may be the more readily understood by those persons especially interested therein, I have written in that curtailed and otherwise maltreated canine Latin, to the writing and reading of which they are accustomed.

OMNIB. PER TOT. ORB. TERRAR. CATALOG. ACADEM. EDD.

Minim. gent. diplom. ab inclytiss. acad. vest. orans,

vir. honorand. operosiss., at sol. ut sciat. quant. glor.
nom. meum (dipl. fort. concess.) catal. vest. temp.
futur. affer., ill. subjec., addit. omnib. titul. honorar.
qu. adh. non tant. opt. quam probab. put.

*** *Litt. Uncial. distinx. ut Præs. S. Hist. Nat. Jaal.*

HOMERUS WILBUR, Mr., Episc. Jaalam. S. T.
D. 1850, et Yal. 1849, et Neo-Cæs. et Brun. et Gulielm.
1852, et Gul. et Mar. et Bowd. et Georgiop. et Viridi-
mont. et Columb. Nov. Ebor. 1853, et Amherst. et
Watervill. et S. Jarlath. Hib. et S. Mar. et S. Joseph.
et S. And. Scot. 1854, et Nashvill. et Dart. et. Dickins.
et Concord. et Wash. et Columbian. et Charlest. et Jeff.
et Dubl. et Oxon. et Cantab. et cæt. 1855, P. U. N. C. H.
et J. U. D. Gott. et Osnab. et Heidelb. 1860, et
Acad. Bore us. Berolin. Soc. et SS. RR. Lugd. Bat.
et Patav. et Lond. et Edinb. et Ins. Feejee. et Null.
Terr. et Pekin. Soc. Hon. et S. H. S. et S. P. A. et A.
A. S. et S. Humb. Univ. et S. Omn. Rer. Quarund. q.
Aliar. Promov. Passamaquod. et H. P. C. et I. O. H. et
A. Λ. Φ. et II. K. P. et Φ B. K. et Peucin, et Erosoph.
et Philadelph. et Frat. in Unit. et Σ. T. et S. Archæo-
log. Athen. et Acad. Scient. et Lit. Panorm. et SS. R.
H. Matrit. et Beeloochist. et Caffrar. et Caribb. et M.
S. Reg. Paris. et S. Am. Antiserv. Soc. Hon. et P. D.
Gott. et LL. D. 1852, et D. C. L. et Mus. Doc. Oxon.
1860, et M. M. S. S. et M. D. 1854, et Med. Fac. Univ.
Harv. Soc. et S. pro Convers. Pollywog. Soc. Hon. et
Higgl. Piggl. et LL. B. 1853, et S. pro Christianiz.
Moschet. Soc., et SS. Ante-Diluv. ubiq. Gent. Soc.
Hon. et Civit. Cleric. Jaalam. et S. pro Diffus. Gen-
eral. Tenebr. Secret. Corr.

NOTICES OF AN INDEPENDENT PRESS.

[I HAVE observed, reader, (bene- or male-volent, as it may happen,) that it is customary to append to the second editions of books, and to the second works of authors, short sentences commendatory of the first, under the title of *Notices of the Press.* These, I have been given to understand, are procurable at certain established rates, payment being made either in money or advertising patronage by the publisher, or by an adequate outlay of servility on the part of the author. Considering these things with myself, and also that such notices are neither intended, nor generally believed, to convey any real opinions, being a purely ceremonial accompaniment of literature, and resembling certificates to the virtues of various morbiferal panaceas, I conceived that it would be not only more economical to prepare a sufficient number of such myself, but also more immediately subservient to the end in view to prefix them to this our primary edition rather than await the contingency of a second, when they would seem to be of small utility. To delay attaching the *bobs* until the second attempt at flying the kite would indicate but a slender experience in that useful art. Neither has it escaped my notice, nor failed to afford me matter of reflection, that, when a circus or a caravan is about to visit Jaalam, the initial step is to send forward large and highly ornamented bills of perform-

7

ance to be hung in the bar-room and the post-office. These having been sufficiently gazed at, and beginning to lose their attractiveness except for the flies, and, truly, the boys also, (in whom I find it impossible to repress, even during school hours, certain oral and telegraphic correspondences concerning the expected show,) upon some fine morning the band enters in a gaily-painted wagon, or triumphal chariot, and with noisy advertisement, by means of brass, wood, and sheepskin, makes the circuit of our startled village streets. Then, as the exciting sounds draw nearer and nearer, do I desiderate those eyes of Aristarchus, " whose looks were as a breeching to a boy." Then do I perceive, with vain regret of wasted opportunities, the advantage of a pancratic or pantechnic education, since he is most reverenced by my little subjects who can throw the cleanest summerset or walk most securely upon the revolving cask. The story of the Pied Piper becomes for the first time credible to me, (albeit confirmed by the Hameliners dating their legal instruments from the period of his exit,) as I behold how those strains, without pretence of magical potency, bewitch the pupillary legs, nor leave to the pedagogic an entire self-control. For these reasons, lest my kingly prerogative should suffer diminution, I prorogue my restless commons, whom I also follow into the street, chiefly lest some mischief may chance befall them. After the manner of such a band, I send forward the following notices of domestic manufacture, to make brazen proclamation, not unconscious of the advantage which will accrue, if our little craft, *cymbula sutilis*, shall seem to leave port with a clipping breeze, and to carry, in nautical phrase, a bone in her mouth. Nevertheless, I have chosen, as being more equitable, to prepare some also sufficiently objurgatory, that readers of every taste may find a dish to their palate. I have modelled them upon actually existing specimens, preserved in my own cabinet of natural curiosities. One, in particular, I had copied with tolerable exactness from a notice of one of my own discourses, which, from its superior tone and appearance of vast experience, I concluded to have been written by a man at least three hundred years of age, though I recollected no existing instance of such antediluvian longevity. Nevertheless, I afterward discovered the author to be a young gentleman preparing for the ministry under the direction of one of my brethren in a neighboring town, and whom I had once instinctively corrected in a Latin quantity. But this I have been forced to omit, from its too great length.—H. W.]

From the Universal Littery Universe.

Full of passages which rivet the attention of the reader. . . . Under a rustic garb, sentiments are conveyed which should be committed to the memory and engraven on the heart of every moral and social being . . . We consider this a *unique* performance . . . We hope to see it soon introduced into our common schools . . . Mr. Wilbur has performed his duties as editor with excellent taste and judgment . . . This is a vein which we hope to see successfully prosecuted . . . We hail the appearance of this work as a long stride toward the formation of a purely aboriginal, indigenous, nati e and American literature. We rejoice to meet with an author national enough to break away from the slavish deference, too common among us, to English grammar and orthography . . . Where all is so good, we are at a loss how to make extracts, . . . On the whole, we may call it a volume which no library, pretending to entire completeness, should fail to place upon its shelves.

From the Higginbottomopolis Snapping-turtle.

A collection of the merest balderdash and doggerel that it was ever our bad fortune to lay eyes on. The author is a vulgar buffoon, and the editor a talkative, tedious old fool. We use strong language, but should any of our readers peruse the book, (from which calamity Heaven preserve them!) they will find reasons for it thick as the leaves of Vallumbrozer, or, to use a still more expressive comparison, as the combined heads of author and editor. The work is wretchedly got up . . . We should like to know how much *British gold* was pocketed by this libeller of our country and her purest patriots.

From the Oldfogrumville Mentor.

We have not had time to do more than glance through this handsomely printed volume, but the name of its respectable editor, the Rev. Mr. Wilbur, of Jaalam, will afford a sufficient guaranty for the worth of its contents . . . The paper is white, the type clear, and the volume of a convenient and attractive size . . . In reading this elegantly executed work, it has seemed to us that a passage or two might have been retrenched with advantage, and that the general style of diction was susceptible of a higher polish . . . On the whole, we may safely leave the ungrateful task of criticism to the reader. We will barely suggest, that in volumes intended, as this is, for the illustration of a provincial dialect and turns of expression, a dash of humor or satire might be thrown in with advantage . . . The work is admirably got up . . . This work will form an appropriate ornament to the centre-table. It is beautifully printed, on paper of an excellent quality.

From the Dekay Bulwark.

We should be wanting in our duty as the conductor of that tremendous engine, a public press, as an American, and as a man, did we allow such an opportunity as is presented to us by "The Biglow Papers" to pass by without entering our earnest protest against such attempts (now, alas! too common) at demoralizing the public sentiment. Under a wretched mask of stupid drollery, slavery, war, the social glass, and, in short, all the valuable and time-honored institutions justly dear to our common humanity and especially to republicans, are made the butt of coarse and senseless ribaldry by this low-minded scribbler. It is time that the respectable and religious portion of our community should be aroused to the alarming inroads of foreign Jacobinism, sansculottism, and infidelity. It is a fearful proof of the widespread nature of this contagion, that these secret stabs at religion and virtue are given from under the cloak (*credite, posteri!*) of a clergyman. It is a mournful spectacle indeed to the patriot and the Christian to see liberality and new ideas (falsely so called,—they are as old as Eden) invading the sacred precincts of the pulpit . . . On the whole, we consider this volume as one of the first shocking results which we predicted would spring out of the late French " Revolution " (!)

From the Bungtown Copper and Comprehensive Tocsin (a try-weakly family journal).

Altogether an admirable work . . . Full of humor, boisterous, but delicate,—of wit withering and scorching, yet combined with a pathos cool as morning dew,—of satire ponderous as the mace of Richard, yet keen as the scymitar of Saladin . . . A work full of "mountain mirth," mischievous as Puck and lightsome as Ariel . . . We know not whether to admire most the genial, fresh, and discursive concinnity of the author, or his playful fancy, weird imagination, and compass of style, at once both objective and subjective . . . We might indulge in some criticisms, but, were the author other than he is, he would be a different being. As it is, he has a wonderful *pose*, which flits from flower to flower, and bears the reader irresistibly along on its eagle pinions (like Ganymede) to the " highest heaven of invention." . . . We love a book so purely objective . . Many of his pictures of natural scenery have an extraordinary subjective clearness and fidelity . . . In fine, we consider this as one of the most extraordinary volumes of this or any age. We know of no English author who could have written it. It is a work to which the proud genius of our country, standing with one foot on the Aroostook and the other on the Rio Grande, and holding up the star-spangled banner amid the wreck of matter and the crush of worlds. may point with bewildering scorn of the punier efforts of enslaved Europe . . . We hope soon to encounter our author among those higher walks of literature in which he is evidently capable of achieving enduring fame. Already we should be inclined to assign him a high position in the bright galaxy of our American bards.

From the *Saltriver Pilot and Flag of Freedom.*

A volume of bad grammar and worse taste . . . While the pieces here collected were confined to their appropriate sphere in the corners of obscure newspapers, we considered them wholly beneath contempt, but. as the author has chosen to come forward in this public manner, he must expect the lash he so richly merits . . . Contemptible slanders . . . Vilest Billingsgate . . . Has raked all the gutters of our language . . . The most pure, upright, and consistent politicians not safe from his malignant venom . . . General Cushing comes in for a share of his vile calumnies . . . the *Reverend* Homer Wilbur is a disgrace to his cloth . . .

From the *World-Harmonic-Æolian-Attachment.*

Speech is silver : silence is golden. No utterance more Orphic than this. While, therefore, as highest author, we reverence him whose works continue heroically unwritten, we have also our hopeful word for those who with pen (from wing of goose loud-cackling, or seraph God-commissioned) record the thing that is revealed . . . Under mask of quaintest irony, we detect here the deep. storm-tost (nigh shipwrecked) soul, thunder-scarred, semiarticulate, but ever climbing hopefully toward the peaceful summits of an Infinite Sorrow . . . Yes, thou poor, forlorn Hosea, with Hebrew fire-flaming soul in thee, for thee also this life of ours has not been without its aspects of heavenliest pity and laughingest mirth. Conceivable enough ! Through coarse Thersites-cloak, we have revelation of the heart, wild-glowing, world-clasping, that is in him. Bravely he grapples with the life-problem as it presents itself to him, uncombed, shaggy, careless of the "nicer proprieties," inexpert of "elegant diction," yet with voice audible enough to whoso hath ears, up there on the gravelly side-hills, or down on the splashy, India-rubber-like salt-marshes of native Jaalam. To this soul also the *Necessity of Creating* somewhat has unveiled its awful front. If not Œdipuses and Electras and Alcestises, then in God's name Birdofredum Sawins ! These also shall get born into the world, and filch (if so need) a Zingali subsistence therein, these lank, omnivorous Yankees of his. He shall paint the Seen, since the Unseen will not sit to him. Yet in him also are Nibelungen-lays, and Iliads, and Ulysses-wanderings, and Divine Comedies,—if only once he could come at them ! Therein lies much, nay all : for what truly is this which we name *All*, but that which we do *not* possess ? . . . Glimpses also are given us of an old father Ezekiel, not without paternal pride, as is the wont of such. A brown, parchment-hided old man of the geoponic or bucolic species, gray-eyed, we fancy, *queued* perhaps, with much weather-cunning and plentiful September-gale memories, bidding fair in good time to become the Oldest Inhabitant. After such hasty apparition, he vanishes and is seen no more . . . Of "Rev. Homer Wilbur, A. M., Pastor of the First Church in Jaalam," we have small care to speak here. Spare touch in him of his Melesigenes namesake, save haply, the—blindness ! A tolerably caliginose, nephelegeretous elderly gentleman, with infinite faculty of sermonizing, muscularized by long practice, and excellent digestive apparatus, and, for the rest, well-meaning enough, and with small private illuminations (somewhat tallowy, it is to be feared) of his own. To him, there, "Pastor of the First Church in Jaalam," our Hosea presents himself as a quiet inexplicable Sphinx-riddle. A rich poverty of Latin and Greek,—so far is clear enough, even

to eyes peering myopic through horn-lensed editorial specta-
cles,—but naught farther?   O pur-blind, well-meaning, alto-
gether fuscous Melesigenes-Wilbur, there are things in him
incommunicable by stroke of birch!   Did it ever enter that
old bewildered head of thine that there was the *Possibility of
the Infinite* in him?   To thee, quite wingless (and even feath-
erless) biped, has not so much even as a dream of wings ever
come?   "Talented young parishioner"?   Among the Arts
whereof thou art *Magister*, does that of *seeing* happen to be
one?   Unhappy *Artium Magister!*   Somehow a Nemean lion,
fulvous, torrid-eyed, dry-nursed in broad-howling sand-wil-
dernesses of a sufficiently rare spirit-Libya (it may be supposed)
has got whelped among the sheep.   Already he stands wild-
glaring, with feet clutching the ground as with oak-roots,
gathering for a Remus-spring over the walls of thy little fold.
In Heaven's name, go not near him with that fly-bite crook
of thine!   In good time, thou painful preacher, thou wilt go
to the appointed place of departed Artillery-Election Sermons,
Right-Hands of Fellowship, and Results of Councils, gathered
to thy spiritual fathers with much Latin of the Epitaphial sort;
thou, too, shalt have thy reward; but on him the Eumenides
have looked, not Xantippes of the pit, snake-tressed, finger-
threatening, but radiantly calm as on antique gems; for him
paws impatient the winged courser of the gods, champing un-
welcome bit; him the starry deeps, the empyrean glooms,
and far-flashing splendors await.

———

From the Onion Grove Phœnix.

A talented young townsman of ours, recently returned
from a Continental tour, and who is already favorably known
to our readers by his sprightly letters from abroad which
have graced our columns, called at our office yesterday.   We
learn from him, that, having enjoyed the distinguished privi-
lege, while in Germany, of an introduction to the celebrated
Von Humbug, he took the opportunity to present that emi-
nent man with a copy of the "Biglow Papers."   The next
morning he received the following note, which he has kindly

furnished us for publication. We prefer to print *verbatim*, knowing that our readers will readily forgive the few errors into which the illustrious writer has fallen, through ignorance of our language.

" HIGH-WORTHY MISTER !

" I shall also now especially happy starve, because I have more or less a work of one of those aboriginal Red-Men seen in which have I so deaf an interest ever taken fullworthy on the self shelf with our Gootsched to be upset.

" Pardon my in the English-speech unpractice !

" VON HUMBUG."

He also sent with the above note a copy of his famous work on " Cosmetics," to be presented to Mr. Biglow ; but this was taken from our friend by the English customhouse officers, probably through a petty national spite.   No doubt, it has by this time found its way into the British Museum.   We trust this outrage will be exposed in all our American papers.   We shall do our best to bring it to the notice of the State Department.   Our numerous readers will share in the pleasure we experience at seeing our young and vigorous national literature thus encouragingly patted on the head by this venerable and world-renowned German.   We love to see these reciprocations of good-feeling between the different branches of the great Anglo-Saxon race.

[The following genuine "notice" having met my eye, I gladly insert a portion of it here, the more especially as it contains a portion of one of Mr. Biglow's poems not elsewhere printed.—H. W.]

———

From the Jaalam Independent Blunderbuss.

. . . But, while we lament to see our young townsman thus mingling in the heated contests of party politics, we think we detect in him the presence of talents which, if properly directed, might give an innocent pleasure to many.   As a proof that he is competent to the production of other kinds of poetry, we copy for our readers a short fragment of a pastoral by him, the manuscript of which was loaned us by a friend. The title of it is "The Courtin'."

ZEKLE crep' up, quite unbeknown,
  An' peeked in thru the winder,
An' there sot Huldy all alone,
  'ith no one nigh to hender.

Agin' the chimbly crooknecks hung,
  An' in amongst 'em rusted
The old queen's arm thet gran'ther Young
  Fetched back frum Concord busted.

The wannut logs shot sparkles out
  Toward the pootiest, bless her !
An' leetle fires danced all about
  The chiny on the dresser.

The very room, coz she wuz in,
  Looked warm frum floor to ceilin',
An' she looked full ez rosy agin
  Ez th' apples she wuz peelin'.

She heerd a foot an' knowed it, tu,
  Araspin' on the scraper,—
All ways to once her feelins flew
  Like sparks in burnt-up paper.

He kin' o' l'itered on the mat.
  Some doubtfle o' the seekle ;
His heart kep' goin' pitypat,
  But hern went pity Zekle.

     •   •   •   •   •

SATIS multis sese emptores futuros libri professis, Georgius Nichols, Cantabrigiensis, opus emittet de parte gravi sed adhuc neglecta historiæ naturalis, cum titulo sequenti, videlicet :

Conatus ad Delineationem naturalem nonnihil perfectiorem Scarabæi Bombilatoris, vulgo dicti HUMBUG, ab HOMERO WILBUR, Artium Magistro, Societatis historico-naturalis Jaalamensis Præside, (Secretario, Socioque (eheu !) singulo,) multarumque aliarum Societatum eruditarum (sive ineruditarum) tam domesticarum quam transmarinarum Socio—forsitan futuro.

PROEMIUM.

LECTORI BENEVOLO S.

Toga scholastica nondum deposita, quum systemata varia entomologica, a viris ejus scientiæ cultoribus studiosissimis summa diligentia ædificata, penitus indagâssem, non fuit quin luctuose omnibus in iis, quamvis aliter laude dignissimis, hiatum magni momenti perciperem. Tunc, nescio quo motu superiore impulsus, aut qua captus dulcedine operis, ad eum implendum (Curtius alter) me solemniter devovi. Nec ab isto labore, δαιμονιως imposito, abstinui antequam tractatulum sufficienter inconcinnum lingua vernacula perfeceram. Inde, juveniliter tumefactus, et barathro ineptiæ τῶν βιβλιοπωλῶν (necnon " Publici Legentis ") nusquam explorato, me composuisse quod quasi placentas præfervidas (ut sic dicam) homines ingurgitarent

17

credidi. Sed, quum huic et alii bibliopolæ MSS. mea
submisissem et nihil solidius responsione valde negativa
in Musæum meum retulissem, horror ingens atque
misericordia, ob crassitudinem Lambertianam in cere-
bris homunculorum istius muneris cœlesti quadam ira
infixam, me invasere. Extemplo mei solius impensis
librum edere decrevi, nihil omnino dubitans quin
"Mundus Scientificus" (ut aiunt) crumenam meam
ampliter repleret. Nullam, attamen, ex agro illo meo
parvulo segetem demessui, præter gaudium vacuum bene
de Republica merendi. Iste panis meus pretiosus super
aquas literarias fæculentas præfidenter jactus, quasi
Harpyiarum quarundam (scilicet bibliopolarum istorum
facinorosorum supradictorum) tactu rancidus, intra
perpaucos dies mihi domum rediit. Et, quum ipse
tali victu ali non tolerarem, primum in mentem venit
pistori (typographo nempe) nihilominus solvendum
esse. Animum non idcirco demisi, imo æque ac pueri
naviculas suas penes se lino retinent (eo ut e recto cursu
delapsas ad ripam retrahant), sic ego Argô meam char-
taceam fluctibus laborantem a quæsitu velleris aurei,
ipse potius tonsus pelleque exutus, mente solida revo-
cavi. Metaphoram ut mutem, *boomarangam* meam a
scopo aberrantem retraxi, dum majore vi, occasione
ministrante, adversus Fortunam intorquerem. Ast
mihi, ¿talia volventi, et, sicut Saturnus ille παιδοβόρος,
liberos intellectus mei depascere fidenti, casus mise-
randus, nec antea inauditus, supervenit. Nam, ut
ferunt Scythas pietatis causa et parsimoniæ, parentes
suos mortuos devorâsse, sic filius hic meus primogenitus,
Scythis ipsis minus mansuetus, patrem vivum totum et
calcitrantem exsorbere enixus est. Nec tamen hac de
causa sobolem meam esurientem exheredavi. Sed

famem istam pro valido testimonio virilitatis roborisque potius habui, cibumque ad eam satiandam, salva paterna mea carne, petii. Et quia bilem illam scaturientem ad æs etiam concoquendum idoneam esse estimabam, unde æs alienum, ut minoris pretii, haberem, circumspexi. Rebus ita se habentibus, ab avunculo meo Johanne Doolittle, Armigero, impetravi ut pecunias necessarias suppeditaret, ne opus esset mihi universitatem relinquendi antequam ad gradum primum in artibus pervenissem. Tunc ego, salvum facere patronum meum munificum maxime cupiens, omnes libros primæ editionis operis mei non venditos una cum privilegio in omne ævum ejusdem imprimendi et edendi avunculo meo dicto pigneravi. Ex illo die, atro lapide notando, curae vociferantes familiæ singulis annis crescentis eo usque insultabant ut nunquam tam carum pignus e vinculis istis aheneis solvere possem.

Avunculo vero nuper mortuo, quum inter alios consanguineos testamenti ejus lectionem audiendi causa advenissem, erectis auribus verba talia sequentia accepi : —"Quoniam persuasum habeo meum dilectum nepotem Homerum, longa et intima rerum angustarum domi experientia, aptissimum esse qui divitias tueatur, beneficenterque ac prudenter iis divinis creditis utatur,— ergo, motus hisce cogitationibus, exque amore meo in illum magno, do, legoque nepoti caro meo supranominato omnes singularesque istas possessiones nec ponderabiles nec computabiles meas quæ sequuntur, scilicet : quingentos libros quos mihi pigneravit dictus Homerus, anno lucis 1792, cum privilegio edendi et repetendi opus istud 'scientificum' (quod dicunt) suum, si sic elegerit. Tamen D. O. M. precor oculos Homeri nepotis mei ita aperiat eumque moveat, ut libros istos in bibliotheca unius e plurimis castellis suis Hispaniensibus tuto abscondat."

His verbis (vix credibilibus) auditis, cor meum in pectore exsultavit. Deinde, quoniam tractatus Anglice scriptus spem auctoris fefellerat, quippe quum studium Historiæ Naturalis in Republica nostra inter factionis strepitum languescat, Latine versum edere statui, et eo potius quia nescio quomodo disciplina academica et duo diplomata proficiant, nisi quod peritos linguarum omnino mortuarum (et damnandarum, ut dicebat iste πανοῦργος Gulielmus Cobbett) nos faciant.

Et mihi adhuc superstes est tota illa editio prima, quam quasi crepitaculum per quod dentes caninos dentibam retineo.

OPERIS SPECIMEN.

(Ad exemplum Johannis Physiophili speciminis Monachologiæ.

12. S. B. *Militaris*, WILBUR. *Carnifex*, JABLONSK. *Profanus*, DESPONT.

[Male hancce speciem *Cyclopem* Fabricius vocat, ut qui singulo oculo ad quod sui interest distinguitur. Melius vero Isaacus Outis nullum inter S. milit. S. que Belzebul (Fabric. 152) discrimen esse defendit.]

Habitat civitat. Americ. austral.

Aureis lineis splendidus; plerumque tamen sordidus, utpote lanienas valde frequentans, fœtore sanguinis allectus. Amat quoque insuper septa apricari, neque inde, nisi maxima conatione, detruditur. *Candidatus* ergo populariter vocatus. Caput cristam quasi pennarum ostendit. Pro cibo vaccam publicam callide mulget; abdomen enorme; facultas suctus haud facile estimanda. Otiosus, fatuus; ferox nihilominus, semperque dimicare paratus. Tortuose repit.

Capite sæpe maxima cum cura dissecto, ne illud rudimentum etiam cerebri commune omnibus prope insectis detegere poteram.

Unam de hoc S. milit. rem singularem notavi ; nam S. Guineens. (Fabric. 143) servos facit, et idcirco a multis summa in reverentia habitus, quasi scintillas rationis pæne humanæ demonstrans.

24 S. B. *Criticus*, WILBUR. *Zoilus*, FABRIC. *Pygmœus,* CARLSEN.

[Stultissime Johannes Stryx cum S. punctato (Fabric. 64–109) confundit. Specimina quamplurima scrutationi microscopicæ subjeci, nunquam tamen unum ulla indicia puncti cujusvis prorsus ostendentem inveni.]

Præcipue formidolosus, insectatusque, in proxima rima anonyma sese abscondit, *we, we*, creberrime stridens. Ineptus, segnipes.

Habitat ubique gentium ; in sicco ; nidum suum terebratione indefessa ædificans. Cibus. Libros depascit ; siccos præcipue seligens, et forte succidum.

INTRODUCTION.

WHEN, more than three years ago, my talented young parishioner, Mr. Biglow, came to me and submitted to my animadversions the first of his poems which he intended to commit to the more hazardous trial of a city newspaper, it never so much as entered my imagination to conceive that his productions would ever be gathered into a fair volume, and ushered into the august presence of the reading public by myself. So little are we short-sighted mortals able to predict the event! I confess that there is to me a quite new satisfaction in being associated (though only as sleeping partner) in a book which can stand by itself in an independent unity on the shelves of libraries. For there is always this drawback from the pleasure of printing a sermon, that, whereas the queasy stomach of this generation will not bear a discourse long enough to make a separate volume, those religious and godly-minded children (those Samuels, if I may call them so) of the brain must at first lie buried in an undistinguished heap, and then get such resurrection as is vouchsafed to them, mummy-wrapt with a score of others in a cheap binding, with no other mark of distinction than the word " *Miscellaneous* " printed upon the back. Far be it from me to claim any credit for the quite unexpected popularity which I am pleased to find these bucolic strains have attained unto. If I know myself, I am measurably free from the itch of

23

vanity ; yet I may be allowed to say that I was not backward to recognize in them a certain wild, puckery, acidulous (sometimes even verging toward that point which, in our rustic phrase, is termed *shut-eye*) flavor, not wholly unpleasing, nor unwholesome, to palates cloyed with the sugariness of tamed and cultivated fruit. It may be, also, that some touches of my own, here and there, may have led to their wider acceptance, albeit solely from my larger experience of literature and authorship.*

I was, at first, inclined to discourage Mr. Biglow's attempts, as knowing that the desire to poetize is one of the diseases naturally incident to adolescence, which, if the fitting remedies be not at once and with a bold hand applied, may become chronic, and render one, who might else have become in due time an ornament of the social circle, a painful object even to nearest friends and relatives. But thinking, on a further experience, that there was a germ of promise in him which required only culture and the pulling up of weeds from around it, I thought it best to set before him the acknowledged examples of English compositions in verse, and leave the rest to natural emulation. With this view, I accordingly lent him some volumes of Pope and Goldsmith, to the assiduous study of which he promised to devote his evenings. Not long afterward, he brought me some verses written upon that model,

---

* The reader curious in such matters may refer (if he can find them) to "A Sermon Preached on the Anniversary of the Dark Day," "An Artillery Election Sermon," "A Discourse on the Late Eclipse," "Dorcas, a Funeral Sermon on the Death of Madam Submit Tidd, Relict of the late Experience Tidd, Esq.," &c., &c.

a specimen of which I subjoin, having changed some phrases of less elegancy, and a few rhymes objectionable to the cultivated ear. The poem consisted of childish reminiscences, and the sketches which follow will not seem destitute of truth to those whose fortunate education began in a country village. And, first, let us hang up his charcoal portrait of the schooldame.

"Propt on the marsh, a dwelling now, I see
The humble schoolhouse of my A, B, C,
Where well-drilled urchins, each behind his tire,
Waited in ranks the wished command to fire,
Then all together, when the signal came,
Discharged their *a-b abs* against the dame,
Who, 'mid the volleyed learning, firm and calm,
Patted the furloughed ferule on her palm,
And, to our wonder, could detect at once
Who flashed the pan, and who was downright dunce.
There young Devotion learned to climb with ease
The gnarly limbs of Scripture family-trees,
And he was most commended and admired
Who soonest to the topmost twig perspired;
Each name was called as many various ways
As pleased the reader's ear on different days,
So that the weather, or the ferule's stings,
Colds in the head, or fifty other things,
Transformed the helpless Hebrew thrice a week
To guttural Pequot or resounding Greek,
The vibrant accent skipping here and there,
Just as it pleased invention or despair;
No controversial Hebraist was the Dame:
With or without the points pleased her the same;
If any tyro found a name too tough,
And looked at her, pride furnished skill enough:
She nerved her larynx for the desperate thing,
And cleared the five-barred syllables at a spring.

> Ah, dear old times ! there once it was my hap,
> Perched on a stool, to wear the long-eared cap ;
> From books degraded, there 1 sat at ease,
> A drone, the envy of compulsory bees."

I add only one further extract, which will possess a melancholy interest to all such as have endeavored to gleam the materials of Revolutionary history from the lips of aged persons, who took a part in the actual making of it, and, finding the manufacture profitable, continued the supply in an adequate proportion to the demand.

> " Old Joe is gone, who saw hot Percy goad
> His slow artillery up the Concord road,
> A tale which grew in wonder, year by year,
> As, every time he told it, Joe drew near
> To the main fight, till, faded and grown gray,
> The original scene to bolder tints gave way :
> Then Joe had heard the foe's scared double-quick
> Beat on stove drum with one uncaptured stick,
> And, ere death came the lengthening tale to lop,
> Himself had fired, and seen a red-coat drop ;
> Had Joe lived long enough, that scrambling fight
> Had squared more nearly to his sense of right,
> And vanquished Percy. to complete the tale,
> Had hammered stone for life in Concord jail."

I do not know that the foregoing extracts ought not to be called my own rather than Mr. Biglow's, as indeed, he maintained stoutly that my file had left nothing of his in them.   I should not, perhaps, have felt entitled to take so great liberties with them, had I not more than suspected an hereditary vein of poetry in myself, a very near ancestor having written a Latin poem in the Harvard *Gratulatio* on the accession of George the Third,

Suffice it to say, that, whether not satisfied with such limited approbation as I could conscientiously bestow, or from a sense of natural inaptitude, I know not, certain it is that my young friend could never be induced to any further essays in this kind. He affirmed that it was to him like writing in a foreign tongue,—that Mr. Pope's versification was like the regular ticking of one of Willard's clocks, in which one could fancy, after long listening, a certain kind of rhythm or tune, but which yet was only a poverty-stricken *tick, tick,* after all,—and that he had never seen a sweet-water on a trellis growing so fairly, or in forms so pleasing to his eye, as a fox-grape over a scrub-oak in a swamp. He added I know not what, to the effect that the sweet-water would only be the more disfigured by having its leaves starched and ironed out, and that Pegāsus (so he called him) hardly looked right with his mane and tail in curl-papers. These and other such opinions I did not long strive to eradicate, attributing them rather to a defective education and senses untuned by too long familiarity with purely natural objects, than to a perverted moral sense. I was the more inclined to this leniency since sufficient evidence was not to seek, that his verses, as wanting as they certainly were in classic polish and point, had somehow taken hold of the public ear in a surprising manner. So, only setting him right as to the quantity of the proper name Pegasus, I left him to follow the bent of his natural genius.

There are two things upon which it would seem fitting to dilate somewhat more largely in this place,—the Yankee character and the Yankee dialect. And, first, of the Yankee character, which has wanted neither open maligners, nor even more dangerous enemies in

the persons of those unskilful painters who have given
to it that hardness, angularity, and want of proper per-
spective, which, in truth, belonged, not to their sub-
ject, but to their own niggard and unskilful pencil.

New England was not so much the colony of a mother
country, as a Hagar driven forth into the wilderness.
The little self-exiled band which came hither in 1620
came, not to seek gold, but to found a democracy.
They came that they might have the privilege to work
and pray, to sit upon hard benches and listen to pain-
ful preachers as long as they would, yea, even unto
thirty-seventhly, if the spirit so willed it.   And surely,
if the Greek might boast his Thermopylæ, where three
hundred men fell in resisting the Persian, we may well
be proud of our Plymouth Rock, where a handful of
men, women, and children not merely faced, but van-
quished, winter, famine, the wilderness, and the yet
more invincible *storge* that drew them back to the green
island far away.   These found no lotus growing upon
the surly shore, the taste of which could make them
forget their little native Ithaca ; nor were they so
wanting to themselves in faith as to burn their ship,
but could see the fair west wind belly the homeward
sail, and then turn unrepining to grapple with the
terrible Unknown.

As Want was the prime foe these hardy exodists had
to fortress themselves against, so it is little wonder if
that traditional feud is long in wearing out of the stock.
The wounds of the old warfare were long ahealing, and
an east wind of hard times puts a new ache in every one
of them.   Thrift was the first lesson in their horn-book,
pointed out, letter after letter, by the lean finger of the
hard schoolmaster, Necessity.   Neither were those

plump, rosy-gilled Englishmen that came hither, but a hard-faced, atrabilious, earnest-eyed race, stiff from long wrestling with the Lord in prayer, and who had taught Satan to dread the new Puritan hug. Add two hundred years' influence of soil, climate, and exposure, with its necessary result of idiosyncrasies, and we have the present Yankee, full of expedients, half master of all trades, inventive in all but the beautiful, full of shifts, not yet capable of comfort, armed at all points against the old enemy Hunger, longanimous, good at patching, not so careful for what is best as for what will *do,* with a clasp to his purse and a button to his pocket, not skilled to build against Time, as in old countries, but against sore-pressing Need, accustomed to move the world with no ποῦ στῶ but his own two feet, and no lever but his own long forecast. A strange hybrid, indeed, did circumstances beget, here in the New World, upon the old Puritan stock, and the earth never before saw such mystic-practicalism, such niggard-geniality, such calculating-fanaticism, such cast-iron-enthusiasm, such unwilling-humor, such close-fisted-generosity. This new *Græculus esuriens* will make a living out of any thing. He will invent new trades as well as tools. His brain is his capital, and he will get education at all risks. Put him on Juan Fernandez, and he would make a spelling-book first, and a salt-pan afterward. *In cœlum jusseris, ibit,*—or the other way either,—it is all one, so any thing is to be got by it. Yet, after all, thin, speculative Jonathan is more like the Englishman of two centuries ago than John Bull himself is. He has lost somewhat in solidity, has become fluent and adaptable, but more of the original groundwork of character remains. He feels more at home with Fulke Greville, Herbert of Cherbury, Quarles, George Herbert, and Browne, than with his modern English cousins. He is nearer than John, by at least a hundred years, to Naseby, Marston Moor, Worcester, and the time when, if ever, there were true Englishmen. John Bull has suffered the idea of the Invisible to be very much fattened out of him. Jonathan is conscious still that he lives in the world of the Unseen as well as of the Seen. To move John, you must make your fulcrum of solid beef and pudding; an abstract idea will do for Jonathan.

⁎ TO THE INDULGENT READER.

My friend, the Reverend Mr. Wilbur, having been seized with a dangerous fit of illness, before this Introduction had passed through the press, and being incapacitated for all literary exertion, sent to me his notes, memoranda, &c., and requested me to fashion them into some shape more fitting for the general eye. This, owing to the fragmentary and disjointed state of his manuscripts, I have felt wholly unable to do; yet, being unwilling that the reader should be deprived of such parts of his lucubrations as seemed more finished, and not well discerning how to segregate these from the rest, I have concluded to send them all to the press precisely as they are.

COLUMBUS NYE, *Pastor of a Church in Bungtown Corner.*

It remains to speak of the Yankee dialect. And, first, it may be premised, in a general way, that any one much read in the writings of the early colonists need not be told that the far greater share of the words and phrases now esteemed peculiar to New England, and local there, were brought from the mother country. A person familiar with the dialect of certain portions of Massachusetts will not fail to recognize, in ordinary discourse, many words now noted in English vocabularies as archaic, the greater part of which were in common use about the time of the King James translation of the Bible. Shakspeare stands less in need of a glossary to most New Englanders than to many a native of the Old Country. The peculiarities of our speech, however, are rapidly wearing out. As there is no country where reading is so universal and newspapers are so multitudinous, so no phrase remains long local, but is transplanted in the mail bags to every remotest corner of the land. Consequently our dialect approaches nearer to uniformity than that of any other nation.

The English have complained of us for coining new words. Many of those so stigmatized were old ones by them forgotten, and all make now an unquestioned part of the currency, wherever English is spoken. Undoubtedly, we have a right to make new words, as they are needed by the fresh aspects under which life presents itself here in the New World ; and, indeed, wherever a language is alive, it grows. It might be questioned whether we could not establish a stronger title to the ownership of the English tongue than the mother-islanders themselves. Here, past all question, is to be its great home and centre. And not only is it already spoken here by greater numbers, but with a far higher popular average of correctness, than in Britain. The great writers of it, too, we might claim as ours, were ownership to be settled by the number of readers and lovers.

As regards the provincialisms to be met with in this volume, 1 may say that the reader will not find one which is not (as I believe) either native or imported with the early settlers, nor one which I have not, with my own ears, heard in familiar use. In the metrical portion of the book, I have endeavored to adapt the spelling as nearly as possible to the ordinary mode of pronunciation. Let the reader who deems me over-particular remember this caution of Martial :—

> " *Quem recitas, meus est, O Fidentine libellus ;*
> *Sed male cum recitas, incipit esse tuus.*"

A few further explanatory remarks will not be impertinent.

I shall barely lay down a few general rules for the reader's guidance.

1. The genuine Yankee never gives the rough sound to the *r* when he can help it, and often displays considerable ingenuity in avoiding it even before a vowel.

2. He seldom sounds the final *g*, a piece of self-denial, if we consider his partiality for nasals. The same of the final *d*. as *han'* and *stan'* for *hand* and *stand.*

3. The *h* in such words as *while, when, where*, he omits altogether.

4. In regard to *a*, he shows some inconsistency, sometimes giving a close and obscure sound. as *hev* for *have*, *hendy* for *handy*, *ez* for *as*, *thet* for *that*, and again giving it the broad sound it has in *father*, as *hánsome* for *handsome.*

5. To the sound *ou* he prefixes an *e* (hard to exemplify otherwise than orally).

The following passage in Shakspeare he would recite thus :—

> Neow is the winta uv eour discontent
> Med glorious summa by this sun o' Yock,
> An' all the cleouds thet leowered upon eour heouse
> In the deep buzzum o' the oshin buried ;
> Neow air eour breows beound 'ith victorious wreaths ;
> Eour breused arms hung up fer monimunce ;
> Eour starn alarums chānged to merry meetins,
> Eour dreffle marches to delightful measures.
> Grim-visaged war heth smeuthed his wrinkled front,
> An' neow. instid o' mountin' barebid steeds
> To fright the souls o' ferfle edverseries,
> He capers nimly in a lady's chāmber,
> To the lascivious pleasin' uv a loot."

6. *Au,* in such words as *daughter* and *slaughter,* he pronounces *ah.*

7. To the dish thus seasoned add a drawl *ad libitum.*

[Mr. Wibur's notes here become entirely fragmentary.—C. N.]

a. Unable to procure a likeness of Mr. Biglow, I thought the curious reader might be gratified with a sight of the editorial effigies. And here a choice between two was offered,—the one a profile (entirely black) cut by Doyle, the other a portrait painted by a native artist of much promise. The first of these seemed wanting in expression, and in the second a slight obliquity of the visual organs has been heightened (perhaps from an over-desire of force on the part of the artist) into too close an approach to actual *strabismus.* This slight divergence in my optical apparatus from the ordinary model—however I may have been taught to regard it in the light of a mercy rather than a cross, since it enabled me to give as much of directness and personal application to my discourses as met the wants of my congregation, without risk of offending any by being supposed to have him or her in my eye (as the saying is)—seemed yet to Mrs. Wilbur a sufficient objection to the engraving of the aforesaid painting. We read of many who either absolutely refused to allow the copying of their features, as especially did Plotinus and Agesilaus among the ancients, not to mention the more modern instances of Scioppius Palæottus, Pinellus, Velserus, Gataker, and others, or were indifferent thereto, as Cromwell.

β. Yet was Cæsar desirous of concealing his baldness. *Per contra*, my Lord Protector's carefulness in the matter of his wart might be cited. Men generally more desirous of being *improved* in their portraits than characters. Shall probably find very unflattered likeness of ourselves in Recording Angel's gallery.

———

γ. Whether any of our national peculiarities may be traced to our use of stoves, as a certain closeness of the lips in pronunciation, and a smothered smoulderingness of disposition, seldom roused to open flame? An unrestrained intercourse with fire probably conducive to generosity and hospitality of soul. Ancient Mexicans used stoves, as the friar Augustin Ruiz reports, Hakluyt, III., 468,—but Popish priests not always reliable authority.

To-day picked my Isabella grapes. Crop injured by attacks of rose-bug in the spring. Whether Noah was justifiable in preserving this class of insects?

δ. Concerning Mr. Biglow's pedigree. Tolerably certain that there was never a poet among his ancestors. An ordination hymn attributed to a maternal uncle, but perhaps a sort of production not demanding the creative faculty.

His grandfather a painter of the grandiose or Michael Angelo school. Seldom painted objects smaller than houses or barns, and these with uncommon expression.

ε. Of the Wilburs no complete pedigree. The crest said to be a *wild boar*, whence, perhaps, the name. (?) A connection with the Earls of Wilbraham (*quasi* wild boar ham) might be made out. This suggestion worth following up. In 1677, John W. m. Expect——, had issue, 1. John, 2. Haggai, 3. Expect, 4. Ruhamah, 5. Desire.

> "Hear lyes yᵉ bodye of Mrs. Expect Wilber,
>   Yᵉ crewell salvages they kil'd her
>   Together wᵗʰ other Christian soles eleaven,
>   October yᵉ ix daye, 1707.
>   Yᵉ stream of Jordan sh' as crost ore
>   And now expeacts me on yᵉ other shore:
>   I live in hope her soon to join ;
>   Her earthlye yeeres were forty and nine."
>   *From Gravestone in Pekussett, North Parish.*

This is unquestionably the same John who afterward (1711) married Tabitha Hagg or Ragg.

But if this were the case, she seems to have died early ; for only three years after, namely, 1714, we have evidence that he married Winifred, daughter of Lieutenant Tipping.

He seems to have been a man of substance, for we find him in 1696 conveying " one undivided eightieth part of a salt-meadow " in Yabbok, and he commanded a sloop in 1702.

Those who doubt the importance of genealogical studies *fuste potius quam argumento erudiendi.*

I trace him as far as 1723, and there lose him. In that year he was chosen selectman.

No gravestone. Perhaps overthrown when new hearse-house was built, 1802.

He was probably the son of John, who came from Bilham Comit. Salop. circa 1642.

This first John was a man of considerable importance, being twice mentioned with the honorable prefix of *Mr.* in the town records. Name spelt with two *l*'s.

> " Hear lyeth ye bod [*stone unhappily broken.*]
>   Mr. Ihon Willber [Esq.] [*I enclose this in brackets*
>   *as doubtful. To me it seems clear.*]
>   Ob't die [*illegible ; looks like xviii.*]. . . . . iii [*prob.* 1693.]
>   .   .   .   .   paynt
>   .   .   .   .   deseased seinte :
>   A friend and [fath]er untoe all ye opreast,
>   Hee gave ye wicked familists noe reast.
>   When Sat[an bl]ewe his Antinomian blaste,
>   Wee clong to [Willber as a steadf]ast maste.
>   [A]gaynst ye horrid Qua[kers] . . . . .

It is greatly to be lamented that this curious epitaph is mutilated. It is said that the sacrilegious British soldiers made a target of this stone during the war of Independence. How odious an animosity which pauses not at the grave ! How brutal that which spares not the monuments of authentic history ! This is not improbably from the pen of Rev. Moody Pyram, who is mentioned by Hubbard as having been noted for a silver vein of poetry. If his papers be still extant, a copy might possibly be recovered.

THE BIGLOW PAPERS.

No. I.

A LETTER

FROM MR. EZEKIEL BIGLOW OF JAALAM TO THE HON. JOSEPH T. BUCKINGHAM, EDITOR OF THE BOSTON COURIER, INCLOSING A POEM OF HIS SON, MR. HOSEA BIGLOW.

JAYLEM, june 1846.

MISTER EDDYTER :—Our Hosea wuz down to Boston last week, and he see a cruetin Sarjunt a struttin round as popler as a hen with 1 chicking, with 2 fellers a drummin and fifin arter him like all nater. the sarjunt he thout Hosea hedn't gut his i teeth cut cos he looked a kindo's though he's jest com down, so he cal'lated to hook him in, but Hosy woodn't take none o' his sarse for all he hed much as 20 Rooster's tales stuck onto his hat and eenamost enuf brass a bobbin up and down on his shoulders and figureed onto his coat and trousis, let alone wut nater hed sot in his featers, to make a 6 pounder out on.

wal, Hosea he com home considerabal riled, and arter I 'd gone to bed I heern Him a thrashin round like a short-tailed Bull in fli-time. The old Woman ses she

37

to me ses she, Zekle, ses she. our Hosee's gut the chol-
lery or suthin anuther ses she, don't you Bee skeered,
ses I, he's oney amakin pottery * ses i, he's ollers on
hand at that ere busynes like Da & martin, and shure
enuf, cum mornin, Hosy he cum down stares full chiz-
zle, hare on eend and cote tales flyin, and sot rite of to
go reed his varses to Parson Wilbur bein he hain't aney
grate shows o' book larnin himself, bimeby he cum back
and sed the parson wuz dreffle tickled with 'em as i
hoop you will Be, and said they wuz True grit.

Hosea ses, tain't hardly fair to call 'em hisn now, cos
the parson kind o' slicked off sum o' the last varses, but
he told Hosee he didn't want to put his ore in to tetch
to the Rest on 'em, bein they wuz verry well As thay
wuz, and then Hosy ses he sed suthin a nuther about
Simplex Mundishes or sum sech feller, but I guess Hosea
kind o' didn't hear him. for I never hearn o' nobody o'
that name in this villadge, and I've lived here man and
boy 76 year cum next tater diggin, and thair ain't no
wheres a kitting spryer 'n I be.

If you print 'em I wish you'd jest let folks know who
hosy's father is, cos my ant Keziah used to say it's nater
to be curus ses she, she ain't livin though and he's a
likely kind o' lad.

EZEKIEL BIGLOW.

THRASH away, you 'll *hev* to rattle
   On them kittle drums o' yourn,—
'Tain't a knowin' kind o' cattle
   Thet is ketched with mouldy corn ;

* *Aut insanit, aut versos facit.—H. W.*

Put in stiff, you fifer feller,
  Let folks see how spry you be,—
Guess you 'll toot till you are yeller
  'Fore you git ahold o' me !

Thet air flag 's a lettle rotten,
  Hope it ain't your Sunday's best ;—
Fact ! it takes a sight o' cotton
  To stuff out a soger's chest :
Sence we farmers hev to pay fer 't,
  Ef you must wear humps like these,
Sposin' you should try salt hay fer 't,
  It would du ez slick ez grease.

'T would n't suit them Southern fellers,
  They 're a dreffle graspin' set,
We must ollers blow the bellers
  Wen they want their irons het ;
May be it 's all right ez preachin',
  But *my* narves it kind o' grates,
Wen I see the overreachin'
  O' them nigger-drivin' States.

Them thet rule us, them slave-traders,
  Hain't they cut a thunderin' swarth,
(Helped by Yankee renegaders,)
  Thru the vartu o' the North !
We begin to think it 's nater
  To take sarse an' not be riled ;—
Who 'd expect to see a tater
  All on eend at bein' biled ?

Ez fer war, I call it murder, —
  There you hev it plain an' flat;
I don't want to go no furder
  Than my Testyment fer that;
God hez sed so plump an' fairly,
  It 's ez long ez it is broad,
An' you 've gut to git up airly
  Ef you want to take in God.

'T ain't your eppyletts an' feathers
  Make the thing a grain more right;
'Taint afollerin' your bell-wethers
  Will excuse ye in His sight :
Ef you take a sword an' dror it,
  An' go stick a feller thru,
Guv'ment ain't to answer for it,
  God 'll send the bill to you.

Wut 's the use o' meeting-goin'
  Every Sabbath, wet or dry,
Ef it 's right to go amowin'
  Feller-men like oats an' rye ?
I dunno but wut it 's pooty
  Training round in bobtail coats,—
But it 's curus Christian dooty
  This ere cuttin' folks's throats.

They may talk o' Freedom's airy
  Tell they 're pupple in the face,—
It 's a grand gret cemetary
  Fer the barthrights of our race;

They jest want this Californy
  So 's to lug new slave-states in
To abuse ye, an' to scorn ye,
  An' to plunder ye like sin.

Ain't it cute to see a Yankee
  Take sech everlastin' pains,
All to git the Devil's thankee,
  Helpin' on 'em weld their chains?
Wy, it 's jest ez clear ez figgers,
  Clear ez one an' one make two,
Chaps thet make black slaves o' niggers
  Want to make wite slaves o' you.

Tell me jest the eend I 've come to
  Arter cipherin' plaguy smart,
An' it makes a handy sum, tu,
  Any gump could larn by heart;
Laborin' man an' laborin' woman
  Hev one glory an' one shame,
Ev'y thin' thet 's done inhuman
  Injers all on 'em the same.

'Tain't by turnin' out to hack folks
  You 're goin' to git your right,
Nor by lookin' down on black folks
  Coz you 're put upon by wite;
Slavery ain't o' nary color,
  'Tain't the hide thet makes it wus,
All it keers fer in a feller
  'S jest to make him fill its pus.

Want to tackle *me* in, du ye ?
  I expect you 'll hev to wait ;
Wen cold lead puts daylight thru ye
  You 'll begin to kal'late ;
'Spose the crows wun't fall to pickin'
  All the carkiss from your bones,
Coz you helped to give a lickin'
  To them poor half-Spanish drones ?

Jest go home an' ask our Nancy
  Wether I 'd be sech a goose
Ez to jine ye,—guess you 'd fancy
  The etarnal bung wuz loose !
She wants me fer home consumption,
  Let alone the hay 's to mow,—
Ef you 're arter folks o' gumption,
  You 've a darned long row to hoe.

Take them editors thet 's crowin'
  Like a cockerel three months old,—
Don't ketch any on 'em goin',
  Though they *be* so blasted bold ;
Ain't they a prime set o' fellers ?
  'Fore they think on 't they will sprout,
(Like a peach thet's got the yellers,)
  With the meanness bustin' out.

Wal, go 'long to help 'em stealin'
  Bigger pens to cram with slaves,
Help the men thet 's ollers dealin'
  Insults on your fathers' graves ;

Help the strong to grind the feeble,
   Help the many agin the few,
Help the men thet call your people
   Witewashed slaves an' peddling crew !

Massachusetts, God forgive her,
   She 's akneelin' with the rest,
She, thet ough' to ha' clung fer ever
   In her grand old eagle-nest ;
She thet ough' to stand so fearless
   Wile the wracks are round her hurled,
Holdin' up a beacon peerless
   To the oppressed of all the world !

Hain't they sold your colored seamen ?
   Hain't they made your env'ys wiz ?
Wut 'll make ye act like freemen ?
   Wut 'll git your dander riz ?
Come, I 'll tell ye wut I 'm thinkin'
   Is our dooty in this fix,
They 'd ha' done 't ez quick ez winkin'
   In the days o' seventy-six.

Clang the bells in every steeple,
   Call all true men to disown
The tradoocers of our people,
   The enslavers o' their own ;
Let our dear old Bay State proudly
   Put the trumpet to her mouth,
Let her ring this messidge loudly
   In the ears of all the South :—

" I 'll return ye good fer evil
  Much ez we frail mortils can,
But I wun't go help the Devil
  Makin' man the cus o' man ;
Call me coward, call me traiter,
  Jest ez suits your mean idees,—
Here I stand a tyrant-hater,
  An' the friend o' God an' Peace ! "

Ef I 'd *my* way I hed ruther
  We should go to work an' part,—
They take one way, we take t'other,—
  Guess it would n't break my heart ;
Man hed ough' to put asunder
  Them thet God has noways jined ;
An' I should n't gretly wonder
  Ef there 's thousands o' my mind.

[The first recruiting sergeant on record I conceive
to have been that individual who is mentioned in the
Book of Job as *going to and fro in the earth, and walk-
ing up and down in it.* Bishop Latimer will have him
to have been a bishop, but to me that other calling
would appear more congenial. The sect of Cainites is
not yet extinct, who esteemed the firstborn of Adam
to be the most worthy, not only because of that priv-
ilege of primogeniture, but inasmuch as he was able to
overcome and slay his younger brother. That was a
wise saying of the famous Marquis Pescara to the Papal
Legate, that *it was impossible for men to serve Mars
and Christ at the same time.* Yet in time past the pro-
fession of arms was judged to be κατ' ἐξοχήν that of a
gentleman, nor does this opinion want for strenuous

upholders even in our day. Must we suppose, then, that the profession of Christianity was only intended for losels, or, at best, to afford an opening for plebeian ambition ? Or shall we hold with that nicely meta- physical Pomeranian, Captain Vratz, who was Count Königsmark's chief instrument in the murder of Mr. Thynne, that the Scheme of Salvation has been ar- ranged with an especial eye to the necessities of the upper classes, and that " God would consider *a gentle- man* and deal with him suitably to the condition and profession he had placed him in ? " It may be said of us all, *Exemplo plus quam ratione vivimus.*—H. W.|

No. II.

A LETTER

FROM MR. HOSEA BIGLOW TO THE HON. J. T. BUCK-
INGHAM, EDITOR OF THE BOSTON COURIER, COVERING
A LETTER FROM MR. B. SAWIN, PRIVATE IN THE
MASSACHUSETTS REGIMENT.

[THIS letter of Mr. Sawin's was not originally written
in verse.   Mr. Biglow, thinking it peculiarly suscep-
tible of metrical adornment, translated it, so to speak,
into his own vernacular tongue.   This is not the time
to consider the question, whether rhyme be a mode of
expression natural to the human race.   If leisure from
other and more important avocations be granted, I
will handle the matter more at large in an appendix to
the present volume.   In this place I will barely remark,
that I have sometimes noticed in the unlanguaged prat-
tlings of infants a fondness for alliteration, assonance,
and even rhyme, in which natural predisposition we
may trace the three degrees through which our Anglo-
Saxon verse rose to its culmination in the poetry of
Pope.   I would not be understood as questioning in
these remarks that pious theory which supposes that
children, if left entirely to themselves, would naturally
discourse in Hebrew.   For this the authority of one
experiment is claimed, and I could, with Sir Thomas
Browne, desire its establishment, inasmuch as the

46

acquirement of that sacred tongue would thereby be facilitated. I am aware that Herodotus states the conclusion of Psammeticus to have been in favor of a dialect of the Phrygian. But, beside the chance that a trial of this importance would hardly be blessed to a Pagan monarch whose only motive was curiosity, we have on the Hebrew side the comparatively recent investigation of James the Fourth of Scotland. I will add to this prefatory remark, that Mr. Sawin, though a native of Jaalam, has never been a stated attendant on the religious exercises of my congregation. I consider my humble efforts prospered in that not one of my sheep hath ever indued the wolf's clothing of war, save for the comparatively innocent diversion of a militia training. Not that my flock are backward to undergo the hardship of *defensive* warfare. They serve cheerfully in the great army which fights even unto death *pro aris et focis,* accoutred with the spade, the axe, the plane, the sledge, the spelling-book, and other such effectual weapons against want and ignorance and unthrift. I have taught them (under God) to esteem our human institutions as but tents of a night, to be stricken whenever Truth puts the bugle to her lips and sounds a march to the heights of wider-viewed intelligence and more perfect organization.—H. W.]

MISTER BUCKINUM, the follerin Billet was writ hum by a Yung feller of our town that wuz cussed fool enuff to goe atrottin inter Miss Chiff arter a Drum and fife. it ain't Nater for a feller to let on that he's sick o' any bizness that He went intu off his own free will and a Cord, but I rather cal'late he's middlin tired o' voluntearin By this Time. I bleeve u may put dependunts on his statemence. For I never heered nothin bad on him let Alone his havin what Parson Wilbur cals a *pongshong* for cocktales, and he ses it wuz a soshiashun of ideas sot him agoin arter the Crootin Sargient cos he wore a cocktale onto his hat.

his Folks gin the letter to me and i shew it to parson Wilbur and he ses it oughter Bee printed. send It to mister Buckinum, ses he. i don't allers agree with him, ses he, but by Time,* ses he, I *du* like a feller that ain't a Feared.

I have intusspussed a Few refleckshuns hear and thair. We're kind o' prest with Hayin.

Ewers respecfly

HOSEA BIGLOW.

THIS kind o' sogerin' ain't a mite like our October
    trainin',
A chap could clear right out from there ef 't only
    looked like rainin'.
An' th' Cunnles, tu, could kiver up their shappoes
    with bandanners,
An' send the insines skootin' to the barroom with their
    banners,
(Fear o' gittin' on 'em spotted,) an' a feller could cry
    quarter

---

* In relation to this expression, I cannot but think that Mr. Biglow has been too hasty in attributing it to me. Though Time be a comparatively innocent personage to swear by, and though Longinus in his discourse Περὶ Ὕψους has commended timely oaths as not only a useful but sublime figure of speech, yet I have always kept my lips free from that abomination. *Odi profanum vulgus*, I hate your swearing and hectoring fellows.—H. W.

Ef he fired away his ramrod arter tu much rum an'
    water.

Recollect wut fun we hed, you 'n I an Ezry Hollis,

Up there to Waltham plain last fall, ahavin' the Corn-
    wallis ? *

This sort o' thing ain't *jest* like thet,—I wish thet I was
    furder,—†

Nimepunce a day fer killin' folks comes kind o' low fer
    murder,

(Wy I 've worked out to slarterin' some fer Deacon Ce-
    phas Billins,

An' in the hardest times there wuz I ollers tetched ten
    shillins,

There's sutthin' gits into my throat thet makes it hard
    to swaller,

It comes so nateral to think about a hempen collar ;

It 's glory,—but, in spite o' all my tryin' to git callous,

I feel a kind o' in a cart, aridin' to the gallus.

But wen it comes to *bein'* killed,—I tell ye I felt
    streaked

The fust time ever I found out **wy baggonets wuz**
    peaked ;

Here 's how it wuz : I started out to go to a fandango,

The sentinul he ups an' sez, "Thet 's furder 'an you
    can go."

"None o' your sarse," sez I ; sez he, "Stan' back !"
    "Ain't you a buster ?"

Sez I, "I 'm up to all thet air, I guess I 've ben to
    muster ;

---

* i hait the Site of a feller with a muskit as I du pizn But
their *is* fun to a cornwallis I ain't agoin' to deny it.—H. B.

† he means Not quite so fur i guess.—H. B.

I know wy sentinuls air sot ; you ain't agoin' to eat
    us ;
Caleb hain't no monopoly to court the scenoreetas ;
My folks to hum air full ez good ez hisn be, by golly !"
An' so ez I wuz goin' by, not thinkin wut would folly,
The everlastin' cus he stuck his one-pronged pitchfork
    in me
An' made a hole right thru my close ez ef I wuz an
    in'my.
Wal, it beats all how big I felt hoorawin' in ole Fun-
    nel
Wen Mister Bolles he gin the sword to our Leftenant
    Cunnle,
(It's Mister Secondary Bolles,* thet writ the prize
    peace essay ;
Thet's why he did n't list himself along o' us, I dessay,)
An' Rantoul, tu, talked pooty loud, but don't put *his*
    foot in it,
Coz human life's so sacred thet he's principled agin'
    it,—
Though I myself can 't rightly see it 's any wus achokin'
    on 'em
Than puttin' bullets thru their lights, or with a bagnet
    pokin' on 'em ;
How dreffle slick he reeled it off, (like Blitz at our
    lyceum
Ahaulin' ribbins from his chops so quick you skeercely
    see 'em,)
About the Anglo-Saxon race (an' saxons would be
    handy
To du the buryin' down here upon the Rio Grandy),

---

* the ignerant creeter meens Sekketary ; but he ollers stuck
to his books like cobbler's wax to an ile-stone.—H. B.

About our patriotic pas an' our star-spangled banner,
Our country's bird alookin' on an' singin' out hosanner,
An' how he (Mister B. himself) wuz happy fer Amer-
    iky,—
I felt, ez sister Patience sez, a leetle mite histericky.
I felt, I swon, ez though it wuz a dreffle kind o' privi-
    lege
A trampin' round thru Boston streets among the gutter's
    drivelage ;
I act'lly thought it wuz a treat to hear a little drum-
    min',
An' it did bonyfidy seem millanyum wuz acomin'
Wen all on us got suits (darned like them wore in the
    state prison)
An' every feller felt ez though all Mexico wuz hisn.*

This 'ere 's about the meanest place a skunk could wal
    diskiver
(Saltillo 's Mexican, I b'lieve, fer wut we call Saltriver).
The sort o' trash a feller gits to eat doos beat all nater,
I 'd give a year's pay fer a smell o' one good bluenose
    tater ;
The country here that Mister Bolles declared to be so
    charmin
Throughout is swarmin' with the most alarmin' kind o'
    varmin'.

   * it must be aloud that thare 's a streak o' nater in lovin' sho,
but it sartinly is 1 of the curusest things in nater to see a ris-
pecktable dri goods dealer (deekon off a chutch mayby) a
riggin' himself out in the Weigh they du and struttin' round
in the Reign aspilin' his trowsis and makin' wet goods of him-
self. Ef any thin 's foolisher and moor dicklus than militerry
gloary it is milishy gloary.—H. B.

He talked about delishis froots, but then it wuz a wopper
    all,
The holl on't 's mud an' prickly pears, with here an'
    there a chapparal ;
You see a feller peekin' out, an', fust you know, a lariat
Is round your throat an' you a copse, 'fore you can say,
    " Wut air ye at ? " *
You never see sech darned gret bugs (it may not be
    irrelevant
To say I 've seen a *scarabæus pilularius* † big ez a year
    old elephant,)
The rigiment come up one day in time to stop a red
    bug
From runnin' off with Cunnle Wright,—'t wuz jest a
    common *cimex lectularius.*
One night I started up on eend an' thought I wuz to
    hum agin,
I heern a horn, thinks I it 's Sol the fisherman hez come
    agin,
His bellowses is sound enough,—ez I 'm a livin creeter,
I felt a thing go thru my leg,—'t wuz nothin' more 'n
    a skeeter !
Then there 's the yaller fever, tu, they call it here el
    vomito,—
(Come, thet wun't du, you landcrab there, I tell ye to
    le' *go* my toe !

* these fellers are verry proppilly called Rank Heroes, and
the more tha kill the ranker and more Herowick tha bekum.
—H. B.

† it wuz " tumblebug " as he Writ it, but the parson put the
Latten instid. i sed tother maid better meeter, but he said
tha was eddykated peepl to Boston and tha would n't stan' it
no how. idnow as tha *wood* and idnow *as* tha wood.—H. B.

My gracious! it 's a scorpion thet 's took a shine to
    play with 't,
I dars n't skeer the tarnal thing fer fear he 'd run away
    with 't.)
Afore I come away from hum I hed a strong persuasion
Thet Mexicans worn't human beans,*—an ourang
    outang nation,
A sort o' folks a chap could kill an' never dream on 't
    arter,
No more 'n a feller 'd dream o' pigs thet he hed hed to
    slarter ;
I 'd an idee thet they were built arter the darkie fashion
    all,
An' kickin' colored folks about, you know, 's a kind o'
    national ;
But when I jined I worn't so wise ez thet air queen o'
    Sheby,
Fer, come to look at 'em, they ain't much diff'rent from
    wut we be,
An' here we air ascrougin' 'em out o' thir own do-
    minions,
Ashelterin' 'em, ez Caleb sez, under our eagle's pin-
    ions,
Wich means to take a feller up jest by the slack o' 's
    trowsis
An' walk him Spanish clean right out o' all his homes
    an' houses ;
Wal, it doos seem a curus way, but then hooraw fer
    Jackson !
It must be right, fer Caleb sez it 's reglar Anglo-saxon.

---

* he means human beins, that 's wut he means. I spose he
kinder thought tha wuz human beans ware the Xisle Poles
comes from.—H. B.

The Mex'cans don't fight fair, they say, they piz'n all
 the water,
An' du amazin' lots o' things thet is n't wut they ough' to ;
Bein' they hain't no lead, they make their bullets out o'
 copper
An' shoot the darned things at us, tu, wich Caleb sez
 ain't proper ;
He sez they 'd ough' to stan' right up an' let us pop 'em
 fairly,
(Guess wen he ketches 'em at thet he 'll hev to git up
 airly,)
Thet our nation 's bigger 'n theirn an' so its rights air
 bigger,
An' thet it 's all to make 'em free thet we air pullin' trig-
 ger.
Thet Anglo Saxondom's idee 's abreakin' 'em to pieces,
An' thet idee 's thet every man doos jest wut he damn
 pleases ;
Ef I don't make his meanin' clear, perhaps in some re-
 spex I can,
I know thet " every man " don't mean a nigger or a
 Mexican ;
An' there 's another thing I know, an' thet is, ef these
 creeturs,
Thet stick an Anglosaxon mask onto State-prison
 feeturs,
Should come to Jaalam Centre fer to argify an' spout
 on 't,
The gals 'ould count the silver spoons the minnit they
 cleared out on 't.

This goin' ware glory waits ye hain't one agreeable
 feetur

An' if it worn't fer wakin' snakes, I'd home agin short
    meter ;

O, would n't I be off, quick time, ef't worn't that I
    wuz sartin

They'd let the daylight into me to pay me fer desartin !

I don't approve o' tellin' tales, but jest to you I may
    state

Our ossifers ain't wut they wuz afore they left the Bay-
    state ;

Then it wuz " Mister Sawin, sir, you're middlin' well
    now, be ye ?

Step up an' take a nipper, sir ; I'm dreffle glad to see
    ye " ;

But now it's " Ware's my eppylet ? here, Sawin, step
    an' fetch it !

An' mind your eye, be thund'rin' spry, or, damn ye,
    you shall ketch it ! "

Wal, ez the Doctor sez, some pork will bile so, but by
    mighty,

Ef I hed some on 'em to hum, I'd give 'em linkum vity,

I'd play the rogue's march on their hides an' other
    music follerin'——

But I must close my letter here, for one on 'em's ahol-
    lerin',

These Anglosaxon ossifers,—wal, tain't no use ajawin',

I'm safe enlisted fer the war,

        Yourn,

           BIRDOFREDOM SAWIN.

[Those have not been wanting (as, indeed, when hath
Satan been to seek for attorneys ?) who have maintained
that our late inroad upon Mexico was undertaken, not
so much for the avenging of any national quarrel, as for

the spreading of free institutions and of Protestantism. *Capita vix duabus Anticyris medenda!* Verily I admire that no pious sergeant among these new Crusaders beheld Martin Luther riding at the front of the host upon a tamed pontifical bull, as, in that former invasion of Mexico, the zealous Diaz (spawn though he were of the Scarlet Woman) was favored with a vision of St. James of Compostella, skewering the infidels upon his apostolical lance. We read, also, that Richard of the lion heart, having gone to Palestine on a similar errand of mercy, was divinely encouraged to cut the throats of such Paynims as refused to swallow the bread of life (doubtless that they might be thereafter incapacitated for swallowing the filthy gobbets of Mahound) by angels of heaven, who cried to the king and his knights,—*Seigneurs, tuez! tuez!* providentially using the French tongue, as being the only one understood by their auditors. This would argue for the pantoglottism of these celestial intelligences, while, on the other hand, the Devil *teste* Cotton Mather, is unversed in certain of the Indian dialects. Yet must he be a semeiologist the most expert, making himself intelligible to every people and kindred by signs; no other discourse, indeed, being needful, than such as the mackerel-fisher holds with his finned quarry, who, if other bait be wanting, can by a bare bit of white rag at the end of a string captivate those foolish fishes. Such piscatorial oratory is Satan cunning in. Before one he trails a hat and feather or a bare feather without a hat; before another, a Presidential chair, or a tidewaiter's stool, or a pulpit in the city, no matter what. To us, dangling there over our heads, they seem junkets dropped out of the seventh heaven, sops dipped in nectar, but, once in our mouths, they are all one, bits of fuzzy cotton.

This, however, by the way. It is time now *revocare gradum*. While so many miracles of this sort, vouched by eyewitnesses, have encouraged the arms of Papists, not to speak of those *Dioscuri* (whom we must conclude imps of the pit) who sundry times captained the pagan Roman soldiery, it is strange that our first American crusade was not in some such wise also signalized. Yet it is said that the Lord hath manifestly prospered our armies. This opens the question, whether, when our hands are strengthened to make great slaughter of our enemies, it be absolutely and demonstratively certain that this might is added to us from above, or whether some Potentate from an opposite quarter may not have a finger in it, as there are few pies into which his meddling digits are not thrust. Would the Sanctifier and Setter-apart of the seventh day have assisted in a victory gained on the Sabbath, as was one in the late war ? Or has that day become less an object of his especial care since the year 1697, when so manifest a providence occurred to Mr. William Trowbridge, in answer to whose prayers, when he and all on shipboard with him were starving, a dolphin was sent daily, " which was enough to serve 'em ; only on *Saturdays* they still catched a couple, and on the *Lord's Days* they could catch none at all " ? Haply they might have been permitted, by way of mortification, to take some few sculpins (those banes of the salt-water angler), which unseemly fish would, moreover, have conveyed to them a symbolical reproof for their breach of the day, being known in the rude dialect of our mariners as *Cape Cod Clergymen*.

It has been a refreshment to many nice consciences to know that our Chief Magistrate would not regard with eyes of approval the (by many esteemed) sinful pastime of dancing, and I own myself to be so far of that mind, that I could not but set my face against this Mexican Polka, though danced to the Presidential piping with a Gubernatorial second. If ever the country should be seized with another such mania *de propagandâ fide*, I think it would be wise to fill our bomb-shells with alternate copies of the Cambridge Platform and the Thirty-nine Articles, which would produce a mixture of the highest explosive power, and to wrap every one of our cannon-balls in a leaf of the New Testament, the reading of which is denied to those who sit in the darkness of Popery. Those iron evangelists would thus be able to disseminate vital religion and Gospel truth in quarters inaccessible to the ordinary missionary. I have seen lads, unimpregnate with the more sublimated punctiliousness of Walton, secure pickerel, taking their unwary *siesta* beneath the lily-pads too nigh the surface, with a gun and small shot. Why not, then, since gunpowder was unknown to the Apostles (not to enter here upon the question whether it were discovered before that period by the Chinese), suit our metaphor to the age in which we live and say *shooters* as well as *fishers* of men?

I do much fear that we shall be seized now and then with a Protestant fervor, as long as we have neighbor Naboths whose wallowings in Papistical mire excite our horror in exact proportion to the size and desirableness of their vineyards. Yet I rejoice that some earnest Protestants have been made by this war,—I mean those who protested against it. Fewer they were than I could wish, for one might imagine America to have been colonized by a tribe of those nondescript African animals the Aye-Ayes, so difficult a word is *No* to us all. There is some malformation or defect of the vocal organs, which either prevents our uttering it at all, or gives it so thick a pronunciation as to be unintelligible. A mouth filled with the national pudding, or watering in expectation thereof, is wholly incompetent to this refractory monosyllable. An abject and herpetic Public Opinion is the Pope, the Anti-Christ, for us to protest against *e corde cordium*. And by what College of Cardinals is this our God's-vicar, our binder and looser, elected ? Very like, by the sacred conclave of Tag, Rag, and Bobtail, in the gracious atmosphere of the grog-shop. Yet it is of this that we must all be puppets. This thumps the pulpit-cushion, this guides the editor's pen, this wags the senator's tongue. This decides what Scriptures are canonical, and shuffles Christ away into the Apocrypha. " According to that sentence fathered upon Solon, Οὕτω δημόσιον κακὸν ἔρχεται οἴκαδ' ἑκάστῳ. This unclean spirit is skilful to assume various shapes. I have known it to enter my own study and nudge my elbow of a Saturday, under the semblance of a wealthy member of my congregation. It were a great blessing, if every particular of what in the sum we call popular sentiment could carry about the name of its manufacturer stamped legibly upon it. I gave a stab under the fifth rib to that pestilent fallacy,—" Our country, right or wrong,"—by tracing its original to a speech of Ensign Cilley at a dinner of the Buugtown Fencibles.—H. W.]

No. III.

WHAT MR. ROBINSON THINKS.

[A FEW remarks on the following verses will not be out of place. The satire in them was not meant to have any personal, but only a general, application. Of the gentleman upon whose letter they were intended as a commentary Mr. Biglow had never heard, till he saw the letter itself. The position of the satirist is oftentimes one which he would not have chosen, had the election been left to himself. In attacking bad principles, he is obliged to select some individual who has made himself their exponent, and in whom they are impersonate, to the end that what he says may not, through ambiguity, be dissipated *tenues in auras.* For what says Seneca ? *Longum iter per præcepta, breve et efficace per exempla.* A bad principle is comparatively harmless while it continues to be an abstraction, nor can the general mind comprehend it fully till it is printed in that large type which all men can read at sight, namely, the life and character, the sayings and doings, of particular persons. It is one of the cunningest fetches of Satan, that he never exposes himself directly to our arrows, but, still dodging behind this neighbor or that acquaintance, compels us to wound him through them, if at all. He holds our affections as hostages, the while he patches up a truce with our conscience.

Meanwhile, let us not forget that the aim of the true

60

satirist is not to be severe upon persons, but only upon falsehood, and, as Truth and Falsehood start from the same point, and sometimes even go along together for a little way, his business is to follow the path of the latter after it diverges, and to show her floundering in the bog at the end of it. Truth is quite beyond the reach of satire. There is so brave a simplicity in her, that she can no more be made ridiculous than an oak or pine. The danger of the satirist is, that continual use may deaden his sensibility to the force of language. He becomes more and more liable to strike harder than he knows or intends. He may be careful to put on his boxing-gloves, and yet forget, that, the older they grow, the more plainly may the knuckles inside be felt. Moreover, in the heat of contest, the eye is insensibly drawn to the crown of victory, whose tawdry tinsel glitters through that dust of the ring which obscures Truth's wreath of simple leaves. I have sometimes thought that my young friend, Mr. Biglow, needed a monitory hand laid on his arm,—*aliquid sufflaminandus erat.* I have never thought it good husbandry to water the tender plants of reform with *aqua fortis*, yet, where so much is to do in the beds, he were a sorry gardener who should wage a whole day's war with an iron scuffle on those ill weeds that make the garden-walks of life unsightly, when a sprinkle of Attic salt will wither them up. *Est ars etiam maledicendi*, says Scaliger, and truly it is a hard thing to say where the graceful gentleness of the lamb merges in downright sheepishness. We may conclude with worthy and wise Dr. Fuller, that " one may be a lamb in private wrongs, but in hearing general affronts to goodness they are asses which are not lions."—H. W,]

GUVENER B. is a sensible man ;
  He stays to his home an' looks arter his folks ;
He draws his furrer ez straight ez he can,
  An' into nobody's tater-patch pokes ;—
        But John P.
        Robinson he
      Sez he wunt vote fer Guvener B.

My ! ain't it terrible ?   Wut shall we du ?
  We can't never choose him, o' course,—thet's flat ;
Guess we shall hev to come round, (don't you ?)
An' go in fer thunder an' guns, an' all that ;
        Fer John P.
        Robinson he
      Sez he wunt vote fer Guvener B.

Gineral C. is a dreffle smart man :
  He 's ben on all sides thet give places or pelf ;
But consistency still wuz a part of his plan,—
  He's ben true to *one* party,—an' thet is himself ;—
        So John P.
        Robinson he
      Sez he shall vote fer Gineral C.

Gineral C. he goes in fer the war ;
  He don't vally principle more 'n an old cud ;
Wut did God make us raytional creeturs fer,
  But glory an' gunpowder, plunder an' blood ?
        So John P.
        Robinson he
      Sez he shall vote fer Gineral C.

We were gittin' on nicely up here to our village,
  With good old idees o' wut's right an' wut ain't,

We kind o' thought Christ went agin war an' pil-
  lage,
  An' thet epplyetts worn't the best mark of a saint ;
    But John P.
    Robinson he
    Sez this kind o' thing's an exploded idee.

The side of our country must ollers be took,
  An' Presidunt Polk, you know, *he* is our country ;
An' the angel thet writes all our sins in a book
  Puts the *debit* to him, an' to us the *per contry* ;
    An' John P.
    Robinson he
    Sez this is his view o' the thing to a T.

Parson Wilbur he calls all these argimunts lies ;
  Sez they 're nothin' on airth but jest *fee, faw,
  fum ;*
An' thet all this big talk of our destinies
  Is half on it ignorance, an 't'other half rum ;
    But John P.
    Robinson he
    Sez it ain't no sech thing ; an', of course, so must
    we.

Parson Wilbur sez *he* never heerd in his life
  Thet th' Apostles rigged out in their swaller-tail
  coats,
An' marched round in front of a drum an' a fife,
  To git some on 'em office, an' some on 'em votes ;
    But John P.
    Robinson he
    Sez they did n't know everythin' down in Judee.

Wal, it 's a marcy we 've gut folks to tell us
  The rights an' the wrongs o' these matters, I vow,—
God sends country lawyers, an' other wise fellers,
    To drive the world's team wen it gits in a slough ;
        Fer John P.
        Robinson he
    Sez the world 'll go right, ef he hollers out Gee !

[The attentive reader will doubtless have perceived in
the foregoing poem an allusion to that pernicious sen-
timent,—" Our country, right or wrong." It is an
abuse of language to call a certain portion of land, much
more, certain personages elevated for the time being to
high station, our country. I would not sever nor loosen
a single one of those ties by which we are united to the
spot of our birth, nor minish by a tittle the respect
due to the Magistrate. I love our own Bay State too
well to do the one, and as for the other, I have myself
for nigh forty years exercised, however unworthily, the
function of Justice of the Peace, having been called
thereto by the unsolicited kindness of that most excellent
man and upright patriot, Caleb Strong. *Patriæ fumus
igne alieno luculentior* is best qualified with this,—*Ubi
libertas, ibi patria.* We are inhabitants of two worlds,
and owe a double, but not a divided, allegiance. In vir-
tue of our clay, this little ball of earth exacts a certain
loyalty of us, while, in our capacity as spirits, we are
admitted citizens of an invisible and holier fatherland.
There is a patriotism of the soul whose claim absolves
us from our other and terrene fealty. Our true coun-
try is that ideal realm which we represent to ourselves
under the names of religion, duty, and the like. Our
terrestrial organizations are but far-off approaches to so

fair a model, and they all are verily traitors who resist not any attempt to divert them from this their original intendment. When, therefore, one would have us to fling up our caps and shout with the multitude,—" *Our country, however bounded!*" he demands of us that we sacrifice the larger to the less, the higher to the lower, and that we yield to the imaginary claims of a few acres of soil our duty and privilege as liegemen of Truth. Our true country is bounded on the north and the south, on the east and the west, by Justice, and when she oversteps that invisible boundary-line by so much as a hair's breadth, she ceases to be our mother, and chooses rather to be looked upon *quasi noverca.* That is a hard choice, when our earthly love of country calls upon us to tread one path and our duty points us to another. We must make as noble and becoming an election as did Penelope between Icarius and Ulysses. Veiling our faces, we must take silently the hand of Duty to follow her.

Shortly after the publication of the foregoing poem, there appeared some comments upon it in one of the public prints which seemed to call for some animadversion. I accordingly addressed to Mr. Buckingham, of the Boston Courier, the following letter.

" JAALAM, November 4, 1847.

" *To the Editor of the Courier:*

" RESPECTED SIR,—Calling at the post office this morning, our worthy and efficient postmaster offered for my perusal a paragraph in the Boston Morning Post of the 3d instant, wherein certain effusions of the pastoral muse are attributed to the pen of Mr. James Russell Lowell. For aught I know or can affirm to the contrary, this Mr. Lowell may be a very deserving person and a youth of parts (though I have seen verses of his which I could never rightly understand) ; and if he be such, he, I am certain, as well as I, would be free from any proclivity to appropriate to himself whatever of credit (or discredit) may honestly belong to another. I am confident, that, in penning these few lines, I am only forestalling a disclaimer from that young gentleman, whose silence hitherto, when rumor pointed to himward, has excited in my bosom mingled emotions of sorrow and surprise. Well may my young parishioner, Mr. Biglow, exclaim with the poet.

'Sic vos non vobis,' &c. ;

though, in saying this, I would not convey the impression that he is a proficient in the Latin tongue,—the tongue, I might add, of a Horace and a Tully.

" Mr. B. does not employ his pen, I can safely say, for any lucre of worldly gain, or to be exalted by the carnal plaudits of men, *digito monstrari*, &c. He does not wait upon Providence for mercies, and in his heart mean *merces*. But I should esteem myself as verily deficient in my duty (who am his friend and in some unworthy sort his spiritual *fidus Achates*, &c.), if I did not step forward to claim for him whatever measure of applause might be assigned to him by the judicious.

" If this were a fitting occasion, I might venture here a brief dissertation touching the manner and kind of my young friend's poetry. But I dubitate whether this abstruser sort of speculation (though enlivened by some apposite instances from Aristophanes) would sufficiently interest your oppidan readers. As regards their satirical tone, and their plainness of speech, I will only say, that, in my pastoral experience, I have found that the Arch-Enemy loves nothing better than to be treated as a religious, moral, and intellectual being, and that there is no *apage Sathanas!* so potent as ridicule. But it is a kind of weapon that must have a button of good-nature on the point of it.

" The productions of Mr. B. have been stigmatized in some quarters as unpatriotic ; but I can vouch that he loves his native soil with that hearty, though discriminating, attachment which springs from an intimate social intercourse of many years' standing. In the ploughing season, no one has a deeper share in the well-being of the country than he. If Dean Swift were right in saying that he who makes two blades of grass grow where one grew before confers a greater benefit on the state than he who taketh a city, Mr. B. might exhibit a fairer claim to the Presidency than General Scott himself. I think that some of those disinterested lovers of the hard-handed democracy, whose fingers have never touched anything rougher than the dollars of our common country, would hesitate to compare palms with him. It would do your heart good, respected Sir, to see that young man mow. He cuts a cleaner and wider swarth than any in his town.

" But it is time for me to be at my Post. It is very clear that my young friend's shot has struck the lintel, for the Post is shaken (Amos ix. 1). The editor of that paper is a strenuous advocate of the Mexican war, and a colonel, as I am given to understand. I presume, that, being necessarily absent in Mexico, he has left his journal in some less judicious hands. At any rate the Post has been too swift on this occasion. It could hardly have cited a more incontrovertible line from

any poem than that which it has selected for animad-
version, namely,—

    ' We kind o' thought Christ went agin war an' pillage.'

    " If the Post maintains the converse of this propo-
sition, it can hardly be considered as a safe guidepost
for the moral and religious portions of its party, how-
ever many other excellent qualities of a post it may be
blessed with. There is a sign in London on which is
painted,—' The Green Man.' It would do very well as
a portrait of any individual who would support so un-
scriptural a thesis. As regards the language of the
line in question, 1 am bold to say that He who readeth
the hearts of men will not account any dialect unseemly
which conveys a sound and pious sentiment. I could
wish that such sentiments were more common, how-
ever uncouthly expressed. Saint Ambrose affirms, that
veritas a quocunque (why not, then, *quomodocunque?*)
dicatur a spiritu sancto est. Digest also this of Bax-
ter :—' The plainest words are the most profitable
oratory in the weightiest matters."

    " When the paragraph in question was shown to Mr.
Biglow, the only part of it which seemed to give him
any dissatisfaction was that which classed him with the
Whig party. He says, that, if resolutions are a nour-
ishing kind of diet, that party must be in a very hearty
and flourishing condition ; for that they have quietly
eaten more good ones of their own baking than he could
have conceived to be possible without repletion. He
has been for some years past (I regret to say) an ardent
opponent of those sound doctrines of protective policy
which form so prominent a portion of the creed of that
party. I confess, that, in some discussions which I

have had with him on this point in my study, he has displayed a vein of obstinacy which I had not hitherto detected in his composition. He is also (*horresco referens* infected in no small measure with the peculiar notions of a print called the Liberator, whose heresies I take every proper opportunity of combating, and of which, I thank God, I have never read a single line.

" I did not see Mr. B.'s verses until they appeared in print, and there *is* certainly one thing in them which I consider highly improper. I allude to the personal references to myself by name. To confer notoriety on an humble individual who is laboring quietly in his vocation, and who keeps his cloth as free as he can from the dust of the political arena (though *væ mihi si non evangelizavero*), is no doubt an indecorum. The sentiments which he attributes to me I will not deny to be mine. They were embodied, though in a different form, in a discourse preached upon the last day of public fasting, and were acceptable to my entire people (of whatever political views), except the postmaster, who dissented *ex officio*. I observe that you sometimes devote a portion of your paper to a religious summary. I should be well pleased to furnish a copy of my discourse for insertion in this department of your instructive journal. By omitting the advertisements, it might easily be got within the limits of a single number, and I venture to insure you the sale of some scores of copies in this town. I will cheerfully render myself responsible for ten. It might possibly be advantageous to issue it as an *extra*. But perhaps you will not esteem it an object, and I will not press it. My offer does not spring from any weak desire of seeing my name in print; for I can enjoy this satisfaction at any time by turning to the Triennial Catalogue of the University, where it also possesses that added emphasis of Italics with which those of my calling are distinguished.

" I would simply add, that I continue to fit ingenuous youth for college, and that I have two spacious and airy sleeping apartments at this moment unoccupied. *Ingenuas didicisse*, &c. Terms, which vary according to the circumstances of the parents, may be known on application to me by letter, post paid. In all cases the lad will be expected to fetch his own towels. This rule, Mrs. W. desires me to add, has no exceptions.

" Respectfully, your obedient servant,
" HOMER WILBUR, A. M."

" P. S. Perhaps the last paragraph may look like an attempt to obtain the insertion of my circular gratuitously. If it should appear to you in that light. I desire that you would erase it. or charge for it at the usual rates, and deduct the amount from the proceeds in your hands from the sale of my discourse, when it shall be printed. My circular is much longer and more explicit, and will be forwarded without charge to any who may desire it. It has been very neatly executed on a letter sheet, by a very deserving printer, who attends upon my ministry, and is a creditable specimen of the typographic art. I have one hung over my mantelpiece in a neat frame, where it makes a beautiful and appropriate ornament, and balances the profile of Mrs. W., cut with her toes by the young lady born without arms.

" H. W."

I have in the foregoing letter mentioned General Scott in connection with the Presidency, because I have been given to understand that he has blown to pieces and otherwise caused to be destroyed more Mexicans than any other commander. His claim would therefore be deservedly considered the strongest. Until accurate returns of the Mexicans killed, wounded, and maimed be obtained, it will be difficult to settle these nice points of precedence. Should it prove that any other officer has been more meritorious and destructive than General S., and has thereby rendered himself more worthy of the confidence and support of the conservative portion of our community, I shall cheerfully insert his name, instead of that of General S., in a future edition. It may be thought, likewise, that General S. has invalidated his claims by too much attention to the decencies of apparel, and the habits belonging to a gentleman. These abstruser points of statesmanship are beyond my scope. I wonder not that successful military achievement should attract the admiration of the multitude. Rather do I rejoice with wonder to behold how rapidly this sentiment is losing its hold upon the popular mind. It is related of Thomas Warton, the second of that honored name who held the office of Poetry Professor at Oxford, that, when one wished to find him, being absconded, as was his wont, in some obscure alehouse, he was counselled to traverse the city with a drum and fife, the sound of which inspiring music would be sure to draw the Doctor from his retirement into the street. We are all more or less bitten with this martial insanity. *Nescio quâ dulcedine. . . . . cunctos ducit.* I confess to some infection of that itch myself. When I see a Brigadier-General maintaining his insecure elevation in the saddle under the severe fire of the training-field, and when I remember that some military enthusiasts, through haste, inexperience, or an over-desire to lend reality to those fictitious combats, will sometimes discharge their ramrods, I cannot but admire, while I deplore, the mistaken devotion of those heroic officers. *Semel insanivimus omnes.* I was myself, during the late war with Great Britain, chaplain of a regiment, which was fortunately never called to active military duty. I mention this circumstance with regret rather than pride. Had I been summoned to actual warfare, I trust that I might have been strengthened to bear myself after the manner of that reverend father in our New England Israel, Dr. Benjamin Colman, who, as we are told in Turell's life of him, when the vessel in which he had taken passage for England was attacked by a French privateer, "fought like a philosopher and a Christian, ... and prayed all the while he charged and fired." As this note is already long, I shall not here enter upon a discussion of the question, whether Christians may lawfully be soldiers. I think it sufficiently evident, that, during the first two centuries of the Christian era, at least, the two professions were esteemed incompatible. Consult Jortin on this head.—H. W.

No. IV.

REMARKS OF INCREASE D. O'PHACE, ESQUIRE, AT AN
EXTRUMPERY CAUCUS IN STATE STREET, REPORTED
BY MR. H. BIGLOW.

[THE ingenious reader will at once understand that
no such speech as the following was ever *totidem verbis*
pronounced. But there are simpler and less guarded
wits, for the satisfying of which such an explanation
may be needful. For there are certain invisible lines,
which as Truth successively overpasses, she becomes
Untruth to one and another, of us, as a large river,
flowing from one kingdom into another, sometimes
takes a new name, albeit the waters undergo no change,
how small soever. There is, moreover, a truth of fic-
tion more veracious than the truth of fact, as that of
the Poet, which represents to us things and events as
they ought to be, rather than servilely copies them as
they are imperfectly imaged in the crooked and smoky
glass of our mundane affairs. It is this which makes
the speech of Antonius, though originally spoken in no
wider a forum than the brain of Shakspeare, more
historically valuable than that other which Appian
has reported, by as much as the understanding of the
Englishman was more comprehensive than that of the
Alexandrian. Mr. Biglow, in the present instance,
has only made use of a license assumed by all the his-
torians of antiquity, who put into the mouths of various

73

characters such words as seem to them most fitting to
the occasion and to the speaker.   If it be objected
that no such oration could ever have been delivered, I
answer, that there are few assemblages for speech-mak-
ing which do not better deserve the title of *Parliamen-
tum Indoctorum* than did the sixth Parliament of
Henry the Fourth, and that men still continue to have
as much faith in the Oracle of Fools as ever Pantagruel
had.   Howell, in his letters, recounts a merry tale of
a certain ambassador of Queen Elizabeth, who, having
written two letters, one to her Majesty and the other
to his wife, directed them at cross-purposes, so that the
Queen was beducked and bedeared and requested to send
a change of hose, and the wife was beprincessed and
otherwise unwontedly besuperlatived, till the one feared
for the wits of her ambassador, the other for those of
her husband.   In like manner it may be presumed that
our speaker has misdirected some of his thoughts, and
given to the whole theatre what he would have wished
to confide only to a select auditory at the back of the
curtain.   For it is seldom that we can get any frank
utterance from men, who address, for the most part, a
Buncombe either in this world or the next.   As for
their audiences, it may be truly said of our people,
that they enjoy one political institution in common
with the ancient Athenians : I mean a certain profitless
kind of *ostracism*, wherewith, nevertheless, they seem
hitherto well enough content.   For in Presidential
elections, and other affairs of the sort, whereas I ob-
serve that the *oysters* fall to the lot of comparatively
few, the *shells* (such as the privileges of voting as they
are told to do by the *ostrivori* aforesaid, and of huzzaing
at public meetings) are very liberally distributed

among the people, as being their prescriptive and quite sufficient portion.

The occasion of the speech is supposed to be Mr. Palfrey's refusal to vote for the Whig candidate for the Speakership.—H. W.]

No? Hez he? He hain't, though? Wut? Voted
  agin him?
Ef the bird of our country could ketch him, she 'd
  skin him;
I seem 's though I see her, with wrath in each quill,
Lake a chancery lawyer, afilin' her bill,
An' grindin' her talents ez sharp ez all nater,
To pounce like a writ on the back o' the traiter.
Forgive me, my friends, ef I seem to be het,
But a crisis like this must with vigor be met;
Wen an Arnold the star-spangled banner bestains,
Holl Fourth o' Julys seem to bile in my veins.

Who ever 'd ha' thought sech a pisonous rig
Would be run by a chap thet wuz chose fer a Wig?
" We knowed wut his principles wuz 'fore we sent
  him"?
Wut wuz ther in them from this vote to pervent him?
A marciful Providunce fashioned us holler
O' purpose thet we might our principles swaller;
It can hold any quantity on 'em, the belly can,
An' bring 'em up ready fer use like the pelican,
Or more like the kangaroo, who (wich is stranger)
Puts her family into her pouch wen there 's danger.
Ain't principle precious? then, who 's goin' to use it
Wen there 's resk o' some chap's gittin' up to abuse it.

I can't tell the wy on 't, but nothin' is *so* sure
Ez thet principle kind o' gits spiled by exposure ; *
A man thet lets all sorts o' folks git a sight on 't
Ough' to hev it all took right away, every mite on 't ;
Ef he can't keep it to himself when it 's wise to,
He ain't one it 's fit to trust nothin' so nice to.

Besides, ther 's a wonderful power in latitude
To shift a man's morril relations an' attitude ;
Some flossifers think thet a fakkilty 's granted
The minnit it 's proved to be thoroughly wanted,
Thet a change o' demand makes a change o' condi-
　　　tion,
An' thet everythin' 's nothin' except by position ;
Ez, fer instance, thet rubber-trees fust begun bearin'
Wen p'litickle conshunces come into wearin',—
Thet the fears of a monkey, whose holt chanced to
　　　fail,
Drawed the vertibry out to a prehensile tail ;
So, wen one 's chose to Congriss, ez soon ez he 's in it,
A collar grows right round his neck in a minnit,
An' sartin it is thet a man cannot be strict
In bein' himself, wen he gits to the Deestrict,

---

* The speaker is of a different mind from Tully, who, in his recently discovered tractate *De Rupublica*, tells us,—*Nec vero haberc vietutem satis est, quasi artem aliqam, nisi utare*, and from our Milton, who says,—"I cannot praise a fugitive and cloistered virtue, unexercised and unbreathed, that never sallies out and sees her adversary, but slinks out of the race where that immortal garland is to be run for, *not without dust and heat.*"—*Arèop.* He had taken the words out of the Roman's mouth, without knowing it, and might well exclaim with Austin (if a saint's name may stand sponsor for a curse), *Pereant qui ante nos nostra dixerint !*—H. W.

Fer a coat thet sets wal here in ole Massachusetts,
Wen it gits on to Washinton, somehow askew sets.

Resolves, do you say, o' the Springfield Convention ?
Thet 's percisely the pint I was goin' to mention ;
Resolves air a thing we most gen'ally keep ill,
They 're a cheap kind o' dust fer the eyes o' the people ;
A parcel o' delligits jest git together
An' chat fer a spell o' the crops an' the weather,
Then, comin' to order, they squabble awile
An' let off the speeches they 're ferful 'll spile ;
Then—Resolve,—That we wunt hev an inch o' slave
    territory ;
Thet President Polk's holl perceedins air very tory ;
Thet the war 's a damned war, an' them thet enlist in it
Should hev a cravat with a dreffle tight twist in it ;
Thet the war is a war fer the spreadin' o' slavery ;
Thet our army desarves our best thanks fer their
    bravery ;
Thet we 're the original friends o' the nation,
All the rest air a paltry an' base fabrication ;
Thet we highly respect Messrs. A, B, an' C,
An' ez deeply despise Messrs. E, F, an' G.

In this way they go to the eend o' the chapter,
An' then they bust out in a kind of a raptur
About their own vartoo, an' folk's stone-blindness
To the men thet 'ould actilly do 'em a kindness,—
The American eagle, the Pilgrims thet landed,
Till on ole Plymouth Rock they git finally stranded.
Wal, the people they listen and say, " Thet 's the
    ticket ;
Ez fer Mexico, 'tain't no great glory to lick it,

But 't would be a darned shame to go pullin' o' **triggers**
To extend the aree of abusin' the niggers."
So they march in percessions, an' git up hooraws,
An' tramp thru the mud fer the good o' the cause,
An' think they 're a kind o' fulfilliu' the prophecies,
Wen they 're on'y jest changin' the holders of offices:
Ware A sot afore, B is comf'tably seated,
One humbug 's victor'ous, an' t'other defeated.
Each honnable doughface gits jest wut he axes,
An' the people---their annooal soft sodder an' taxes.

Now, to keep unimpaired all these glorious feeturs
Thet characterize morril an' reasonin' creeturs,
Thet give every paytriot all he can cram,
Thet oust the untrustworthy Presidunt Flam,
And stick honest Presidunt Sham in his place,
To the manifest gain o' the holl human race,
An' to some indervidgewals on 't in partickler,
Who love Public Opinion an' know how to tickle
     her,—
I say thet a party with great aims liks these
Must stick jest ez close ez a hive full o' bees.

I 'm willin' a man should go tollable strong
Agin wrong in the abstract, fer thet kind o' wrong
Is ollers unpop'lar an' never gits pitied,
Because it 's a crime no one never committed ;
But he mus' n't be hard on partickler sins,
Coz then he'll be kickin' the people's own shins ;
On'y look at the Demmercrats, see wut they 've done
Jest simply by stickin' together like fun ;
They 've sucked us right into a mis'able war
Thet no one on airth ain't responsible for ;

They 've run us a hunderd cool millions in debt,
(An' fer Demmercrat Horners ther 's good plums left
     yet);
They talk agin tayriffs, but act fer a high one,
An' so coax all parties to build up their Zion ;
To the people they 're ollers ez slick ez molasses,
An' butter their bread on both sides with The Masses,
Half o' whom they 've persuaded, by way of a joke,
Thet Washinton's mantelpiece fell upon Polk.

Now all o' these blessins the Wigs might enjoy,
Ef they 'd gumption enough the right means to imploy ; *
Fer the silver spoon born in Dermocracy's mouth
Is a kind of a scringe thet they hev to the South ;
Their masters can cuss 'em an' kick 'em an' wale 'em,
An' they notice it less 'an the ass did to Balaam ;
In this way they screw into second-rate offices
Wich the slaveholder thinks 'ould substract too much
     off his ease ;
The file-leaders, I mean, du, fer they, by their wiles,
Unlike the old viper, grow fat on their files.
Wal, the Wigs hev been tryin' to grab all this prey
     frum 'em
An' to hook his nice spoon o' good fortin' away
     frum 'em,
An' they might ha' succeeded, ez likely ez not
In lickin' the Demmercrats all round the lot,
Ef it warn't thet, wile all faithful Wigs were their
     knees on,

---

* That was a pithy saying of Persius, and fits our politicians
without a wrinkle,—*Magister artis, ingeniique largitor venter.*
—H. W.

Some stuffy old codger would holler out,— "Treason!
You must keep a sharp eye on a dog thet hez bit you
    once,
An' *I* ain't a goin' to cheat my constitoounts,"—
Wen every fool knows thet a man represents
Not the fellers thet sent him, but them on the fence,—
Impartially ready to jump either side
An' make the fust use of a turn o' the tide,—
The waiters on Providunce here in the city,
Who compose wut they call a State Centerl Committy.
Constitoounts air henny to help a man in,
But arterwards don't weigh the heft of a pin.
Wy, the people can't all live on Uncle Sam's pus,
So they 've nothin' to du with 't fer better or wus ;
It 's the folks thet air kind o' brought up to depend
    on 't
Thet hev any consarn in 't, an' thet is the end on 't.

Now here wuz New England ahevin' the honor
Of a chance at the Speakership showered upon her ;—
Do you say,—" She don't want no more Speakers, but
    fewer ;
She's hed plenty o' them, wut she wants is a *doer* "?
Fer the matter o' thet, it 's notorous in town
Thet her own representatives du her quite brown.
But thet 's nothin' to du with it ; wut right hed Pal-
    frey
To mix himself up with fanatical small fry ?
Warn't we gittin' on prime with our hot an' cold blowin',
Acondemnin' the war wilst we kep' it agoin' ?
We 'd assumed with gret skill a commandin' position,
On this side or thet, no one could n't tell wich one,

So, wutever side wipped, we'd a chance at the plunder
An' could sue fer infringin' our paytented thunder ;
We were ready to vote fer whoever wuz eligible,
Ef on all pints at issoo he'd stay unintelligible.
Wal, sposin' we hed to gulp down our perfessions,
We were ready to come out next mornin' with fresh
    ones ;
Besides, ef we did, 't was our business alone,
Fer could n't we du wut we would with our own ?
An' ef a man can, wen pervisions hev riz so,
Eat up his own words, it 's a marcy it is so.

Wy, these chaps frum the North, with back-bones to
    'em, darn 'em,
'Ould be wuth more 'an Gennle Tom Thumb is to Bar-
    num ;
Ther's enough thet to office on this very plan grow,
By exhibitin' how very small a man can grow ;
But an M. C. frum here ollers hastens to state he
Belongs to the order called invertebraty,
Wence some gret filologists judge primy fashy
Thet M. C. is M. T. by paronomashy ;
An' these few exceptions air *loosus naytury*
Folks 'ould put down their quarters to stare at, like
    fury.
It 's no use to open the door o' success,
Ef a member can bolt so fer nothin' or less ;
Wy, all o' them grand constitootional pillers
Our four fathers fetched with 'em over the billers,
Them pillers the people so soundly hev slept on,
Wile to slav'ry, invasion, an' debt they were swept on,
Wile our Destiny higher an' higher kep' mountin',

(Though I guess folks 'll stare wen she hends her ac-
 count in,)
Ef members in this way go kickin' agin 'em,
They wunt hev so much ez a feather left in 'em.

An', ez fer this Palfrey,* we thought wen we 'd gut
 him in,
He 'd go kindly in wutever harness we put him in ;
Supposin' we *did* know thet he wuz a peace man ?
Doos he think he can be Uncle Samwell's policeman,
An' wen Sam gits tipsy an' kicks up a riot,
Lead him off to the lockup to snooze till he 's quiet ?
Wy, the war is a war thet true paytriots can bear, ef
It leads to the fat promised land of a tayriff ;
We don't go an' fight it, nor ain't to be driv on,
Nor Demmercrats nuther, thet hev wut to live on ;
Ef it ain't jest the thing thet 's well pleasin' to God,
It makes us thought highly on elsewhere abroad ;
The Rooshian black eagle looks blue in his eerie
An' shakes both his heads wen he hears o' Monteery ;
In the Tower Victory sets, all of a fluster,
An' reads, with locked doors, how we won Cherry
 Buster ;
An' old Philip Lewis—thet come an' kep' school here
Fer the mere sake o' scorin' his ryalist ruler
On the tenderest part of our kings *in futuro*—
Hides his crown underneath an old shut in his
 bureau,
Breaks off in his brags to a suckle o' merry kings,
How he often hed hided young native Amerrikins,

 *There is truth yet in this of Juvenal,—

  "Dat veniam corvis, vexat censura columbas."

An', turnin' quite faint in the midst of his fooleries,
Sneaks down stairs to bolt the front door o' the Tool-
　　eries.*
You say,—" We 'd ha' scared 'em by growin' in peace,
A plaguy sight more then by bobberies like these " ?
Who is it dares say thet " our naytional eagle
Wunt much longer be classed with the birds thet air
　　regal,
Coz theirn be hooked beaks, an' she, arter this slaughter,
'll bring back a bill ten times longer 'n she oug't to ? "
Wut 's your name ?　Come, I see ye, you up-country
　　feller,
You 've put me out severil times with your beller ;
Out with it !　Wut ?　Biglow ?　I say nothin' furder,
Thet feller would like nothin' better 'n a murder ;
He 's a traiter, blasphemer, an' wut ruther worse is,
He puts all his ath'ism in dreffle bad verses ;

* Jortin is willing to allow of other miracles besides those
recorded in Holy Writ, and why not of other prophecies ?　It
is granting too much to Satan to suppose him, as divers of the
learned have done, the inspirer of the ancient oracles.　Wiser,
I esteem it, to give chance the credit of the successful ones.
What is said here of Louis Philippe was verified in some of its
minute particulars within a few months' time.　Enough to
have made the fortune of Delphi or Hammon, and no thanks
to Beelzebub neither !　That of Seneca in Medea will suit
here :—

" Rapida fortuna ac levis,
Præcepsque regno eripuit, exsilio dedit."

Let us allow, even to richly deserved misfortune, our com-
miseration, and be not over-hasty meanwhile in our censure
of the French people, left for the first time to govern them-
selves, remembering that wise sentence of Æschylus,—

Ἄπας δὲ τραχυς ὅστις ἂν νεον κρατῇ.

H. W.

Socity ain't safe till sech monsters air out on it,
Refer to the Post, ef you hev the least doubt on it ;
Wy, he goes agin war, agin indirect taxes,
Agin sellin' wild lands 'cept to settlers with axes,
Agin holdin' o' slaves, though he knows it 's the corner
Our libbaty rests on, the mis'able scorner !
In short, he would wholly upset with his ravages
All thet keeps us above the brute critters an' savages,
An' pitch into all kinds o' briles an' confusions
The holl of our civilized, free institutions ;
He writes fer thet rather unsafe print, the Courier,
An' likely ez not hez a squintin' to Foorier ;
I 'll be ——, thet is, I mean I 'll be blest,
Ef I hark to a word frum so noted a pest ;
I shan't talk with *him*, my religion 's too fervent.—
Good mornin', my friends, I 'm your most humble
    servant.

[Into the question, whether the ability to express our-
selves in articulate language has been productive of
more good or evil, I shall not here enter at large. The
two faculties of speech and of speech-making are wholly
diverse in their natures. By the first we make our-
selves intelligible, by the last unintelligible, to our
fellows. It has not seldom occurred to me (noting
how in our national legislature every thing runs to
talk, as lettuces, if the season or the soil be unpropi-
tious, shoot up lankly to seed, instead of forming hand-
some heads) that Babel was the first Congress, the
earliest mill erected for the manufacture of gabble. In
these days, what with Town Meetings, School Com-
mittees, Boards (lumber) of one kind and another,
Congresses, Parliaments, Diets, Indian Councils, Pala-

vers, and the like, there is scarce a village which has not its factories of this description driven by (milk-and-) water power. I cannot conceive the confusion of tongues to have been the curse of Babel, since I esteem my ignorance of other languages as a kind of Martello-tower, in which I am safe from the furious bombardments of foreign garrulity. For this reason I have ever preferred the study of the dead languages, those primitive formations being Ararats upon whose silent peaks I sit secure and watch this new deluge without fear, though it rain figures (*simulacra*, semblances) of speech forty days and nights together, as it not uncommonly happens. Thus is my coat, as it were, without buttons by which any but a vernacular wild bore can seize me. Is it not possible that the Shakers may intend to convey a quiet reproof and hint, in fastening their outer garments with hooks and eyes?

This reflection concerning Babel, which I find in no Commentary, was first thrown upon my mind when an excellent deacon of my congregation (being infected with the Second Advent delusion) assured me that he had received a first instalment of the gift of tongues as a small earnest of larger possessions in the like kind to follow. For, of a truth, I could not reconcile it with my ideas of the Divine justice and mercy that the single wall which protected people of other languages from the incursions of this otherwise well-meaning propagandist should be broken down.

In reading Congressional debates, I have fancied, that, after the subsidence of those painful buzzings in the brain which result from such exercises, I detected a slender residuum of valuable information. I made the discovery that *nothing* takes longer in the saying than any thing else, for, as *ex nihilo nihil fit,* so from one polypus *nothing* any number of similar ones may be produced. I would recommend to the attention of *vivâ voce* debaters and controversialists the admirable example of the monk Copres, who, in the fourth century, stood for half an hour in the midst of a great fire, and thereby silenced a Manichæan antagonist who had less of the salamander in him. As for those who quarrel in print, I have no concern with them here, since the eyelids are a Divinely-granted shield against all such. Moreover, I have observed in many modern books that the printed portion is becoming gradually smaller, and the number of blank or fly-leaves (as they are called) greater. Should this fortunate tendency of literature continue, books will grow more valuable from year to year, and the whole Serbonian bog yield to the advances of firm arable land.

I have wondered, in the Representatives' Chamber of our own Commonwealth, to mark how little impression seemed to be produced by that emblematic fish suspended over the heads of the members. Our wiser ancestors, no doubt, hung it there as being the animal which the Pythagoreans reverenced for its silence, and which certainly in that particular does not so well merit the epithet *cold-blooded,* by which naturalists distinguish it, as certain bipeds, afflicted with ditch-water on the brain, who take occasion to tap themselves in Fanueil Halls, meeting-houses, and other places of public resort.—H. W.]

No. V.

THE DEBATE IN THE SENNIT.

SOT TO A NUSRY RHYME.

THE incident which gave rise to the debate satirized in the following verses was the unsuccessful attempt of Drayton and Sayres to give freedom to seventy men and women, fellow-beings and fellow-Christians. Had Tripoli, instead of Washington, been the scene of this undertaking, the unhappy leaders in it would have been as secure of the theoretic as they now are of the practical part of martyrdom. I question whether the Dey of Tripoli is blessed with a District Attorney so benighted as ours at the seat of government. Very fitly is he named Key, who would allow himself to be made the instrument of locking the door of hope against sufferers in such a cause. Not all the waters of the ocean can cleanse the vile smutch of the jailer's fingers from off that little Key. *Ahenea clavis,* a brazen Key indeed!

Mr. Calhoun, who is made the chief speaker in this burlesque, seems to think that the light of the nineteenth century is to be put out as soon as he tinkles his little cow-bell curfew. Whenever slavery is touched, he sets up his scare-crow of dissolving the Union. This may do for the North, but I should conjecture that something more than a pumpkin-lantern is required to scare manifest and irretrievable Destiny out of her path. Mr. Calhoun cannot let go the apron-string of the Past. The Past is a good nurse, but we must be weaned from her sooner or later, even though, like Plotinus, we should run home from school to ask the breast, after we are tolerably well-grown youths. It will not do for us to hide our faces in her lap, whenever the strange Future holds out her arms and asks us to come to her.

But we are all alike. We have all heard it said, often enough, that little boys must not play with fire, and yet, if the matches be taken away from us and put out of reach upon the shelf, we must needs get into our little corner, and scowl and stamp and threaten the dire revenge of going to bed without our supper. The world shall stop till we get our dangerous plaything again. Dame Earth, meanwhile, who has more than enough household matters to mind, goes bustling hither and thither as a hiss or a sputter tells her that this or that kettle of hers is boiling over, and before bedtime we are glad to eat our porridge cold, and gulp down our dignity along with it.

Mr. Calhoun has somehow acquired the name of a great statesman, and, if it be great statesmanship to put lance in rest and run a tilt at the Spirit of the Age with the certainty of being next moment hurled neck and heels into the dust amid universal laughter, he deserves the title. He is the Sir Kay of our modern chivalry. He should remember the old Scandinavian mythus. Thor was the strongest of gods, but he could not wrestle with Time, nor so much as lift up a fold of the great snake which knit the universe together ; and when he smote the Earth, though with his terrible mallet, it was but as if a leaf had fallen. Yet all the while it seemed to Thor that he had only been wrestling with an old woman, striving to lift a cat, and striking a stupid giant on the head.

And in old times, doubtless, the giants *were* stupid, and there was no better sport for the Sir Launcelots and Sir Gawains than to go about cutting off their great blundering heads with enchanted swords. But things have wonderfully changed. It is the giants, nowadays, that have the science and the intelligence, while the chivalrous Don Quixotes of Conservatism still cumber themselves with the clumsy armor of a bygone age. On whirls the restless globe through unsounded time, with its cities and its silences, its births and funerals, half light, half shade, but never wholly dark, and sure to swing round into the happy morning at last. With an involuntary smile, one sees Mr. Calhoun letting slip his pack-thread cable with a crooked pin at the end of it to anchor South Carolina upon the bank and shoal of the Past.—H. W.]

TO MR. BUCKENAM.

MR. EDITER, As i wuz kinder prunin round, in a little nussry sot out a year or 2 a go, the Dbait in the sennit cum inter my mine An so i took & Sot it to wut I call a nussry rime. I hev made sum onnable Gentlemun speak that dident speak in a Kind uv Poetikul lie sense the seeson is dreffle backerd up This way

ewers as ushul
 HOSEA BIGLOW.

" HERE we stan' on the Constitution, by thunder !
It 's a fact o' wich ther 's bushils o' proofs ;
Fer how could we trample on 't so, I wonder,
Ef 't worn't thet it 's ollers under our hoofs ?"

Sez John C. Calhoun, sez he ;
    " Human rights hain't no more
    Right to come on this floor,
No more 'n the man in the moon," sez he.

" The North hain't no kind o' bisness with nothin',
    An' you 've no idee how much bother it saves ;
We ain't none riled by their frettin' an' frothin',
    We 're *used* to layin' the string on our slaves,"
      Sez John C. Calhoun, sez he ;—
        Sez Mister Foote,
        " l should like to shoot
The holl gang, by the gret horn spoon ! " sez he.

" Freedom's Keystone is Slavery, thet ther 's no doubt
      on,
    It 's sutthin' thet 's—wha' d' ye call it ?—divine,—
An' the slaves thet we ollers *make* the most out on
    Air them north o' Mason an' Dixon's line,"
      Sez John C. Calhoun, sez he ;—
        " Fer all thet," sez Mangum,
        " 'T would be better to hang 'em,
    An' so git red on 'em soon," sez he.

" The mass ough' to labor an' we lay on soffies,
    Thet 's the reason I want to spread Freedom's aree ;
It puts all the cunninest on us in office,
    An' reelises our Maker's orig'nal idee,"
      Sez John C. Calhoun, sez he ;—
        " Thet 's ez plain," sez Cass,
        " Ez thet some one's an ass,
    It 's ez clear ez the sun is at noon," sez he.

" Now don't go to say I 'm the friend of oppression,
  But keep all your spare breath fer coolin' your broth,
Fer I ollers hev strove (at least thet 's my impression)
  To make cussed free with the rights o' the North,"
    Sez John C. Calhoun, sez he ;—
      " Yes," sez Davis o' Miss.,
      "The perfection o' bliss
    Is in skinnin' thet same old coon," sez he.

" Slavery 's a thing thet depends on complexion,
  It 's God's law thet fetters on black skins don't chafe ;
Ef brains wuz to settle it (horrid reflection !)
  Wich of our onnable body 'd be safe ? "
    Sez John C. Calhoun, sez he ;—
      Sez Mister Hannegan,
      Afore he began agin,
    " Thet exception is quite oppertoon," sez he.

" Gen'nle Cass, Sir, you need n't be twitchin' your col-
      lar,
  Your merit 's quite clear by the dut on your knees,
At the North we don't make no distinctions o' color ;
  You can all take a lick at our shoes wen you please,"
    Sez John C. Calhoun, sez he ;—
      Sez Mister Jarnagin,
      " They wunt hev to larn agin,
    They all on 'em know the old toon," sez he.

" The slavery question ain't no ways bewilderin'.
  North an' South hev one int'rest, it 's plain to a glance ;
No'thern men, like us patriarchs, don't sell their chil-
      drin,
  But they *du* sell themselves, ef they git a good
      chance,"

Sez John C. Calhoun, sez he ;—
  Sez Atherton here,
  " This is gittin' severe,
I wish I could dive like a loon," sez he.

" It'll break up the Union, this talk about freedom,
  An' your fact'ry gals (soon ez we split) 'll make head,
An' gittin' some Miss chief or other to lead 'em,
  'll go to work raisin' promiscoous Ned,"
    Sez John C. Calhoun, sez he ;—
      " Yes, the North," sez Colquitt,
      " Ef we Southerners all quit,
    Would go down like a busted balloon," sez he.

" Jest look wut is doin', wut annyky 's brewin'
  In the beautiful clime o' the olive an' vine,
All the wise aristoxy is tumblin' to ruin,
  An' the sankylots drorin' an' drinkin' their wine,"
    Sez John C. Calhoun, sez he ;—
      " Yes," sez Johnson, " in France
      They 're beginnin' to dance
    Beelzebub's own rigadoon," sez he.

" The South 's safe enough, it don't feel a mite skeery,
  Our slaves in their darkness an' dut air tu blest
Not to welcome with proud hallylugers the ery
  Wen our eagle kicks yourn from the naytional nest,"
    Sez John C. Calhoun, sez he ;—
      " O," sez Westcott o' Florida,
      " Wut treason is horrider
    Then our priv'leges tryin' to proon ?" sez he.

" It 's 'coz they 're so happy, thet, wen crazy sarpints
  Stick their nose in our bizness, we git so darned riled ;

We think its our dooty to give pooty sharp hints,
　Thet the last crumb of Edin on airth shan't be spiled,"
　　Sez John C. Calhoun, sez he ;—
　　　" Ah," sez Dixon H. Lewis,
　　　" It perfectly true is
　　Thet slavery's airth 's grettest boon," sez he.

[It was said of old time, that riches have wings ; and
though this be not applicable in a literal strictness to
the wealth of our patriarchal brethren of the South,
yet it is clear that their possessions have legs, and an
unaccountable propensity for using them in a northerly
direction.　I marvel that the grand jury of Washington
did not find a true bill against the North Star for aid-
ing and abetting Drayton and Sayres.　It would have
been quite of a piece with the intelligence displayed by
the South on other questions connected with slavery.
I think that no ship of state was ever freighted with a
more veritable Jonah than this same domestic institu-
tion of ours.　Mephistopheles himself could not feign
so bitterly, so satirically sad a sight as this of three
millions of human beings crushed beyond help or hope
by this one mighty argument,—*Our fathers knew no
better !*　Nevertheless, it is the unavoidable destiny of
Jonahs to be cast overboard sooner or later.　Or shall
we try the experiment of hiding our Jonah in a safe
place, that none may lay hands on him to make jetsam
of him ?　Let us, then, with equal forethought and
wisdom, lash ourselves to the anchor, and await, in
pious confidence, the certain result.　Perhaps our sus-
picious passenger is no Jonah after all, being black.
For it is well known that a superintending Providence

made a kind of sandwich of Ham and his descendants, to be devoured by the Caucasian race.

In God's name, let all, who hear nearer and nearer the hungry moan of the storm and the growl of the breakers, speak out! But, alas! we have no right to interfere. If a man pluck an apple of mine, he shall be in danger of the justice; but if he steal my brother I must be silent. Who says this? Our Constitution, consecrated by the callous suetude of sixty years, and grasped in triumphant argument in the left hand of him whose right hand clutches the clotted slave-whip. Justice, venerable with the undethronable majesty of countless æons, says,—SPEAK! The Past, wise with the sorrows and desolations of ages, from amid her shattered fanes and wolf-housing palaces, echoes,— SPEAK! Nature, through her thousand trumpets of freedom, her stars, her sunrises, her seas, her winds, her cataracts, her mountains blue with cloudy pines, blows jubilant encouragement, and cries,—SPEAK! From the soul's trembling abysses the still, small voice not vaguely murmurs,—SPEAK! But alas! the Constitution and the Honorable Mr. Bagowind, M. C., say,—BE DUMB!

It occurs to me to suggest, as a topic of inquiry in this connection, whether, on that momentous occasion when the goats and the sheep shall be parted, the Constitution and the Honorable Mr. Bagowind, M. C., will be expected to take their places on the left as our hircine vicars.

> *Quid sum miser tunc dicturus?*
> *Quem patronum rogaturus?*

There is a point where toleration sinks into sheer baseness and poltroonery. The toleration of the worst leads us to look on what is barely better as good enough and to worship what is only moderately good. Woe to that man, or that nation, to whom mediocrity has become an ideal !

Has our experiment of self-government succeeded, if it barely manage to *rub and go?* Here, now, is a piece of barbarism which Christ and the nineteenth century say shall cease, and which Messrs. Smith, Brown, and others say shall *not* cease. I would by no means deny the eminent respectability of these gentlemen, but I confess, that, in such a wrestling-match, 1 cannot help having my fears for them.

Discite justitiam, moniti, et non temnere divos.

H. W.]

No. VI.

THE PIOUS EDITOR'S CREED.

[AT the special instance of Mr. Biglow, I preface the following satire with an extract from a sermon preached during the past summer, from Ezekiel xxxiv. 2 :— " Son of man, prophesy against the shepherds of Israel." Since the Sabbath on which this discourse was delivered, the editor of the " Jaalam Independent Blunderbuss " has unaccountably absented himself from our house of worship.

" I know of no so responsible position as that of the public journalist. The editor of our day bears the same relation to his time that the clerk bore to the age before the invention of printing. Indeed, the position which he holds is that which the clergyman should hold even now. But the clergyman chooses to walk off to the extreme edge of the world, and to throw such seed as he has clear over into that darkness which he calls the Next Life. As if *next* did not mean *nearest*, and as if any life were nearer than that immediately present one which boils and eddies all around him at the caucus, the ratification meeting, and the polls ! Who taught him to exhort men to prepare for eternity, as for some future era of which the present forms no integral part ? The furrow which Time is even now turning runs through the Everlasting, and in that must he plant, or nowhere. Yet he would fain believe and teach that we are *going* to have more of eternity than we have now. This *going* of his is like that of the auctioneer, on which *gone* follows before we have made up our minds to bid,—in which manner, not three months back, I lost an excellent copy of Chappelow on Job. So it has come to pass that the preacher, instead of being a living force, has faded into an emblematic figure at christenings, weddings, and funerals. Or, if he exercise any other function, it is as keeper and feeder of certain theologic dogmas, which, when occasion offers, he unkennels with a *staboy!* " to bark and bite as 't is their nature to," whence that reproach of *odium theologicum* has arisen.

"Meanwhile, see what a pulpit the editor mounts daily, sometimes with a congregation of fifty thousand within reach of his voice, and never so much as a nodder, even, among them ! And from what a Bible can he choose his text,—a Bible which needs no translation, and which no priestcraft can shut and clasp from the laity,—the open volume of the world, upon which, with a pen of sunshine or destroying fire, the inspired Present is even now writing the annals of God ! Methinks the editor who should understand his calling, and be equal thereto, would truly deserve that title of ποιμὴν λαῶν, which Homer bestows upon princes. He would be the Moses of our nineteenth century, and whereas the old Sinai, silent now, is but a common mountain stared at by the elegant tourist and crawled over by the hammering geologist, he must find his tables of the new law here among factories and cities in this Wilderness of Sin (Numbers xxxiii. 12), called Progress of

Civilization, and be the captain of our Exodus into the Canaan of a truer social order.

" Nevertheless, our editor will not come so far within even the shadow of Sinai as Mahomet did, but chooses rather to construe Moses by Joe Smith.   He takes up the crook, not that the sheep may be fed, but that he may never want a warm woollen suit and a joint of mutton.

Immemor, O, fidei pecorumque oblite tuorum!

For which reason I would derive the name *editor* not so much from *edo,* to publish, as from *edo,* to eat, that being the peculiar profession to which he esteems himself called.   He blows up the flames of political discord for no other occasion than that he may thereby handily boil his own pot.   I believe there are two thousand of these mutton-loving shepherds in the United States, and of these, how many have even the dimmest perception of their immense power, and the duties consequent thereon ?   Here and there, haply, one.   Nine hundred and ninety-nine labor to impress upon the people the great principles of *Tweedledum,* and other nine hundred and ninety-nine preach with equal earnestness the gospel according to *Tweedledee.*"—H. W.]

> I DU believe in Freedom's cause,
>   Ez fur away ez Paris is ;
> I love to see her stick her claws
>   In them infarnal Pharisees ;
> It 's wal enough agin a king
>   To dror resolves an' triggers,—
> But libbaty 's a kind o' thing
>   **Thet don't agree with niggers.**

I du believe the people want
   A tax on teas an' coffees,
Thet nothin' ain't extravygunt,—
   Purvidin' I 'm in office ;
Fer I hev loved my country sence
   My eye-teeth filled their sockets,
An' Uncle Sam I reverence,
   Partic'larly his pockets.

I du believe in *any* plan
   O' levyin' the taxes,
Ez long ez, like a lumberman,
   I git jest wut I axes :
I go free-trade thru thick an' thin,
   Because it kind o' rouses
The folks to vote,—an' keeps us in
   Our quiet customhouses.

I du believe it 's wise an' good
   To sen' out furrin missions,
Thet is, on sartin understood
   An' orthydox conditions ;—
I mean nine thousan' dolls. per ann.,
   Nine thousan' more fer outfit,
An' me to recommend a man
   The place 'ould jest about fit.

I du believe in special ways
   O' prayin' an' convartin' ;
The bread comes back in many days,
   An' buttered, tu, fer sartin ;—

I mean in preyin' till one busts
  On wut the party chooses,
An' in convartin' public trusts
  To every privit uses.

I du believe hard coin the stuff
  Fer 'lectioneers to spout on ;
The people's ollers soft enough
  To make hard money out on ;
Dear Uncle Sam pervides fer his,
  An' gives a good-sized junk to all,—
I don't care *how* hard money is,
  Ez long ez mine's paid punctooal.

I du believe with all my soul
  In the gret Press's freedom,
To pint the people to the goal
  An' in the traces lead 'em ;
Palsied the arm thet forges yokes
  At my fat contracts squintin',
An' withered be the nose thet pokes
  Inter the gov'ment printin' !

I du believe thet I should give
  Wut's his'n unto Cæsar,
Fer it 's by him I move an' live,
  Frum him my bread an' cheese air ;
I du believe thet all o' me
  Doth bear his souperscription,—
Will, conscience, honor, honesty,
  An' things o' thet description.

I du believe in prayer an' praise
  To him thet hez the grantin'
O' jobs,—in every thin' thet **pays,**
  But most of all in CANTIN' ;
This doth my cup with marcies fill,
  This lays all thought o' sin to **rest,—**
I *don't* believe in princerple,
  But, O, I *du* in interest.

I du believe in bein' this
  Or thet, ez it may happen
One way or t'other hendiest **is**
  To ketch the people nappin' ;
It ain't by princerples nor men
  My preudunt course is steadied,—
I scent wich pays the best, an' **then**
  Go into it baldheaded.

I du believe thet holdin' **slaves**
  Comes nat'ral tu a Presidunt,
Let 'lone the rowdedow it saves
  To hev a wal-broke precedunt ;
Fer any office, small or gret,
  I could n't ax with no face,
Without I'd ben, thru dry an' **wet,**
  Th' unrizzest kind o' doughface.

I du believe wutever trash
  'll keep the people in blindness,—
Thet we the Mexicuns can thrash
  Right inter brotherly kindness,

Thet bombshells, grape, an' powder 'n' ball
  Air good-will's strongest magnets,
Thet peace, to make it stick at all,
  Must be druv in with bagnets.

In short, I firmly du believe
  In Humbug generally,
Fer it's a thing thet I perceive
  To hev a solid vally ;
This heth my faithful shepherd ben,
  In pasturs sweet heth led me,
An' this 'll keep the people green
  To feed ez they hev fed me.

[I subjoin here another passage from my before-
mentioned discourse.

" Wonderful, to him that has eyes to see it rightly,
is the newspaper. To me, for example, sitting on the
critical front bench of the pit, in my study here in
Jaalam, the advent of my weekly journal is as that of a
strolling theatre, or rather of a puppet-show, on whose
stage, narrow as it is, the tragedy, comedy, and farce
of life are played in little. Behold the whole huge
earth sent to me hebdomadally in a brown paper wrapper !

" Hither, to my obscure corner, by wind or steam, on
horseback or dromedary-back, in the pouch of the In-
dian runner, or clicking over the magnetic wires, troop
all the famous performers from the four quarters of the
globe. Looked at from a point of criticism, tiny pup-
pets they seem all, as the editor sets up his booth upon
my desk and officiates as showman. Now I can truly
see how little and transitory is life. The earth appears
almost as a drop of vinegar, on which the solar micro-

scope of the imagination must be brought to bear in order to make out anything distinctly. That animalcule there, in the pea-jacket, is Louis Philippe, just landed on the coast of England. That other, in the gray surtout and cocked hat, is Napoleon Bonaparte Smith, assuring France that she need apprehend no interference from him in the present alarming juncture. At that spot, where you seem to see a speck of something in motion, is an immense mass meeting. Look sharper, and you will see a mite brandishing his mandibles in an excited manner. That is the great Mr. Soandso, defining his position amid tumultuous and irrepressible cheers. That infinitesimal creature, upon whom some score of others, as minute as he, are gazing in open-mouthed admiration, is a famous ph'losop er, expounding to a select audience their capacity for the Infinite. That scarce discernible pufflet of smoke and dust is a revolution. That speck there is a reformer, just arranging the lever with which he is to move the world. And lo, there creeps forward the shadow of a skeleton that blows one breath between its grinning teeth, and all our distinguished actors are whisked off the slippery stage into the dark Beyond.

" Yes, the little show box has its solemner suggestions. Now and then we catch a glimpse of a grim old man, who lays down a scythe and hour-glass in the corner while he shifts the scenes. There, too, in the dim background, a weird shape is ever delving. Sometimes he leans upon his mattock, and gazes, as a coach whirls by, bearing the newly married on their wedding jaunt, or glances carelessly at a babe brought home from christening. Suddenly (for the scene grows larger and larger as we look) a bony hand snatches back a performer in the midst of his part, and him, whom yesterday two infinities (past and future) would not suffice, a handful of dust is enough to cover and silence forever. Nay, we see the same fleshless fingers opening to clutch the showman himself, and guess, not without a shudder, that they are lying in wait for spectators also.

" Think of it : for three dollars a year I buy a season ticket to this great Globe Theatre, for which God would write the dramas (only that we like farces, spectacles, and the tragedies of Apollyon better), whose scene-shifter is Time, and whose curtain is rung down by Death.

" Such thoughts will occur to me sometimes as I am tearing off the wrapper of my newspaper. Then suddenly that otherwise too often vacant sheet becomes invested for me with a strange kind of awe. Look ! deaths and marriages, notices of inventions, discoveries and books, lists of promotions, of killed, wounded, and missing, news of fires, accidents, of sudden wealth and as sudden poverty ;—I hold in my hand the ends of myriad invisible electric conductors, along which tremble the joys, sorrows, wrongs, triumphs, hopes, and despairs of as many men and women everywhere. So that upon that mood of mind which seems to isolate me from mankind as a spectator of their puppet-pranks, another supervenes, in which I feel that I, too, unknown and unheard of, am yet of some import to my fellows. For, through my newspaper here, do not families take pains to send me, an entire stranger, news of a death among them ? Are not here two who would have me know of their marriage ? And, strangest of all, is not this singular person anxious to have me informed that he has received a fresh supply of Dimitry Bruisgins ?

But to none of us does the Present (even if for a moment discerned as such) continue miraculous. We glance carelessly at the sunrise, and get used to Orion and the Pleiades. The wonder wears off, and to-morrow this sheet, in which a vision was let down to me from Heaven, shall be the wrappage to a bar of soap or the platter for a beggar's broken victuals."—H. W.]

No. VII.

A LETTER

FROM A CANDIDATE FOR THE PRESIDENCY IN ANSWER
TO SUTTIN QUESTIONS PRCPOSED BY MR. HOSEA BIG-
LOW, INCLOSED IN A NOTE FROM MR. BIGLOW TO S. H.
GAY, ESQ., EDITOR OF THE NATIONAL ANTI-SLAVERY
STANDARD.

[CURIOSITY may be said to be the quality which pre-
eminently distinguishes and segregates man from the
lower animals.   As we trace the scale of animated nature
downward, we find this faculty of the mind (as it may
truly be called) diminished in the savage, and quite
extinct in the brute.   The first object which civilized
man proposes to himself I take to be the finding out
whatsoever he can concerning his neighbors.   *Nihil
humanum a me alienum puto ;* I am curious about even
John Smith.   The desire next in strength to this (an
opposite pole, indeed, of the same magnet) is that of
communicating intelligence.

Men in general may be divided into the inquisitive
and the communicative.   To the first class belong Peep-
ing Toms, eavesdroppers, navel-contemplating Brah-
mins, metaphysicians, travelers, Empedocleses, spies,
the various societies for promoting Rhinothism, Colum-
buses, Yankees, discoverers, and men of science, who
present themselves to the mind as so many marks of

106

interrogation wandering up and down the world, or sitting in studies and laboratories. The second class I should again subdivide into four. In the first subdivision I would rank those who have an itch to tell us about themselves,—as keepers of diaries, insignificant persons generally, Montaignes, Horace Walpoles, autobiographers, poets. The second includes those who are anxious to impart information concerning other people, —as historians, barbers, and such. To the third belong those who labor to give us intelligence about nothing at all,—as novelists, political orators, the large majority of authors, preachers, lecturers, and the like. In the fourth come those who are communicative from motives of public benevolence,—as finders of mares'-nests and bringers of ill news. Each of us two-legged fowls without feathers embraces all these subdivisions in himself to a greater or less degree, for none of us so much as lays an egg, or incubates a chalk one, but straightway the whole barnyard shall know it by our cackle or our cluck. *Omnibus hoc vitium est.* There are different grades in all these classes. One will turn his telescope toward a backyard, another toward Uranus ; one will tell you that he dined with Smith, another that he supped with Pl.to. In one particular, all men may be considered as belonging to the first grand division, inasmuch as they all seem equally desirous of discovering the mote in their neighbor's eye.

To one or another of these species every human being may safely be referred. I think it beyond a peradventure that Jonah prosecuted some inquiries into the digestive apparatus of whales, and that Noah sealed up a letter in an empty bottle, that news in regard to him might not be wanting in case of the worst. They had else been super or subter human. I conceive, also, that, as there are certain persons who continually peep and pry at the keyhole of that mysterious door through which, sooner or later, we all make our exits, so there are doubtless ghosts fidgeting and fretting on the other side of it, because they have no means of conveying back to the world the scraps of news they have picked up. For there is an answer ready somewhere to every question, the great law of *give and take* runs through all nature, and if we see a hook, we may be sure that an eye is waiting for it. I read in every face I meet a standing advertisement of information wanted in regard to A. B., or that the friends of C. D. can hear of him by application to such a one.

It was to gratify the two great passions of asking and answering that epistolary correspondence was first invented. Letters (for by this usurped title epistles are now commonly known) are of several kinds. First, there are those which are not letters at all,—as letters patent, letters dismissory, letters inclosing bills, letters of administration, Pliny's letters, letters of diplomacy, of Cato, of Mentor, of Lords Lyttelton, Chesterfield, and Orrery, of Jacob Behmen, Seneca (whom St. Jerome includes in his list of sacred writers), letters from abroad, from sons in college to their fathers, letters of marque, and letters generally, which are in no wise letters of mark. Second, are real letters, such as those of Gray, Cowper, Walpole, Howel, Lamb, the first letters from children (printed in staggering capitals) Letters from New York, letters of credit, and others, interesting for the sake of the writer or the thing written. I have read also letters from Europe by a gentleman named Pinto, containing some curious gossip, and which I hope to see collected for the benefit of the curious. There are, besides, letters addressed to posterity,—as epitaphs, for example, written for their own monuments, by monarchs, whereby we have lately become possessed of the names of several great conquerors and kings of kings, hitherto unheard of and still unpronounceable, but valuable to the student of the entirely dark ages. The letter which St. Peter sent to King Pepin in the year of grace 755 I would place in a class by itself, as also the letters of candidates, concerning which I shall dilate more fully in a note at the end of the following poem. At present, *sat prata biberunt.* Only, concerning the shape of letters, they are all either square or oblong, to which general figures, circular letters and round-robins also conform themselves.—H. W.]

DEER SIR its gut to be the fashun now to rite letters to the candid 8s and i wus chose at a publick Meetin in Jaalam to du wut wus nessary fur that town. i writ to 271 ginerals and gut ansers to 209. tha air called candid 8s but I don't see nothin candid about em. this here I wich I send wus thought satty's factory. I dunno as it's ushle to print Poscrips, but as all the ansers I got hed the saim, I sposed it wus best. times has gretly changed. Formaly to knock a man into a cocked hat wus to use him up, but now it ony gives him a chance fur the cheef madgustracy.—H. B.

DEAR SIR,—You wish to know my notions
  On sartin pints thet rile the land ;
There 's nothin' thet my natur so shuns
  Ez bein' mum or underhand ;

I 'm a straight-spoken kind o' creetur
  Thet blurts right out wut 's in his head,
An' ef I 've one pecooler feetur,
  It is a nose thet wunt be led.

So, to begin at the beginnin',
  An' come direcly to the pint,
I think the country's underpinnin'
  Is some consid'ble out o' jint ;
I ain't agoin' to try your patience
  By tellin' who done this or thet,
I don't make no insinooations,
  I jest let on I smell a rat.

Thet is, I mean, it seems to me so,
  But, ef the public think I 'm wrong,
I wunt deny but wut I be so,—
  An', fact, it don't smell very strong ;
My mind 's tu fair to lose its balance
  An' say wich party hez most sense ;
There may be folks o' greater talence
  Thet can't set stiddier on the fence.

I 'm an eclectic ; ez to choosin'
  'Twixt this an' thet, I 'm plaguy lawth ;
I leave a side thet looks like losin',
  But (wile there 's doubt) I stick to both ;
I stan' upon the Constitution,
  Ez preudunt statesmun say, who 've planned
A way to git the most profusion
  O' chances ez to *ware* they 'll stand.

Ez fer the war, I go agin it,—
  I mean to say I kind o' du,—

Thet is, I mean thet, bein' in it,
　　The best way wuz to fight it thru ;
Not but wut abstract war is horrid,
　　I sign to thet with all my heart,—
But civlyzation *doos* git forrid
　　Sometimes upon a powder-cart.

About thet darned Proviso matter
　　I never hed a grain o' doubt,
Nor I ain't one my sense to scatter
　　So 's no one could n't pick it out ;
My love fer North an' South is equil,
　　So I 'll jest answer plump an' frank,
No matter wut may be the sequil,—
　　Yes, Sir, I *am* agin a Bank.

Ez to the answerin' o' questions,
　　I 'm an off ox at bein' druv,
Though I ain't one thet ary test shuns
　　'll give our folks a helpin' shove ;
Kind o' promiscoous I go it
　　Fer the holl country, an' the ground
I take, ez nigh ez I can show it,
　　Is pooty gen'ally all round.

I don't appruve o' givin' pledges ;
　　You 'd ough' to leave a feller free,
An' not go knockin' out the wedges
　　To ketch his fingers in the tree ;
Pledges air awfle breachy cattle
　　Thet preudent farmers don't turn out,—
Ez long 'z the people git their rattle,
　　Wut is there fer 'm to grout about ?

Ez to the slaves, there's no confusion
  In *my* idees consarnin' them,—
I think they air an Institution,
  A sort of—yes—yes, jest so,—ahem :
Do *I* own any ? Of my merit
  On thet pint you yourself may jedge :
All is, I never drink no sperit,
  Nor I hain't never signed no pledge.

Ez to my principles, I glory
  In hevin' nothin' o' the sort.
I ain't a Wig, I ain't a Tory,
  I'm jest a candidate, in short ,
Thet 's fair an' square an' parpendicler,
  But, ef the Public cares a fig
To hev me an'thin' in particler,
  Wy, I 'm a kind o' peri-wig.

P. S.

Ez we 're a sort o' privateerin',
  O' course, you know, it 's sheer an' sheer,
An' there is sutthin' wuth your hearin'
  I 'll mention in *your* privit ear ;
Ef you git *me* inside the White House,
  Your head with ile I 'll kin' o' 'nint
By gittin' *you* inside the Lighthouse
  Down to the eend o' Jaalam Pint.

An' ez the North hez took to brustlin'
  At bein' scrouged frum off the roost,
I 'll tell ye wut 'll save all tusslin'
  An' give our side a harnsome boost,—

Tell 'em thet on the Slavery question
I 'm RIGHT, although to speak I 'm lawth;
This gives you a safe pint to rest on,
An' leaves me frontin' South by North.

[And now of epistles candidatial, which are of two kinds,—namely, letters of acceptance, and letters definitive of position. Our republic, on the eve of an election, may safely enough be called a republic of letters. Epistolary composition becomes then an epidemic, which seizes one candidate after another, not seldom cutting short the thread of political life. It has come to such a pass that a party dreads less the attacks of its opponents than a letter from its candidate. *Litera scripta manet,* and it will go hard if something bad cannot be made of it. General Harrison, it is well understood, was surrounded, during his candidacy, with the *cordon sanitaire* of a vigilance committee. No prisoner in Spielberg was ever more cautiously deprived of writing materials. The soot was scraped carefully from the chimney-places ; outposts of expert rifle-shooters rendered it sure death for any goose (who came clad in feathers) to approach within a certain limited distance of North Bend ; and all domestic fowls about the premises were reduced to the condition of Plato's original man. By these precautions the General was saved. *Parva componere magnis,* I remember, that, when party-spirit once ran high among my people, upon occasion of the choice of a new deacon, I, having my preferences, yet not caring too openly to express them, made use of an innocent fraud to bring about that result which I deemed most desirable. My stratagem was no other than the throwing a copy of the Complete Letter-Writer in the way of the candidate whom I wished to d feat. He caught the infection, and addressed a short note to his constituents, in which the opposite party detected so many and so grave improprieties, (he had modelled it upon the letter of a young lady accepting a proposal of marriage,) that he not only lost his election, but, falling under a suspicion of Sabellianism and I know not what, (the widow Endive .assured me that he was a Paralipomenon, to her certain knowledge,) was forced to leave the town. Thus it is that the letter killeth.

The object which candidates propose to themselves in writing is to convey no meaning at all. And here is a quite unsuspected pitfall into which they successively plunge headlong. For it is prec.sely in such cryptographies that mankind are prone to seek for and find a wonderful amount and variety of significance. *Omne ignotum pro mirifico.* How do we admire at the antique world striving to crack those oracular nuts from Delphi, Hammon, and elsewhere, in only one of which can I so much as surmise that any kernel had ever lodged ; that, namely, wherein Apollo confessed that he was mortal. One Didymus is, moreover, relaced to have written six thousand books on the single subject of grammar, a topic rendered only more tenebrific by the labors of his successors, and which seems still to possess an attraction for authors in proportion as they can make nothing of it. A singular loadstone for theologians, also, is the Beast in the Apocalypse, whereof, in the course of my studies, I have noted two hundred and three several interpretations, each lethiferal to all the rest. *Non nostrum est tantas componere lites,* yet I have myself ventured upon a two hundred and fourth, which I embodied in a discourse preached on occasion of the demise of the late usurper, Napoleon Bonaparte, and which quieted, in a large measure, the minds of my people. It is true that my views on this important point were ardently controverted by Mr. Shearjashub Holden, the then preceptor of our academy, and in other particulars a very deserving and sensible young man, though possessing a somewhat limited knowledge of the Greek tongue. But his heresy struck down no deep root, and, he having been lately removed by the hand of Providence, I had the satisfaction of reaffirming my cherished sentiments in a sermon preached upon the Lord's day immediately succeeding his funeral. This might seem like taking an unfair advantage, did I not add that he had made provision in his last will (being celibate) for the publication of a posthumous tractate in support of his own dangerous opinions.

I know of nothing in our modern times which approaches so nearly to the ancient oracle as the letter of a Presidential candidate. Now, among the Greeks, the eating of beans was strictly forbidden to all such as had it in mind to consult those expert amphibologists, and this same prohibition on the part of Pythagoras to his disciples is understood to imply an abstinence from politics, beans having been used as ballots. That other explication, *quod videlicet sensus eo cibo obtundi existimaret*, though supported *pugnis et calcibus* by many of the learned, and not wanting the countenance of Cicero, is confuted by the larger experience of New England. On the whole, I think it safer to apply here the rule of interpretation which now generally obtains in regard to antique cosmogonies, myths, fables, proverbial expressions, and knotty points generally, which is, to find a common-sense meaning, and then select whatever can be imagined the most opposite thereto. In this way we arrive at the conclusion, that the Greeks objected to the questioning of candidates. And very properly, if, as I conceive, the chief point be not to discover what a person in that position is, or what he will do, but whether he can be elected. *Vos exemplaria Græca nocturna versate manu, versate diurna.*

But, since an imitation of the Greeks in this particular (the asking of questions being one chief privilege of freemen) is hardly to be hoped for, and our candidates will answer, whether they are questioned or not, I would recommend that these ante-electionary dialogues should be carried on by symbols, as were the diplomatic correspondences of the Scythians and Macrobii, or confined to the language of signs, like the famous interview of Panurge and Goatsnose. A candidate might then convey a suitable reply to all committees of inquiry by closing one eye, or by presenting them with a phial of Egyptian darkness to be speculated upon by their respective constituencies. These answers would be susceptible of whatever retrospective construction the exigencies of the political campaign might seem to demand, and the candidate could take his position on either side of the fence with entire consistency. Or, if letters must be written, profitable use might be made of the Dighton rock hieroglyphic or the cuneiform script, every fresh decipherer of which is enabled to educe a different meaning, whereby a sculptured stone or two supplies us, and will probably continue to supply posterity, with a very vast and various body of authentic history. For even the briefest epistle in the ordinary chirography is dangerous. There is scarce any style so compressed that superfluous words may not be detected in it. A severe critic might curtail that famous brevity of Cæsar's by two-thirds, drawing his pen through the supererogatory *veni* and *vidi*. Perhaps, after all, the surest footing of hope is to be found in the rapidly increasing tendency to demand less and less of qualification in candidates. Already have statesmanship, experience, and the possession (nay, the profession, even) of principles been rejected as superfluous, and may not the patriot reasonably hope that the ability to write will follow ? At present, there may be death in pot-hooks as well as pots, the loop of a letter may suffice for a bow-string, and all the dreadful heresies of Anti-slavery may lurk in a flourish.—H. W.]

No. VIII.

A SECOND LETTER FROM B. SAWIN, Esq.

[IN the following epistle, we behold Mr. Sawin returning, a *miles emeritus*, to the bosom of his family. *Quantum mutatus!* The good Father of us all had doubtless intrusted to the keeping of this child of his certain faculties of a constructive kind. He had put in him a share of that vital force, the nicest economy of every minute atom of which is necessary to the perfect development of Humanity. He had given him a brain and heart, and so had equipped his soul with the two strong wings of knowledge and love. whereby it can mount to hang its nest under the eaves of heaven. And this child, so dowered, he had intrusted to the keeping of his vicar, the State. How stands the account of that stewardship? The State, or Society, (call her by what name you will,) had taken no manner of thought of him till she saw him swept out into the street, the pitiful leavings of last night's debauch, with cigar-ends, lemon-parings, tobacco-quids, slops, vile stenches, and the whole loathsome next-morning of the barroom,—an own child of the Almighty God! I remember him as he was brought to be christened, a ruddy, rugged babe; and now there he wallows, reeking, seething,—the dead corpse, not of a man, but of a soul, —a putrefying lump, horrible for the life that is in it. Comes the wind of heaven, that good Samaritan, and

118

parts the hair upon his forehead, nor is too nice to kiss those parched, cracked lips , the morning opens upon him her eyes full of pitying sunshine, the sky yearns down to him,—and ther he lies fermenting. O sleep ! let me not profane thy holy name by calling that stertorous unconsciousness a slumber ! By and by comes along the State, God's vicar. Does she say,— " My poor, forlorn foster-child ! Behold here a force which I will make dig and plant and build for me ? " Not so, but,—" Here is a recruit ready-made to my hand, a piece of destroying energy lying uprofitably idle." So she claps an ugly gray suit on him, puts a musket in his grasp, and sends him off, with Gubernatorial and other godspeeds, to do duty as a destroyer.

I made one of the crowd at the last Mechanics' Fair, and, with the rest, stood gazing in wonder at a perfect machine, with its soul of fire, its boiler-heart that sent the hot blood pulsing along the iron arteries, and its thews of steel. And while I was admiring the adaptation of means to end, the harmonious involutions of contrivance, and the never-bewildered complexity, 1 saw a grimed and greasy fellow, the imperious engine's lackey and drudge, whose sole office was to let fall, at intervals, a drop or two of oil upon a certain joint. Then my soul said within me, See there a piece of mechanism to which that other you marvel at is but as the rude first effort of a child,—a force which not merely suffices to set a few wheels in motion, but which can send an impulse all through the infinite future,—a contrivance, not for turning out pins, or stitching buttonholes, but for making Hamlets and Lears. And yet this thing of iron shall be housed, waited on, guarded from rust and dust, and it shall be a crime but so much as to scratch it with

a pin ; while the other, with its fire of God in it shall
be buffeted hither and thither, and finally sent carefully
a thousand miles to be the target for a Mexican cannon-
ball. Unthrifty Mother State ! My heart burned
within me for pity and indignation, and I renewed this
covenant with my own soul,—*In aliis mansuetus ero,
at, in blasphemiis contra Christum, non ita.*—H. W.]

I spose you wonder ware I be ; I can't tell, fer the soul
    o' me,
Exacly ware I be myself,—meanin' by thet the holl o'
    me.
Wen I left hum, I hed two legs, an' they worn't bad
    ones neither,
(The scaliest trick they ever played wuz bringin' on me
    hither,)
Now one on 'em 's I dunno ware ;—they thought I wuz
    adyin',
An' sawed it off because they said 'twuz kin' o' mor-
    tifyin' ;
I'm willin' to believe it wuz, an' yit I don't see, nuther,
Wy one should take to feelin' cheap a minnit sooner 'n
    t'other,
Sence both wuz equilly to blame ; but things is ez they
    be :
It took on so they took it off, an' thet 's enough fer me :
There 's one good thing, though, to be said about my
    wooden new one.—
The liquor can't git into it ez 't used to in the true one ;
So it saves drink ; an' then, besides, a feller could n't
    beg
A gretter blessin' then to hev one ollers sober peg ;

It 's true a chap 's in want o' two fer follerin' a drum,
But all the march I 'm up to now is jest to **Kingdom
Come.**

I 've lost one eye, but thet 's a loss it 's easy to supply
Out o' the glory thet I 've gut, fer thet is all my eye ;
An' one is big enough, I guess, by diligently usin' it,
To see all I shall ever git by way o' pay fer losin' it ;
Off'cers, I notice, who git paid fer all our thumps an'
   kickins,
Du wal by keepin' single eyes arter the fattest pickins ;
So, ez the eye 's put fairly out, I 'll larn to go with-
   out it,
An' not allow *myself* to be no gret put out about it.
Now, le' me see, thet is n't all ; I used, 'fore leavin'
   Jaalam,
To count things on my finger-eends, but sutthin' seems
   to ail 'em :
Ware 's my left hand ?   O, darn it, yes, I recollect wut 's
   come on 't ;
I hain't no left arm but my right, an' thet 's gut jest a
   thumb on 't ;
It ain't so hendy ez it wuz to cal'late a sum on 't.
I 've had some ribs broke,—six (I b'lieve),—I hain't
   kep' no account on 'em ;
Wen pensions git to be the talk, I 'll settle the amount
   on 'em.
An' now I 'm speakin' about ribs, it kin' o' brings to'
   mind
One thet I could n't never break,—the one I lef' be-
   hind ;
Ef you should see her, jest clear out the spout o' your
   invention

An' pour the longest sweetnin' in about an annooal
    pension,
An' kin o' hint (in case, you know, the critter should
    refuse to be
Consoled) I ain't so 'xpensive now to keep ez wut I used
    to be ;
There 's one arm less, ditto one eye, an' then the leg
    thet 's wooden
Can be took off an' sot away wenever ther' 's a puddin'.

I spose you think I 'm comin' back ez opperlunt ez
    thunder,
With shiploads o' gold images an' varus sorts o' plunder ;
Wal, 'fore I vullinteered, I thought this country wuz a
    sort o'
Canaan, a reg'lar Promised Land flowin' with rum an'
    water,
Ware propaty growed up like time, without no cultiva-
    tion,
An' gold wuz dug ez taters be among our Yankee
    nation,
Ware nateral advantages were pufficly amazin',
Ware every rock there wuz about with precious stuns
    wuz blazin',
Ware mill-sites filled the country up ez thick ez you
    could cram 'em,
An' desput rivers run about abeggin' folks to dam 'em ;
Then there were meetinhouses, tu, chockful o' gold an'
    silver
Thet you could take, an' no one could n't hand ye in no
    bill fer ;—
Thet 's wut I thought afore I went, thet 's wut them
    fellers told us

Thet stayed to hum an' speechified an' to the buzzards
    sold us ;
I thought thet gold mines could be gut cheaper than
    china asters,
An' see myself acomin' back like sixty Jacob Astors ;
But sech idees soon melted down an' did n't leave a
    grease-spot ;
I vow my holl sheer o' the spiles would n't come nigh
    a V spot ;
Although, most anywares we 've ben, you need n't break
    no locks,
Nor run no kin' o' risks, to fill your pocket full o'
    rocks.
I guess I mentioned in my last some o' the nateral
    feeturs
O' this all-fiered buggy hole in th' way o' awfle cree-
    turs,
But I fergut to name (new things to speak on so
    abounded)
How one day you 'll most die o' thust, an' 'fore the next
    git drownded.
The clymit seems to me just like a teapot made o'
    pewter
Our Prudence hed, thet would n't pour (all she could
    du) to suit her ;
Fust place the leaves 'ould choke the spout, so 's not a
    drop 'ould dreen out,
Then Prude 'ould tip an' tip an' tip, till the holl kit
    bust clean out,
The kiver-hinge-pin bein' lost, tea-leaves an' tea an'
    kiver
'ould all come down *kerswosh !* ez though the dam broke
    in a river.

Jest so 't is here ; holl months there ain't a day o' rainy
　　　　weather,
An' jest ez th' officers 'ould be alayin' heads to-
　　　　gether
Ez t' how they 'd mix their drink at sech a milingtary
　　　　deepot,—
'T 'ould pour ez though the lid wuz off the everlastin'
　　　　teapot.
The cons'quence is, thet I shall take, wen I'm allowed
　　　　to leave here,
One piece o' propaty along,—an' thet 's the shakin'
　　　　fever ;
It 's reggilar employment, though, an' thet ain't thought
　　　　to harm one,
Nor 't ain't so tiresome ez it wuz with t' other leg an'
　　　　arm on ;
An' it 's a consolation, tu, although it does n't pay,
To hev it said you're some gret shakes in any kin' o'
　　　　way.
'T worn't very long, I tell ye wut, I thought o' fortin-
　　　　makin',—
One day a reg'lar shiver-de-freeze, an' next ez good ez
　　　　bakin',—
One day abrilin' in the sand, then smoth'rin' in the
　　　　mashes,—
Git up all sound, be put to bed a mess o' hacks an'
　　　　smashes.
But then, thinks I, at any rate there 's glory to be
　　　　hed,—
Thet 's an investment, arter all, that may n't turn out
　　　　so bad ;
But somehow, wen we 'd fit an' licked, I ollers found
　　　　the thanks

Gut kin' o' lodged afore they come ez low down ez the
     ranks ;
The Gin'rals gut the biggest sheer, the Cunnles next,
     an' so on,—
We never gut a blasted mite o' glory ez I know on ;
An' spose we hed, I wonder how you're goin' to con-
     trive its
Division so 's to give a piece to twenty thousand
     privits ;
Ef you should multiply by ten the portion o' the brav'st
     one,
You would n't git more 'n half enough to speak of on a
     grave-stun ;
We git the licks,—we 're jest the grist thet 's put into
     War's hoppers ;
Leftenants is the lowest grade thet helps pick up the
     coppers.
It may suit folks thet go agin a body with a soul in 't,
An' ain't contented with a hide without a bagnet hole
     in 't ;
But glory is a kin' o' thing *I* shan't pursue no furder,
Coz thet 's the off'cers parquisite,—yourn 's on'y jest
     the murder.
Wal, arter I gin glory up, thinks I at least there 's one
Thing in the bills we ain't hed yit, an' thet 's the GLORI-
     OUS FUN ;
Ef once we git to Mexico, we fairly may presume we
All day an' night shall revel in the halls o' Montezumy.
I 'll tell ye wut *my* revels wuz, an' see how you would
     like 'em ;
We never gut inside the hall : the nighest ever *I* come
Wuz stan'in' sentry in the sun (an', fact, it *seemed* a
     cent'ry)

A ketchin' smells o' biled an' roast thet come out thru
    the entry,
An' hearin', ez I sweltered thru my passes an' repasses,
A rat-tat-too o' knives an' forks, a clinkty-clink o'
    glasses :
I can't tell off the bill o' fare the Gin'rals hed inside ;
All I know is, thet out o' doors a pair o' soles wuz fried,
An' not a hundred miles away frum ware this child wuz
    posted,
A Massachusetts citizen wuz baked an' biled an' roasted ;
The on'y thing like revellin' thet ever come to me
Wuz bein' routed out o' sleep by thet darned revelee.

They say the quarrel 's settled now ; fer my part I 've
    some doubt on 't,
'T 'll take more fish-skin than folks think to take the
    rile clean out on 't ;
At any rate, I 'm so used up I can't do no more fightin',
The on'y chance thet 's left to me is politics or writin' ;
Now, ez the people 's gut to hev a milingtary man,
An' I ain't nothin' else jest now, I 've hit upon a plan ;
The can'idatin' line, you know, 'ould suit me to a T,
An' ef I lose, 't wunt hurt my ears to lodge another
    flea ;
So I 'll set up ez can'idate fer any kin' o' office.
(I mean fer any thet includes good easy-cheers an'
    soffies ;
Fer ez to runnin' fer a place ware work 's the time o'
    day,
You know thet 's wut I never did,—except the other
    way ;)
Ef it 's the Presidential cheer fer wich I 'd better run,

Wut two legs anywares about could keep up with **my**
    one ?
There ain't no kin' o' quality in can'idates, it 's said,
So useful ez a wooden leg,—except a wooden head ;
There's nothin' ain't so poppylar—(wy, it 's a parfect sin
To think wut Mexico hez paid fer Santy Anny's pin ;)—
Then I hain't gut no principles, an', sence I wuz knee-
    high,
I never *did* hev any gret, ez you can testify ;
I'm decided peace-man, tu, an' go agin the war,—
Fer now the holl on 't 's gone an' past, wut is there to
    go *for* ?
Ef, wile you 're 'lectioneerin' round, some curus chaps
    should beg
To know my views o' state affairs, jest answer WOODEN
    LEG !
Ef they ain't settisfied with thet, an' kin' o' pry an'
    doubt
An' ax fer sutthin' deffynit, jest say ONE EYE PUT OUT !
Thet kin' o' talk I guess you 'll find 'll answer to a
    charm,
An' wen you 're druv tu nigh the wall, hol' up my miss-
    in' arm ;
Ef they should nose round fer a pledge, put on a
    vartoou look
An' tell 'em thet 's precisely wut I never gin nor—took !

Then you can call me " Timbertoes."—that's wut the
    people likes ;
Sutthin' combinin' morril truth with phrases sech ez
    strikes ;
Some say the people 's fond o' this, or thet, or wut **you**
    please,—

I tell ye wut the people want is jest correct idees ;
" Old Timbertoes," you see, 's a creed it 's safe to be
    quite bold on,
Ther 's nothin' in 't the other side can any ways git
    hold on ;
It 's a good tangible idee, a sutthin' to embody
Thet valooable class o' men who look thru brandy-
    toddy ;
It gives a Party Platform, tu, jest level with the mind
Of all right-thinkin', honest folks thet mean to go it
    blind ;
Then there air other good hooraws to dror on ez you
    need 'em,
Sech ez the ONE-EYED SLARTERER, the BLOODY BIRDO-
    FREDUM :
Them 's wut takes hold o' folks thet think, ez well ez o'
    the masses,
An' makes you sartin o' the aid o' good men of all
    classes.

There 's one thing I 'm in doubt about ; in order to be
    Presidunt,
It 's absolutely ne'ssary to be a Southern residunt ;
The Constitution settles thet, an' also thet a feller
Must own a nigger o' some sort, jet black, or brown, or
    yeller.
Now I hain't no objections agin particklar climes,
Nor agin ownin' anythin' (except the truth sometimes),
But, ez I hain't no capital, up there among ye, may be,
You might raise funds enough fer me to buy a low-
    priced baby,
An' then, to suit the No'thern folks, who feel obleeged
    to say

They hate an' cuss the very thing they vote fer every
    day,

Say you're assured I go full butt fer Libbaty's diffusion

An' made the purchis on'y jest to spite the Institoo-
    tion ;—

But, golly ! there's the currier's hoss upon the pavement
    pawin' !

I'll be more 'xplicit in my next.

        Yourn,

           BIRDOFREDUM SAWIN.

[We have now a tolerably fair chance of estimating
how the balance-sheet stands between our returned
volunteer and glory. Supposing the entries to be set
down on both sides of the account in fractional parts
of one hundred, we shall arrive at something like the
following result :—

Cr. B. SAWIN, Esq., in account with (BLANK) GLORY. Dr.

By loss of one leg, . .	20	To one 675th three cheers in	
" do. one arm, .	15	Faneuil Hall, . . .	30
" do. four fingers, .	5	" do. do. on	
" do. One eye, .	10	occasion of presentation of	
"the breaking of six ribs,	6	sword to Colonel Wright,	25
"having served under		" one suit of gray clothes	
Colonel Cushing one		(ingeniously unbecoming),	15
month,	44	" musical entertainments	
		(drum and fife six months),	5
		" one dinner after return,	1
		" chance of pension, .	1
		" privilege of drawing long-	
		bow during rest of natural	
		life, ...	23
	100		100

E. E.

It would appear that Mr. Sawin found the actual feast curiously the reverse of the bill of fare advertised in Faneuil Hall and other places. His primary object seems to have been the making of his fortune. *Quœrenda pecunia primum, virtus post nummos.* He hoisted sail for Eldorado, and shipwrecked on Point Tribulation. *Quid non mortalia pectora cogis auri sacra fames?* The speculation has sometimes crossed my mind, in that dreary interval of drought which intervenes between quarterly stipendiary showers, that Providence, by the creation of a money-tree, might have simplified wonderfully the sometimes perplexing problem of human life. We read of bread-trees, the butter for which lies ready churned in Irish bogs. Milk-trees we are assured of in South America, and stout Sir John Hawkins testifies to water-trees in the Canaries. Boot-trees bear abundantly in Lynn and elsewhere ; and I have seen, in the entries of the wealthy, hat-trees with a fair show of fruit. A family-tree I once cultivated myself, and found therefrom but a scanty yield, and that quite tasteless and innutritious. Of trees bearing men we are not without examples ; as those in the park of Louis the Eleventh of France. Who has forgotten, moreover, that olive-tree, growing in the Athenian's back-garden with its strange uxorious crop, for the general propagation of which, as of a new and precious variety, the philosopher Diogenes, hitherto uninterested in arboriculture, was so zealous ? In the *sylva* of our own Southern States, the females of my family have called my attention to the china-tree. Not to multiply examples, I will barely add to my list the birch-tree, in the smaller branches of which has been implanted so miraculous a virtue for communicating the Latin and

Greek languages, and which may well, therefore, be classed among the trees producing necessaries of life,— *venerabile donum fatalis virgæ*. That money-trees existed in the golden age there want not prevalent reasons for our believing. For does not the old proverb, when it asserts that money does not grow on *every* bush, imply *a fortiori* that there were certain bushes which did produce it ? Again, there is another ancient saw to the effect that money is the *root* of all evil. From which two adages it may be safe to infer that the aforesaid species of tree first degenerated into a shrub, then absconded underground, and finally, in our iron age, vanished altogether. In favorable exposures it may be conjectured that a specimen or two survived to a great age, as in the garden of the Hesperides ; and, indeed, what else could that tree in the Sixth Æneid have been, with a branch whereof the Trojan hero procured admission to a territory, for the entering of which money is a surer passport than to a certain other more profitable (too) foreign kingdom ? Whether these speculations of mine have any force in them, or whether they will not rather, by most readers, be deemed impertinent to the matter in hand, is a question which I leave to the determination of an indulgent posterity. That there were, in more primitive and happier times, shops where money was sold,—and that, too, on credit and at a bargain,—I take to be matter of demonstration. For what but a dealer in this article was that Æolus who supplied Ulysses with motive power for his fleet in bags ? What that Ericus, king of Sweden, who is said to have kept the winds in his cap ? What, in more recent times, those Lapland Nornas who traded in favorable breezes ? All which will appear the more clearly when we consider, that, even to this day, *rais-ing the wind* is proverbial for raising money, and that brokers and banks were invented by the Venetians at a later period.

And now for the improvement of this digression. I find a parallel to Mr. Sawin's fortune in an adventure of my own. For, shortly after I had first broached to myself the before-stated natural-historical and archæo-logical theories, as I was passing, *hæc negotia penitus mecum revolvens*, through one of the obscure suburbs of our New England metropolis, my eye was attracted by these words upon a signboard,—CHEAP CASH-STORE. Here was at once the confirmation of my speculations, and the substance of my hopes. Here lingered the fragment of a happier past, or stretched out the first tremulous organic filament of a more fortunate future. Thus glowed the distant Mexico to the eyes of Sawin, as he looked through the dirty pane of the recruiting-office window, or speculated from the summit of that mirage-Pisgah which the imps of the bottle are so cun-ning in raising up. Already had my Alnaschar-fancy (even during that first half-believing glance) expended in various useful directions the funds to be obtained by pledging the manuscript of a proposed volume of discourses. Already did a clock ornament the tower of the Jaalam meeting-house, a gift appropriately, but modestly, commemorated in the parish and town records, both, for now many years, kept by myself. Already had my son Seneca completed his course at the University. Whether, for the moment, we may not be considered as actually lording it over those Baratarias with the viceroyalty of which Hope invests us, and whether we are ever so warmly housed as in our Span-

ish castles, would afford matter of argument.   Enough
that I found that signboard to be no other than a bait
to the trap of a decayed grocer.   Nevertheless, I bought
a pound of dates (getting short weight by reason of im-
mense flights of harpy flies who pursued and lighted
upon their prey even in the very scales), which pur-
chase I made, not only with an eye to the little ones at
home, but also as a figurative reproof of that too fre-
quent habit of my mind, which, forgetting the due order
of chronology, will often persuade me that the happy
sceptre of Saturn is stretched over this Astræa-forsaken
nineteenth century.

Having glanced at the ledger of Glory under the title
Sawin, B., let us extend our investigations, and dis-
cover if that instructive volume does not contain some
charges more personally interesting to ourselves.   I
think we should be more economical of our resources,
did we thoroughly appreciate the fact, that, whenever
Brother Jonathan seems to be thrusting his hand into
his own pocket, he is, in fact, picking ours.   I confess
that the late *muck* which the country has been running
has materially changed my views as to the best method
of raising revenue.   If, by means of direct taxation,
the bills for every extraordinary outlay were brought
under our immediate eye, so that, like thrifty house-
keepers, we could see where and how fast the money
was going, we should be less likely to commit extrava-
gances.   At present, these things are managed in such
a hugger-mugger way, that we know not what we pay
for ; the poor man is charged as much as the rich ;
and, while we are saving and scrimping at the spigot,
the government is drawing off at the bung.   If we
could know that a part of the money we expend **for**

tea and coffee goes to buy powder and balls, and that it is Mexican blood which makes the clothes on our backs more costly, it would set some of us athinking. During the present fall, I have often pictured to myself a government official entering my study and handing me the following bill :—

WASHINGTON, Sept. 30, 1848.

REV. HOMER WILBUR to Uncle Samuel,   Dr.

To his share of work done in Mexico on partnership account, sundry jobs, as below.

"killing, maiming, and wounding about 5,000 Mexicans, ... $ 2.00

"slaughtering one woman carrying water to wounded, ...10

"extra work on two different Sabbaths (one bombardment and one assault) whereby the Mexicans were prevented from defiling themselves with the idolatries of high mass,   .   .   . 3.50

"throwing an especially fortunate and Protestant bombshell into the Cathedral at Vera Cruz, whereby several female Papists were slain at the altar, ...50

"his proportion of cash paid for conquered territory, ... 1.75

"his proportion do for conquering territory, ... 1.50

"manuring do. with new superior compost called " American Citizen," 50

"extending the area of freedom and Protestantism, .01

"glory, ...01

$ 9.87

Immediate payment is requested.

N. B. Thankful for former favors, U. S. requests a continuance of patronage. Orders executed with neatness and despatch. Terms as low as those of any other contractor for the same kind and style of work.

[I can fancy the official answering my look of horror with,—" Yes, Sir, it looks like a high charge, Sir ; but in these days slaughtering is slaughtering." Verily, I would that every one understood that it was ; for it goes about obtaining money under the false pretence of being glory. For me, I have an imagination which plays me uncomfortable tricks. It happens to me sometimes to see a slaughterer on his way home from his day's work, and forthwith my imagination puts a cocked-hat upon his head and epaulettes upon his shoulders, and sets him up as a candidate for the Presidency. So, also, on a recent public occasion, as the place assigned to the " Reverend Clergy " is just behind that of " Officers of the Army and Navy " in processions, it was my fortune to be seated at the dinner-table over against one of these respectable persons. He was arrayed as (out of his own profession) only kings, court-officers, and footmen are in Europe, and Indians in America. Now what does my over-officious imagination but set to work upon him, strip him of his gay livery, and present him to me coatless, his trowsers thrust into the tops of a pair of boots thick with clotted blood, and a basket on his arm out of which lolled a gore-smeared axe, thereby destroying my relish for the temporal mercies upon the board before me ?—H. W.]

No. IX.

A THIRD LETTER FROM B. SAWIN, Esq.

[UPON the following letter slender comment will be needful. In what river Selemnus has Mr. Sawin bathed, that he has become so swiftly oblivious of his fomer loves ? From an ardent and (as befits a soldier) confident wooer of that coy bride, the popular favor, we see him subside of a sudden into the (I trust not jilted) Cincinnatus, returning to his plough with a goodly-sized branch of willow in his hand ; figuratively returning, however, to a figurative plough, and from no profound affection for that honored implement of husbandry, (for which, indeed, Mr. Sawin never displayed any decided predilection,) but in order to be gracefully summoned therefrom to more congenial labors. It would seem that the character of the ancient Dictator had become part of the recognized stock of our modern political comedy, though, as our term of office extends to a quadrennial length, the parallel is not so minutely exact as could be desired. It is sufficiently so, however, for purposes of scenic representation. An humble cottage (if built of logs, the better) forms the Arcadian background of the stage. This rustic paradise is labelled Ashland, Jaalam, North Bend, Marshfield, Kinderhook, or Bâton Rouge, as occasion demands. Before the door stands a something with one handle (the other painted in proper perspective), which represents, in happy ideal vagueness, the plough.   To this the defeated candidate rushes with delirious joy, welcomed as a father by appropriate groups of happy laborers, or from it the successful one is torn with difficulty, sustained alone by a noble sense of public duty.   Only I have observed, that, if the scene be laid at Bâton Rouge or Ashland, the laborers are kept carefully in the background, and are heard to shout from behind the scenes in a singular tone resembling ululation, and accompanied by a sound not unlike vigorous clapping.   This, however, may be artistically in keeping with the habits of the rustic population of those localities.   The precise connection between agricultural pursuits and statesmanship I have not been able, after diligent inquiry, to discover.   But, that my investigations may not be barren of all fruit, I will mention one curious statistical fact, which I consider thoroughly established, namely, that no real farmer ever attains practically beyond a seat in General Court, however theoretically qualified for more exalted station.

It is probable that some other prospect has been opened to Mr. Sawin, and that he has not made this great sacrifice without some definite understanding in regard to a seat in the cabinet or a foreign mission. It may be supposed that we of Jaalam were not untouched by a feeling of villatic pride in beholding our townsman occupying so large a space in the public eye. And to me, deeply revolving the qualifications necessary to a candidate in these frugal times, those of Mr. S. seemed peculiarly adapted to a successful campaign. The loss of a leg, an arm, an eye, and four fingers, reduced him so nearly to the condition of a *vox et præ-terea nihil*, that I could think of nothing but the loss of his head by which his chance could have been bettered. But since he has chosen to balk our suffrages, we must content ourselves with what we can get, remembering *lactucas non esse dandas, dum cardui sufficiant.*—H. W.]

I spose you recollect thet I explained my gennle views
In the last billet thet I writ, 'way down from Veery
  Cruze,
Jest arter I 'd a kind o' ben spontanously sot up
To run unanimously fer the Presidential cup ;
O' course it worn't no wish o' mine, 't wuz ferflely dis-
  tressin,'
But poppiler enthusiasm gut so almighty pressin'
Thet, though like sixty all along I fumed an' fussed an'
  sorrered.
There did n't seem no ways to stop their bringin' on me
  forrerd:
Fact is, they udged the matter so, I could n't help ad-
  mittin'
The Father o' his Country's shoes no feet but mine
  'ould fit in,
Besides the savin' o' the soles fer ages to succeed,
Seein' thet with one wannut foot, a pair 'd be more 'n I
  need ;
An', tell ye wut, them shoes 'll want a thund'rin' sight
  o' patchin',
Ef this ere fashion is to last we 've gut into o' hatchin'
A pair o' second Washintons fer every new election,—
Though, fur ez number one 's consarned, I don't make
  no objection.

I wuz agoin' on to say thet wen at fust I saw
The masses would stick to 't I wuz the Country's father-
    'n-law,
(They would ha' hed it *Father,* but I told 'em 't would
    n't du,
Coz thet wuz sutthin' of a sort they could n't split in tu,
An' Washinton hed hed the thing laid fairly to his
    door,
Nor dars n't say 't worn't his'n, much ez sixty year
    afore,)
But 't ain't no matter ez to thet ; wen I wuz nomer-
    nated,
'T worn't natur but wut I should feel consid'able elated,
An' wile the hooraw o' the thing wuz kind o' noo an'
    fresh,
I thought our ticket would ha' caird the country with a
    resh.

Sence I 've come hum, though, an' looked round, I think
    I seem to find
Strong argimunts ez thick ez fleas to make me change
    my mind ;
It's clear to any one whose brain ain't fur gone in a
    phthisis,
Thet hail Columby's happy land is goin' thru a crisis,
An' 't would n't noways du to hev the people's mind
    distracted
By bein' all to once by sev'ral pop'lar names attackted ;
'T would save holl haycartloads o' fuss an' three four
    months o' jaw,
Ef some illustrous paytriot should back out an' with-
    draw ;

So, ez I ain't a crooked stick, jest like—like ole (I
    swow,
I dunno ez I know his name)—I 'll go back to my
    plough.
Now, 't ain't no more 'n is proper 'n' right in sech a
    sitooation
To hint the course you think 'll be the savin' o' the
    nation ;
To funk right out o' p'lit'cal strife ain't thought to be
    the thing,
Without you deacon off the toon you want your folks
    should sing ;
So I edvise the noomrous friends thet's in one boat
    with me
To jest up killock, jam right down their hellum hard
    a lee,
Haul the sheets taut, an', laying out upon the Suthun
    tack,
Make fer the safest port they can, wich, *I* think, is Ole
    Zack.
Next thing you'll want to know, I spose, wut argi-
    munts I seem
To see that makes me think this ere 'll be the strong-
    est team ;
Fust place, I've ben consid'ble round in barrooms an'
    saloons
Agethrin' public sentiment, 'mongst Demmercrats and
    Coons,
An' 't ain't ve'y offen thet I meet a chap but wut goes
    in
Fer Rough an' Ready, fair an' square, hufs, taller,
    horns, an' skin ;
I don't deny but wut, fer one, ez fur ez I could see,

I didn't like at fust the Pheladelphy nomernee ;
I could ha' pinted to a man thet wuz, I guess, a peg
Higher than him,—a soger, tu, an' with a wooden leg ;
But every day with more an' more o' Taylor zeal I 'm
    burnin',
Seein' wich way the tide thet sets to office is aturnin' ;
Wy, into Beller's we notched the votes down on three
    sticks,—
'T wuz Birdofredum *one*, Cass *aught*, an' Taylor *twenty-*
    six,
An', bein' the on'y canderdate thet wuz upon the
    ground,
They said 't wuz no more 'n right thet I should pay
    the drinks all round ;
Ef I'd expected sech a trick, I would n't ha' cut my
    foot
By goin' an' votin' fer myself like a consumed coot :
It did n't make no diff'rence, though ; I wish I may be
    cust,
Ef Bellers wuz n't slim enough to say he would n't
    trust !

Another pint thet influences the minds o' sober jedges
Is thet the Gin'ral hez n't gut tied hand an' foot with
    pledges ;
He hez n't told ye wut he is, an' so there ain't no
    knowin'
But wut he may turn out to be the best there is agoin';
This, at the on'y spot thet pinched, the shoe directly
    eases,
Coz every one is free to 'xpect percisely wut he pleases :
I want free-trade ; you don't ; the Gin'ral is n't bound
    to neither ;—

I vote my way ; you, yourn ; an' both air sooted to a
    T there.

Ole Rough an' Ready, tu, 's a Wig, but without bein'
    ultry

(He's like a holsome hayinday, thet 's warm, but is n't
    sultry) ;

He 's jest wut I should call myself, a kin' o' *scratch*, ez
    't ware,

Thet ain't exactly all a wig nor wholly your own
    hair ;

I've ben a Wig three weeks myself, jest o' this mod'rate
    sort,

An' don't find them an' Demmercrats so different ez I
    thought ;

They both act pooty much alike, an' push an' scrouge
    an' cus ;

They 're like two pickpockets in league for Uncle Sam-
    well's pus ;

Each takes a side, an' then they squeeze the old man in
    between 'em,

Turn all his pockets wrong side out an' quick ez light-
    nin' clean 'em ;

To nary one on em I 'd trust a secon'-handed rail

No furder off 'an I could sling a bullock by the tail.

Webster sot matters right in thet air Mashfiel' speech
    o' his'n ;—

" Taylor," sez he, " ain't nary ways the one thet I'd a
    chizzen,

Nor he ain't fittin' fer the place, an' like ez not he ain't

No more 'n a tough ole bullethead, an' no gret of a
    saint ;

But then," sez he, " obsarve my pint, he's jest ez good
    to vote fer

Ez though the greasin' on him worn't a thing to hire
    Choate fer ;
Ain't it ez easy done to drop a ballot in a box
Fer one ez 't is fer t'other, fer the bulldog ez the fox ? "
It takes a mind like Dannel's, fact, ez big ez all ou'
    doors,
To find out thet it looks like rain arter it fairly pours ;
I 'gree with him, it ain't so dreffle troublesome to
    vote
Fer Taylor arter all,—it 's jest to go an' change your
    coat ;
Wen he 's once greased, you'll swaller him an' never
    know on 't, scurce,
Unless he scratches, goin' down, with them air Gin'ral's
    spurs.
I've ben a votin' Demmercrat, ez reg'lar ez a clock,
But don't find goin' Taylor gives my narves no gret 'f a
    shock ;
Truth is, the cutest leadin' Wigs, ever sence fust they
    found
Wich side the bread gut buttered on, hev kep a edgin'
    round ;
They kin' o' slipt the planks frum out th' ole platform
    one by one
An' made it gradooally noo, 'fore folks know'd wut wuz
    done,
Till, fur 'z I know, there ain't an inch thet I could lay
    my han' on,
But I, or any Demmercrat, feels comf'table to stan' on,
An' ole Wig doctrines act'lly look, their occ'pants bein'
    gone,
Lonesome ez staddles on a mash without no hayricks
    on.

I spose it 's time now I shall give my thoughts upon the
    plan,
Thet chipped the shell at Buffalo, o' settin' up ole
    Van.
I used to vote fer Martin, but, I swan, I 'm clean dis-
    gusted,—
He ain't the man thet I can say is fittin' to be trusted ;
He ain't half antislav'ry 'nough, nor I ain't sure, ez some
    be,
He 'd go in fer abolishin' the Deestrick o' Columby ;
An', now I come to recollect, it kin' o' makes me
    sick 'z
A horse, to think o' wut he wuz in eighteen thirty-six.
An' then, another thing ;—1 guess, though mebby I am
    wrong,
This Buff'lo plaster ain't agoin' to dror almighty
    strong ;
Some folks, I know, hev gut th' idee thet No'thun dough
    'll rise,
Though, 'fore I see it riz an' baked, I would n't trust
    my eyes ;
'T will take more emptins, a long chalk, than this noo
    party 's gut,
To give sech heavy cakes ez them a start, I tell ye
    wut.
But even ef they caird the day, there would n't be no
    endurin'
To stand upon a platform with sech critters ez Van
    Buren ;—
An' his son John, tu, I can't think how thet air chap
    should dare
To speak ez he doos ; wy, they say he used to cuss an'
    swear !

I spose he never read the hymn thet tells how down the
    stairs
A feller with long legs wuz throwed thet would n't say
    his prayers.

This brings me to another pint : the leaders o' the party
Ain't jest sech men ez I can act along with free an
    hearty :
They ain't not quite respectable, an' wen a feller's mor-
    rils
Don't toe the straightest kin' o' mark, wy, him an' me
    jest quarrils.
I went to a free soil meetin' once, an' wut d' ye think
    I see ?
A feller wuz aspoutin' there thet act'lly come to me,
About two year ago last spring, ez nigh ez I can jedge,
An' axed me ef I didn't want to sign the Temprunce
    pledge !
He 's one o' them thet goes about an' sez you hed n't
    ough' to
Drink nothin', mornin', noon, or night, stronger 'an
    Taunton water.
There 's one rule I 've ben guided by, in settlin' how
    to vote, ollers,—
I take the side thet *is n't* took by them consarned tee-
    totallers.

Ez fer the niggers, I 've ben South, an' thet hez changed
    my mind ;
A lazier, more ungrateful set you could n't nowers
    find.
You know 1 mentioned in my last thet I should buy a
    nigger,

Ef I could make a purchase at a pooty mod'rate fig-
   ger ;
So, ez there 's nothin' in the world I 'm fonder of 'an
   gunnin',
I closed a bargin finally to take a feller runnin'.
I shou'dered queen's-arm an' stumped out, an' wen I
   come t' th' swamp,
'T worn't very long afore I gut upon the nest o' Pomp ;
I come acrost a kin' o' hut, an', playin' round the door,
Some little woolly-headed cubs, ez many 'z six or more.
At fust I thought o' firin', but *think twice* is safest
   ollers ;
There ain't, thinks I, not one on 'em but 's wuth his
   twenty dollars,
Or would be, ef I hed 'em back into a Christian land,—
How temptin' all on 'em would look upon an auction-
   stand!
(Not but wut *I* hate Slavery in th' abstract, stem to
   starn,—
I leave it ware our fathers did, a privit State consarn.)
Soon 'z they see me, they yelled an' run, but Pomp wuz
   out ahoein'
A leetle patch o' corn he hed, or else there ain 't no
   knowin'
He would n't ha' took a pop at me ; but I hed gut the
   start,
An' wen he looked, I vow he groaned ez though he 'd
   broke his heart ;
He done it like a wite man, tu, ez nat'ral ez a pictur,
The imp'dunt, pis'nous hypocrite ! wus 'an a boy con-
   strictur.
" You can't gum *me*, I tell ye now, an' so you need n't
   try,

I 'xpect my eye-teeth every mail so jest shet up," sez I.
" Don't go to actin' ugly now, or else 1 'll jest let strip,
You 'd best draw kindly, seein' 'z how I 've gut ye on
    the hip ;
Besides, you darned ole fool, it ain't no gret of a dis-
    aster
To be benev'lently druv back to a contented master,
Ware you hed Christian priv'ledges you don't seem
    quite aware of,
Or you 'd ha' never run away from bein' well took care
    of ;
Ez fer kin' treatment, wy, he wuz so fond on ye, he said
He 'd give a fifty spot right out, to git ye,'live or dead ;
Wite folks ain't sot by half ez much ; 'member I run
    away,
Wen I wuz bound to Cap'n Jakes, to Mattysqumscot bay;
Don' know him, likely ? Spose not ; wal, the mean ole
    codger went
An' offered—wut reward, think? Wal, it worn 't no *less*
    'n a cent."

Wal, I jest gut 'em into line, an druv 'em on afore me,
The pis'nous brutes, I 'd no idee o' the ill-will they bore
    me ;
We walked till som'ers about noon, an' then it grew so
    hot
I thought it best to camp awile, so I chose out a spot
Jest under a magnoly tree, an' there right down I sot ;
Then I unstrapped my wooden leg, coz it begun to
    chafe,
An' laid it down jest by my side, supposin' all wuz safe ;
I made my darkies all set down around me in a ring,

An' sot an' kin' o' ciphered up how much the lot would
    bring ;
But, wile I drinked the peaceful cup of a pure heart
    an' mind,
(Mixed with some wiskey, now an' then,) Pomp he
    snaked up behind,
An', creepin, grad'lly close tu, ez quiet ez a mink,
Jest grabbed my leg, and then pulled foot, quicker 'an
    you could wink,
An', come to look, they each on 'em hed gut behin' a
    tree,
An' Pomp poked out the leg a piece, jest so ez I could
    see,
An' yelled to me to throw away my pistils an' my gun,
Or else thet they 'd cair off the leg an' fairly cut the run.
I vow I didn 't b'lieve there wuz a decent alligatur
Thet hed a heart so destitoot o' common human natur ;
However, ez there worn't no help, I finally give in
An, heft my arms away to git my leg safe back agin.
Pomp gethered all the weapins up, an' then he come
    an' grinned,
He showed his ivory some, I guess, an' sez, "You 're
    fairly pinned ;
Jest buckle on your leg agin, an' git right up an' come,
'T wun 't du fer fammerly men like me to be so long
    from hum."
At fust I put my foot right down an' swore I would n't
    budge.
"Jest ez you choose," sez he, quite cool, " either be
    shot or trudge."
So this black-hearted monster took an' act'lly druv me,
    back
Along the very feet marks o' my happy mornin' track

An' kep' me pris'ner 'bout six months, an' worked me,
  tu, like sin,
Till I hed gut his corn an' his Carliny taters in ;
He made me larn him readin', tu, (although the crittur
  saw
How much it hut my morril sense to act agin the law,)
So 'st he could read a Bible he 'd gut ; an' axed ef I
  could pint
The North Star out ; but there I put his nose some
  out o' jint,
Fer I weeled roun' about sou'west, an', lookin' up a bit,
Picked out a middlin' shiny one an' tole him thet wuz it.
Fin'lly, he took me to the door. an', givin' me a kick,
Sez —" Ef you know wut 's best for ye, be off, now,
  double-quick ;
The winter-time 's a comin' on, an', though I gut ye
  cheap,
You 're so darned lazy, I don't think you 're hardly
  wuth your keep ;
Besides, the childrin 's growin' up, an' you ain't jest
  the model
I 'd like to hev 'em immertate, an' so you 'd better
  toddle !"

Now is there any thin' on airth 'll ever prove to me
Thet renegader slaves like him air fit fer bein' free ?
D' you think they 'll suck me in to jine the Buff'lo
  chaps, an' them
Rank infidels thet go agin the Scriptur'l cus o' Shem ?
Not by a jugfull ! sooner 'n thet, I 'd go thru fire an'
  water ;
Wen I hev once made up my mind, a meet'nhus ain't
  sotter ;

No, not though all the crows thet flies to pick my bones
       wuz cawin'—
I guess we 're in a Christian land,—
      Yourn,
           BIRDOFREDUM SAWIN.

[Here, patient reader, we take leave of each other, I
trust with some mutual satisfaction. 1 say *patient*, for I
love not that kind which skims dippingly over the sur-
face of the page, as swallows over a pool before rain.
By such no pearls shall be gathered. But if no pearls
there be (as, indeed the world is not without example of
books wherefrom the longest-winded diver shall bring
up no more than his proper handful of mud), yet let us
hope that an oyster or two may reward adequate perse-
verance. If neither pearls nor oysters, yet is patience
itself a gem worth diving deeply for.

It may seem to some that too much space has been
usurped by my own private lucubrations, and some may
be fain to bring against me that old jest of him who
preached all his hearers out of the meeting-house save
only the sexton, who, remaining for yet a little space,
from a sense of official duty, at last gave out also, and,
presenting the keys, humbly requested our preacher to
lock the doors, when he should have wholly relieved
himself of his testimony. I confess to a satisfaction in
the self act of preaching, nor do I esteem a discourse to
be wholly thrown away even upon a sleeping or unintel-
ligent auditory. I cannot easily believe that the Gos-
pel of Saint John, which Jacques Cartier ordered to be
read in the Latin tongue to the Canadian savages, upon
his first meeting with them, fell altogether upon stony
ground. For the earnestness of the preacher is a sermon

appreciable by dullest intellects and most alien ears.
In this wise did Episcopius convert many to his opin-
ions, who yet understood not the language in which he
discoursed.   The chief thing is, that the messenger be-
lieve that he has an authentic message to deliver.   For
counterfeit messengers that mode of treatment which
Father John de Plano Carpini relates to have prevailed
among the Tartars would seem effectual, and, perhaps,
deserved enough.   For my own part, I may lay claim to
so much of the spirit of martyrdom as would have led
me to go into banishment with those clergymen whom
Alphonso the Sixth of Portugal drave out of his king-
dom for refusing to shorten their pulpit eloquence.   It
is possible, that, having been invited into my brother
Biglow's desk, I may have been too little scrupulous in
using it for the venting of my own peculiar doctrines to
a congregation drawn together in the expectation and
with the desire of hearing him.

I am not wholly unconscious of a peculiarity of mental
organization which impels me, like the railroad-engine
with its train of cars, to run backward for a short distance
in order to obtain a fairer start.   I may compare myself
to one fishing from the rocks when the sea runs high,
who, misinterpreting the suction of the undertow for the
biting of some larger fish, jerks suddenly, and finds that
he has *caught bottom*, hauling in upon the end of his line
a trail of various *algæ*, among which, nevertheless, the
naturalist may haply find somewhat to repay the dis-
appointment of the angler.   Yet have I conscientiously
endeavored to adapt myself to the impatient temper of
the age, daily degenerating more and more from the
high standard of our pristine New England.   To the
catalogue of lost arts I would mournfully add also that

of listening to two-hour sermons. Surely we have been abridged into a race of pigmies. For, truly, in those of the old discourses yet subsisting to us in print, the endless spinal column of divisions and subdivisions can be likened to nothing so exactly as to the vertebræ of the saurians, whence the theorist may conjecture a race of Anakim proportionate to the withstanding of these other monsters. I say Anakim rather than Nephelim, because there seem reasons for supposing that the race of those whose heads (though no giants) are constantly enveloped in clouds (which that name imports) will never become extinct. The attempt to vanquish the innumerable *heads* of one of those aforementioned discourses may supply us with a plausible interpretation of the second labor of Hercules, and his successful experiment with fire affords us a useful precedent.

But while I lament the degeneracy of the age in this regard, I cannot refuse to succumb to its influence. Looking out through my study window, I see Mr. Biglow at a distance busy in gathering his Baldwins, of which, to judge by the number of barrels lying about under the trees, his crop is more abundant than my own, —by which sight I am admonished to turn to those orchards of the mind wherein my labors may be more prospered, and apply myself diligently to the preparation of my next Sabbath's discourse.—H. W.]

A FABLE FOR CRITICS.

Reader ! *walk up at once (it will soon be too late) and buy at a perfectly ruinous rate*

A

FABLE FOR CRITICS;

OR, BETTER,

(I like, as a thing that the reader's first fancy may strike, an old fashioned title-page, such as presents a tabular view of the volume's contents.)

A GLANCE

AT A FEW OF OUR LITERARY PROGENIES

(Mrs. Malaprop's word.)

FROM

THE TUB OF DIOGENES;

A VOCAL AND MUSICAL MEDLEY.

THAT IS,

A SERIES OF JOKES

By A Wonderful Quiz

who accompanies himself with a rub-a-dub-dub, full of spirit and grace, on the top of the tub.

SET FORTH IN

October, the 21st day, in the year '48.

G. P. PUTNAM, BROADWAY,

I<small>T</small> being the commonest mode of procedure, I premise
a few candid remarks

T<small>O</small> <small>THE</small> R<small>EADER</small> :

This trifle, begun to please only myself and my own
private fancy, was laid on the shelf.   But some friends,
who had seen it, induced me, by dint of saying they
liked it, to put it in print.   That is, having come to
that very conclusion, I consulted them when it could
make no confusion.   For, (though in the gentlest of
ways,) they had hinted it was scarce worth the while, I
should doubtless have printed it.

I began it, intending a Fable, a frail, slender thing,
rhyme-ywinged, with a sting in its tail.   But, by add-
ings and alterings not previously planned,—digressions
chance-hatched, like birds' eggs in the sand,—and
dawdlings to suit every whimsy's demand, (always free-
ing the bird which I held in my hand, for the two
perched, perhaps out of reach, in the tree,)—it grew
by degrees to the size which you see.   I was like the
old woman that carried the calf, and my neighbors,
like hers, no doubt, wonder and laugh, and when, my
strained arms with their grown burthen full, I call it
my Fable, they call it a bull.

Having scrawled at full gallop (as far as that goes)
in a style that is neither good verse nor bad prose, and
being a person whom nobody knows, some people will
say I am rather more free with my readers than it is

becoming to be, that I seem to expect them to wait on my leisure in following wherever I wander at pleasure, that, in short, I take more than a young author's lawful ease, and laugh in a queer way so like Mephistopheles, that the public will doubt, as they grope through my rhythm, if in truth I am making fun *at* them or *with* them.

So the excellent Public is hereby assured that the sale of my book is already secured.   For there is not a poet throughout the whole land, but will purchase a copy or two out of hand, in the fond expectation of being amused in it, by seeing his betters cut-up and abused in it.   Now, I find, by a pretty exact calculation, there are something like ten thousand bards in the nation, of that special variety whom the Review and Magazine critics call *lofty* and *true,* and about thirty thousand (*this* tribe is increasing) of the kinds who are termed *full of promise* and *pleasing.*   The Public will see by a glance at this schedule, that they cannot expect me to be over-sedulous about courting *them,* since it seems I have got enough fuel made sure of for boiling my pot.

As for such of our poets as find not their names mentioned once in my pages, with praises or blames, let them SEND IN THEIR CARDS, without further DELAY, to my friend G. P. PUTNAM, Esquire, in Broadway, where a LIST will be kept with the strictest regard to the day and the hour of receiving the card.   Then, taking them up as I chance to have time, (that is, if their names can be twisted in rhyme,) I will honestly give each his PROPER POSITION, at the rate of ONE AUTHOR to each NEW EDITION.   Thus a PREMIUM is offered sufficiently HIGH (as the magazines say when they tell their best lie) to induce bards to CLUB their resources and buy the balance of every edition, until they have all of them fairly been run through the mill.

One word to such readers (judicious and wise) as read books with something behind the mere eyes, of whom in the country, perhaps, there are two, including myself, gentle reader, and you. All the characters sketched in this slight *jeu d'esprit,* though, it may be, they seem, here and there, rather free, and drawn from a Mephistophelian stand-point, are *meant* to be faithful, and that is the grand point, and none but an owl would feel sore at a rub from a jester who tells you, without any subterfuge, that he sits in Diogenes' tub.

A FABLE FOR THE CRITICS.

PHŒBUS, sitting one day in a laurel-tree's shade,
Was reminded of Daphne, of whom it was made,
For the god being one day too warm in his wooing,
She took to the tree to escape his pursuing ;
Be the cause what it might, from his offers she
     shrunk,
And, Ginevra-like, shut herself up in a trunk ;
And, though 't was a step into which he had driven
     her,
He somehow or other had never forgiven her ;
Her memory he nursed as a kind of a tonic,
Something bitter to chew when he 'd play the Byronic,
And I can't count the obstinate nymphs that he
     brought over,
By a strange kind of smile he put on when he thought
     of her.
" My case is like Dido's," he sometimes remark'd,
" When I last saw my love, she was fairly embark'd ;
Let hunters from me take this saw when they need it,
—You 're not always sure of your game when you've
     tree'd it.
Just conceive such a change taking place in one's
     mistress !

What romance would be left ?—who can flatter or
    kiss trees ?
And for mercy's sake, how could one keep up a dia-
    logue
With a dull wooden thing that will live and will die a
    log,—
Not to say that the thought would forever intrude
That you 've less chance to win her the more she is
    wood ?
Ah ! it went to my heart, and the memory still grieves,
To see those loved graces all taking their leaves ;
Those charms beyond speech, so enchanting but
    now,
As they left me forever, each making its bough !
If her tongue *had* a tang sometimes more than was
    right,
Her new bark is worse than ten times her old bite."

Now, Daphne,—before she was happily treeified,—
Over all other flowers the lily had deified,
And when she expected the god on a visit,
('T was before he had made his intentions explicit,)
Some buds she arranged with a vast deal of care,
To look as if artlessly twined in her hair,
Where they seemed, as he said, when he paid his ad-
    dresses,
Like the day breaking through the long night of her
    tresses ;
So, whenever he wished to be quite irresistible,
Like a man with eight trumps in his hand at a whist-
    table,
(I feared me at first that the rhyme was untwistable,

Though I might have lugged in an allusion to Christa-
  bel,)—
He would take up a lily, and gloomily look in it,
As I shall at the ——, when they cut up my book in it.

Well, here, after all the bad rhyme I 've been spinning,
I 've got back at last to my story's beginning :
Sitting there as I say, in the shade of his mistress,
As dull as a volume of old Chester mysteries,
Or as those puzzling specimens, which, in old histories,
We read of his verses—the Oracles, namely,—
(I wonder the Greeks should have swallowed them
      tamely,
For one might bet safely whatever he has to risk,
They were laid at his door by some ancient Miss
      Asterisk,
And so dull that the men who retailed them out doors
Got the ill name of "augurs," because they were
      bores,)—
First, he mused what the animal substance or herb is
Would induce a moustache, for you know he 's *im-
      berbis* ;
Then he shuddered to think how his youthful posi-
      tion
Was assailed by the age of his son the physician ;
At some poems he glanced, had been sent to him
      lately,
And the metre and sentiment puzzled him greatly ;
" Mehercle ! I 'd make such proceedings felonious,—
Have they all of them slept in the cave of Trophonius ?
Look well to your seat, 't is like taking an airing
On a corduroy road, and that out of repairing ;
It leads one, 't is true, through the primitive forest,

Grand natural features—but, then, one has no rest;
You just catch a glimpse of some ravishing distance,
When a jolt puts the whole of it out of existence,—
Why not use their ears, if they happen to have any '"
—Here the laurel-leaves murmured the name of poor
    Daphne.

   "O, weep with me, Daphne," he sighed, "for you
    know it 's
A terrible thing to be pestered with poets !"
But, alas, she is dumb, and the proverb holds good,
She never will cry till she 's out of the wood !
What would n't I give if I never had known of her ?
'T were a kind of relief had I something to groan over ;
If I had but some letters of hers, now, to toss over,
I might turn for the nonce a Byronic philosopher,
And bewitch all the flats by bemoaning the loss of her.
One needs something tangible though to begin on—
A loom, as it were, for the fancy to spin on ;
What boots all your grist ? it can never be ground
Till the breeze makes the arms of the windmill go
    round,
(Or, if 't is a water-mill, alter the metaphor,
And say it won't stir, save the wheel be well wet afore,
Or lug in some stuff about water "so dreamily,"—
It is not a metaphor, though, 't is a simile ;)
A lily, perhaps, would set *my* mill agoing,
For just at this season, I think, they are blowing,
Here, somebody, fetch one, not very far hence
They 're in bloom by the score, 't is but climbing a
    fence ;
There 's a poet hard by, who does nothing but fill his
Whole garden, from one end to t' other, with lilies ;

A very good plan, were it not for satiety,
One longs for a weed here and there, for variety ;
Though a weed is no more than a flower in disguise,
Which is seen through at once, if love gives a man
    eyes.

   Now there happened to be among Phœbus's follow-
    ers,
A gentleman, one of the omnivorous swallowers
Who bolt every book that comes out of the press,
Without the least question of larger or less,
Whose stomachs are strong at the expense of their
    head,—
For reading new books is like eating new bread,
One can bear it at first, but by gradual steps he
Is brought to death's door of a mental dyspepsy.
On a previous stage of existence, our Hero
Had ridden outside, with the glass below zero ;
He had been, 't is a fact you may safely rely on,
Of a very old stock a most eminent scion,—
A stock all fresh quacks their fierce boluses ply on,
Who stretch the new boots Earth 's unwilling to try
    on,
Whom humbugs of all shapes and sorts keep their eye
    on,
Whose hair 's in the mortar of every new Zion,
Who, when whistles are dear, go directly and buy one,
Who think slavery a crime that we must not say fie
    on,
Who hunt, if they e'er hunt at all, with the lion,
(Though they hunt lions also, whenever they spy one,)
Who contrive to make every good fortune a wry one,
And at last choose the hard bed of honor to die on,

Whose pedigree traced to earth's earliest years,
Is longer than any thing else but their ears ;—
In short, he was sent into life with the wrong key,
He unlocked the door, and stept forth a poor donkey.
Though kicked and abused by his bipedal betters,
Yet he filled no mean place in the kingdom of letters ;
Far happier than many a literary hack,
He bore only paper-mill rags on his back ;
(For it makes a vast difference which side the mill
One expends on the paper his labor and skill ;)
So, when his soul waited a new transmigration,
And Destiny balanced 'twixt this and that station,
Not having much time to expend upon bothers,
Remembering he 'd had some connections with authors,
And considering his four legs had grown paralytic,—
She set him on too, and he came forth a critic.

Through his babyhood no kind of pleasure he took
In any amusement but tearing a book ;
For him there was no intermediate stage,
From babyhood up to strait-laced middle age ;
There were years when he did n't wear coat-tails
        behind,
But a boy he could never be rightly defined ;
Like the Irish Good Folk, though in length scarce a
        span,
From the womb he came gravely, a little old man ;
While other boys' trousers demanded the toil
Of the motherly fingers on all kinds of soil,
Red, yellow, brown, black, clayey, gravelly, loamy,
He sat in a corner and read Viri Romæ.
He never was known to unbend or to revel once
In base, marbles, hockey, or kick up the devil once ,

He was just one of those who excite the benevolence
Of old prigs who sound the soul's depths with a
    ledger,
And are on the look out for some young men to
    " edger-
-cate," as they call it, who won't be too costly,
And who 'll afterward take to the ministry mostly ;
Who always wear spectacles, always look bilious,
Always keep on good terms with each *materfamilias*
Throughout the whole parish, and manage to rear
Ten boys like themselves, on four hundred a year ;
Who, fulfilling in turn the same fearful conditions,
Either preach through their noses, or go upon missions.

  In this way our hero got safely to College,
Where he bolted alike both his commons and knowl-
    edge ;
A reading-machine, always wound up and going,
He mastered whatever was not worth the knowing,
Appeared in a gown, and a vest of black satin,
To spout such a Gothic oration in Latin,
That Tully could never have made out a word in it,
(Though himself was the model the author preferred
    in it,)
And grasping the parchment which gave him in fee,
All the mystic and so-forths contained in A. B.,
He was launched (life is always compared to a sea,)
With just enough learning, and skill for the using it,
To prove he 'd a brain, by forever confusing it.
So worthy Saint Benedict, piously burning
With the holiest zeal against secular learning,
Nesciensque scienter, as writers express it,
Indoctusque sapienter á Romá recessit.

'T would be endless to tell you the things that he
  knew,
All separate facts, undeniably true,
But with him or each other they 'd nothing to do ;
No power of combining, arranging, discerning,
Digested the masses he learned into learning ;
There was one thing in life he had practical knowledge
  for,
(And, this you will think, he need scarce go to college
  for,)
Not a deed would he do, not a word would he utter,
Till he 'd weighed its relations to plain bread and
  butter.
When he left Alma Mater, he practised his wits
In compiling the journals' historical bits,—
Of shops broken open, men falling in fits,
Great fortunes in England bequeathed to poor printers,
And cold spells, the coldest for many past winters,—
Then, rising by industry, knack, and address,
Got notices up for an unbiassed press,
With a mind so well poised, it seemed equally made for
Applause or abuse, just which chanced to be paid for ;
From this point his progress was rapid and sure,
To the post of a regular heavy reviewer.

And here I must say, he wrote excellent articles
On the Hebraic points, or the force of Greek particles,
They filled up the space nothing else was prepared for,
And nobody read that which nobody cared for ;
If any old book reached a fiftieth edition,
He could fill forty pages with safe erudition ;
He could gauge the old books by the old set of rules,
And his very old nothings pleased very old fools ;

But give him a new book, fresh out of the heart,
And you put him at sea without compass or chart,—
His blunders aspired to the rank of an art ;
For his lore was engraft, something foreign that grew
in him,
Exhausting the sap of the native and true in him,
So that when a man came with a soul that was new in
him,
Carving new forms of truth out of Nature's old granite,
New and old at their birth, like Le Verrier's planet,
Which, to get a true judgment, themselves must
create
In the soul of their critic the measure and weight,
Being rather themselves a fresh standard of grace,
To compute their own judge, and assign him his place,
Our reviewer would crawl all about it and round it,
And, reporting each circumstance just as he found it,
Without the least malice,—his record would be
Profoundly æsthetic as that of a flea,
Which, supping on Wordsworth, should print, for our
sakes,
Recollections of nights with the Bard of the Lakes,
Or, borne by an Arab guide, ventured to render a
General view of the ruins at Denderah.

As I said, he was never precisely unkind,
The defect in his brain was mere absence of mind ;
If he boasted, 't was simply that he was self-made,
A position which 1, for one, never gainsaid,
My respect for my Maker supposing a skill
In his works which our hero would answer but ill ;
And I trust that the mould which he used may be
cracked, or he,

Made bold by success, may make broad his phylactery,
And set up a kind of a man-manufactory,
An event which I shudder to think about, seeing
That Man is a moral, accountable being.

He meant well enough, but was still in the way,
As a dunce always is, let him be where he may ;
Indeed, they appear to come into existence
To impede other folks with their awkward assistance ;
If you set up a dunce on the very North pole,
All alone with himself, I believe, on my soul,
He 'd manage to get betwixt somebody's shins,
And pitch him down bodily, all in his sins,
To the grave polar bears sitting round on the ice,
All shortening their grace, to be in for a slice ;
Or, if he found nobody else there to pother,
Why, one of his legs would just trip up the other,
For there's nothing we read of in torture's inventions,
Like a well-meaning dunce, with the best of intentions.

A terrible fellow to meet in society,
Not the toast that he buttered was ever so dry at tea ;
There he 'd sit at the table and stir in his sugar,
Crouching close for a spring, all the while, like a
    cougar ;
Be sure of your facts, of your measures and weights,
Of your time—he 's as fond as an Arab of dates ;—
You 'll be telling, perhaps, in your comical way,
Of something you've seen in the course of the day ;
And, just as you 're tapering out the conclusion,
You venture an ill-fated classic allusion,—
The girls have all got their laughs ready, when, whack !
The cougar comes down on your thunderstruck back ;

You had left out a comma,—your Greek 's put in joint,
And pointed at cost of your story's whole point.
In the course of the evening, you venture on certain
Soft speeches to Anne, in the shade of the curtain ;
You tell her your heart can be likened to *one* flower,
" And that, oh most charming of women, 's the sun-
     flower,
Which turns "—here a clear nasal voice, to your terror,
From outside the curtain, says, " that 's all an error."
As for him, he's—no matter, he never grew tender,
Sitting after a ball, with his feet on the fender,
Shaping somebody's sweet features out of cigar smoke,
(Though he 'd willingly grant you that such doings are
     smoke ;)
All women he damns with *mutabile semper*,
And if ever he felt something like love's distemper,
'T was toward a young lady who spoke ancient Mexican,
And assisted her father in making a lexicon ;
Though I recollect hearing him get quite ferocious
About one Mary Clausum, the mistress of Grotius,
Or something of that sort,—but, no more to bore ye.
With character-painting, I 'll turn to my story.

   Now, Apollo, who finds it convenient sometimes
To get his court clear of the makers of rhymes,
The *genus*, I think it is called, *irritabile*,
Every one of whom thinks himself treated most shab-
     bily,
And nurses a—what is it ?—*immedicabile*,
Which keeps him at boiling-point, hot for a quarrel,
As bitter as wormwood, and sourer than sorrel,
If any poor devil but looks at a laurel ;—
Apollo, I say, being sick of their rioting,

(Though he sometimes acknowledged their verse had a
        quieting
Effect after dinner, and seemed to suggest a
Retreat to the shrine of a tranquil siesta,)
Kept our Hero at hand, who, by means of a bray,
Which he gave to the life, drove the rabble away ;
And if that would n't do, he was sure to succeed,
If he took his review out and offered to read ;
Or, failing in plans of this milder description,
He would ask for their aid to get up a subscription,
Considering that authorship was n't a rich craft,
To print the " American drama of Witchcraft."
" Stay, I 'll read you a scene,"—but he hardly began,
Ere Apollo shrieked " Help ! " and the authors all ran :
And once, when these purgatives acted with less spirit,
And the desperate case asked a remedy desperate,
He drew from his pocket a foolscap epistle,
As calmly as if 't were a nine-barrelled pistol,
And threatened them all with the judgment to come,
Of " A wandering Star's first impressions of Rome."
    "Stop ! stop ! " with their hands o'er their ears
        screamed the Muses,
" He may go off and murder himself, if he chooses,
'T was a means self-defence only sanctioned his trying,
'T is mere massacre now that the enemy 's flying ;
If he 's forced to 't again, and we happen to be there,
Give us each a large handkerchief soaked in strong
        ether."

    I called this a " Fable for Critics ; " you think it 's
More like a display of my rhythmical trinkets ;
My plot, like an icicle, 's slender and slippery,
Every moment more slender, and likely to slip awry,

And the reader unwilling *in loco desipere,*
Is free to jump over as much of my frippery
As he fancies, and, if he 's a provident skipper, he
May have an Odyssean sway of the gales,
And get safe into port, ere his patience all fails ;
Moreover, although 't is a slender return
For your toil and expense, yet my paper will burn,
And, if you have manfully struggled thus far with
    me,
You may e'en twist me up, and just light your cigar
    with me :
If too angry for that, you can tear me in pieces,
And my *membra disjecta* consign to the breezes,
A fate like great Ratzau's, whom one of those bores,
Who beflead with bad verses poor Louis Quatorze,
Describes, (the first verse somehow ends with *victoire,*)
As *dispersant partout et ses membres et sa gloire ;*
Or, if I were over-desirous of earning
A repute among noodles for classical learning,
I could pick you a score of allusions, I wis,
As new as the jests of *Didaskalos tis ;*
Better still, I could make out a good solid list
From recondite authors who do not exist,—
But that would be naughty : at least, I could twist
Something out of Absyrtus, or turn your inquiries
After Milton's prose metaphor, drawn from Osiris ;—
But, as Cicero says he won't say this or that,
(A fetch, I must say, most transparent and flat,)
After saying whate'er he could possibly think of,—
I simply will state that I pause on the brink of
A mire, ankle-deep, of deliberate confusion,
Made up of old jumbles of classic allusion,
So, when you were thinking yourselves to be pitied,

Just conceive how much harder your teeth you 'd have
    gritted,
An 't were not for the dulness I 've kindly omitted.

I 'd apologize here for my many digressions,
Were it not that I 'm certain to trip into fresh ones,
('T is so hard to escape if you get in their mesh once ;)
Just reflect, if you please, how 't is said by Horatius,
That Mæonides nods now and then, and, my gracious !
It certainly does look a little bit ominous
When he gets under way with *ton d'apameibomenos.*
(Here a something occurs which I'll just clap a rhyme to,
And say it myself, ere a Zoilus has time to,—
Any author a nap like Van Winkle's may take,
If he only contrive to keep readers awake,
But he 'll very soon find himself laid on the shelf,
If *they* fall a nodding when he nods himself.)

Once for all, to return, and to stay, will I, nill I—
When Phœbus expressed his desire for a lily,
Our hero, whose homœopathic sagacity
With an ocean of zeal mixed his drop of capacity,
Set off for the garden as fast as the wind,
(Or, to take a comparison more to my mind,
As a sound politician leaves conscience behind,)
And leaped the low fence, as a party hack jumps
O'er his principles, when something else turns up
    trumps.

He was gone a long time, and Apollo meanwhile,
Went over some sonnets of his with a file,
For of all compositions, he thought that the sonnet
Best repaid all the toil you expended upon it ;

It should reach with one impulse the end of its course,
And for one final blow collect all of its force ;
Not a verse should be salient, but each one should
    tend
With a wave-like up-gathering to burst at the end ;—
So, condensing the strength here, there smoothing a
    wry kink,
He was killing the time, when up walked Mr. —— ;
At a few steps behind him, a small man in glasses',
Went dodging about, muttering " murderers ! asses ! "
From out of his pocket a paper he 'd take,
With the proud look of martyrdom tied to its stake,
And, reading a squib at himself, he 'd say, " Here I
    see
'Gainst American letters a bloody conspiracy,
They are all by my personal enemies written ;
I must post an anonymous letter to Britain,
And show that this gall is the merest suggestion
Of spite at my zeal on the Copyright question,
For, on this side the water, 't is prudent to pull
O'er the eyes of the public their national wool,
By accusing of slavish respect to John Bull,
All American authors who have more or less
Of that anti-American humbug—success,
While in private we 're always embracing the knees
Of some twopenny editor over the seas,
And licking his critical shoes, for you know 't is
The whole aim of our lives to get one English 'no-
    tice ' ;
My American puffs I would willingly burn all,
(They 're all from one source, monthly, weekly, diur-
    nal)
To get but a kick from a transmarine journal ! "

So, culling the gibes of each critical scorner
As if they were plums. and himself were Jack Horner,
He came cautiously on, peeping round every corner.
And into each hole where a weasel might pass in,
Expecting the knife of some critic assassin,
Who stabs to the heart with a caricature,
Not so bad as those daubs of the Sun, to be sure,
Yet done with a dagger-o-type, whose vile portraits
Disperse all one's good, and condense all one's poor
       traits.

  Apollo looked up, hearing footsteps approaching,
And slipped out of sight the new rhymes he was broach-
      ing,—
" Good day, Mr. ——, I 'm happy to meet
With a scholar so ripe, and a critic so neat,
Who through Grub-street the soul of a gentleman
      carries, —
What news from that suburb of London and Paris
Which latterly makes such shrill claims to monopolize
The credit of being the New World's metropolis ? "

  " Why, nothing of consequence, save this attack
On my friend there, behind, by some pitiful hack,
Who thinks every national author a poor one,
That is n't a copy of something that 's foreign,
And assaults the American Dick—
                        " Nay, 't is clear
That your Damon there 's fond of a flea in his ear,
And, if no one else furnished them gratis, on tick
He would buy some himself, just to hear the old click ;
Why, I honestly think, if some fool in Japan

Should turn up his nose at the ' Poems on Man,'
Your friend there by some inward instinct would know
    it,
Would get it translated, reprinted, and show it ;
As a man might take off a high stock to exhibit
The autograph round his own neck of the gibbet,
Nor would let it rest so, but fire column after column,
Signed Cato, or Brutus, or something as solemn,
By way of displaying his critical crosses,
And tweaking that poor transatlantic proboscis,
His broadsides resulting (and this there's no doubt of,)
In successively sinking the craft they 're fired out of.
Now nobody knows when an author is hit,
If he don't have a public hysterical fit ;
Let him only keep close in his snug garret's dim ether,
And nobody 'd think of his critics—or him either ;
If an author have any least fibre of worth in him,
Abuse would but tickle the organ of mirth in him,
All the critics on earth cannot crush with their ban,
One word that 's in tune with the nature of man."

  " Well, perhaps so ; meanwhile I have brought you a
    book,
Into which if you 'll just have the goodness to look,
You may feel so delighted, when you have got through
    it,
As to think it not unworth your while to review it,
And I think I can promise your thoughts, if you do,
A place in the next Democratic Review."

  " The most thankless of gods you must surely have
    tho't me,
For this is the forty-fourth copy you 've brought me,

I have given them away, or at least I have tried,
But I 've forty-two left, standing all side by side,
(The man who accepted that one copy, died,)—
From one end of a shelf to the other they reach,
'With the author's respects' neatly written in each.
The publisher, sure, will proclaim a Te Deum,
When he hears of that order the British Museum
Has sent for one set of what books were first printed
In America, little or big,—for 't is hinted
That this is the first truly tangible hope he
Has ever had raised for the sale of a copy.
I've thought very often 't would be a good thing
In all public collections of books, if a wing
Were set off by itself, like the seas from the dry
    lands,
Marked *Literature suited to desolate islands,*
And filled with such books as could never be read
Save by readers of proofs, forced to do it for
    bread,—
Such books as one's wrecked on in small country-
    taverns,
Such as hermits might mortify over in caverns,
Such as Satan, if printing had then been invented,
As the climax of woe, would to Job have presented,
Such as Crusoe might dip in, although there are few so
Outrageously cornered by fate as poor Crusoe ;
And since the philanthropists just now are banging
And gibbeting all who 're in favor of hanging,—
(Though Cheever has proved that the Bible and Altar
Were let down from Heaven at the end of a halter,
And that vital religion would dull and grow callous,
Unrefreshed, now and then, with a sniff of the
    gallows,)—

And folks are beginning to think it looks odd,
To choke a poor scamp for the glory of God ;
And that He who esteems the Virginia reel
A bait to draw saints from their spiritual weal,
And regards the quadrille as a far greater knavery
Than crushing His African children with slavery,—
Since all who take part in a waltz or cotillion
Are mounted for hell on the Devil's own pillion,
Who, as every true orthodox Christian well knows,
Approaches the heart through the door of the
    toes,—
That He, I was saying, whose judgments are
    stored
For such as take steps in despite of his word,
Should look with delight on the agonized prancing
Of a wretch who has not the least ground for his
    dancing,
While the State, standing by, sings a verse from the
    Psalter
About offering to God on his favorite halter,
And, when the legs droop from their twitching diver-
    gence,
Sells the clothes to the Jew, and the corpse to the sur-
    geons ;—

    Now, instead of all this, I think I can direct you
        all
To a criminal code both humane and effectual ;—
I propose to shut up every doer of wrong
With these desperate books, for such terms, short
    or long,
As by statute in such cases made and provided,
Shall be by your wise legislators decided

Thus :—Let murderers be shut, to grow wiser and
    cooler,
At hard labor for life on the works of Miss —— ;
Petty thieves, kept from flagranter crimes by their
    fears,
Shall peruse Yankee Doodle a blank term of years,—
That American Punch, like the English, no doubt—
Just the sugar and lemons and spirit left out.

" But stay, here comes Tityrus Griswold, and leads on
The flocks whom he first plucks alive, and then feeds
    on,—
A loud cackling swarm, in whose feathers warm-
    drest,
He goes for as perfect a—swan, as the rest.

"There comes Emerson first, whose rich words,
    every one,
Are like gold nails in temples to hang trophies on,
Whose prose is grand verse, while his verse, the Lord
    knows,
Is some of it pr—— No , 't is not even prose ;
I' m speaking of metres ; some poems have welled
From those rare depths of soul that have ne'er been
    excelled ;
They 're not epics, but that does n't matter a pin,
In creating, the only hard thing 's to begin ;
A grass-blade 's no easier to make than an oak,
If you 've once found the way, you've achieved the
    grand stroke ;
In the worst of his poems are mines of rich matter,
But thrown in a heap with a crush and a clatter ;
Now it is not one thing nor another alone

Makes a poem, but rather the general tone,
The something pervading, uniting the whole,
The before unconceived, unconceivable soul,
So that just in removing this trifle or that, you
Take away, as it were, a chief limb of the statue ;
Roots, wood, bark, and leaves, singly perfect may be,
But, clapt hodge-podge together, they don't make a
  tree.

 " But, to come back to Emerson, (whom by the
  way,
I believe we left waiting,) —his is, we may say,
A Greek head on right Yankee shoulders, whose range
Has Olympus for one pole, for t' other the Exchange ;
He seems, to my thinking, (although I' m afraid
The comparison must, long ere this, have been
  made,)
A Plotinus-Montaigne, where the Egyptian's gold
  mist
And the Gascon's shrewd wit cheek-by-jowl co-exist ;
All admire, and yet scarcely six converts he 's got
To I don't (nor they either) exactly know what ;
For though he builds glorious temples, 't is odd
He leaves never a doorway to get in a god.
'T is refreshing to old-fashioned people like me,
To meet such a primitive Pagan as he,
In whose mind all creation is duly respected
As parts of himself—just a little projected ;
And who 's willing to worship the stars and the sun,
A convert to—nothing but Emerson.
So perfect a balance there is in his head,
That he talks of things sometimes as if they were
  dead ;

Life, nature, love, God, and affairs of that sort,
He looks at as merely ideas ; in short,
As if they were fossils stuck round in a cabinet,
Of such vast extent that our earth 's a mere dab in it ;
Composed just as he is inclined to conjecture her,
Namely, one part pure earth, ninety-nine parts pure
     lecturer ;
You are filled with delight at his clear demonstration,
Each figure, word, gesture, just fits the occasion,
With the quiet precision of science he 'll sort 'em,
But you can't help suspecting the whole a *post mor-*
     tem.

   " There are persons, mole-blind to the soul's make
     and style,
Who insist on a likeness 'twixt him and Carlyle ;
To compare him with Plato would be vastly fairer,
Carlyle 's the more burly, but E. is the rarer ;
He sees fewer objects, but clearlier, truelier,
If C. 's as original, E. 's more peculiar ;
That he 's more of a man you might say of the one,
Of the other he 's more of an Emerson ;
C. 's the Titan, as shaggy of mind as of limb,—
E. the clear-eyed Olympian, rapid and slim ;
The one 's two-thirds Norseman, the other half Greek,
Where the one 's most abounding, the other 's to seek ;
C.'s generals require to be seen in the mass,—
E.'s specialties gain if enlarged by the glass ;
C. gives nature and God his own fits of the blues,
And rims common-sense things with mystical hues,—
E. sits in a mystery calm and intense,
And looks coolly around him with sharp common-
     sense ;

C. shows you how every-day matters unite
With the dim transdiurnal recesses of night,—
While E., in a plain, preternatural way,
Makes mysteries matters of mere every day ;
C. draws all his characters quite *à la* Fuseli,—
He don't sketch their bundles of muscles and thews
    illy,
But he paints with a brush so untamed and profuse,
They seem nothing but bundles of muscles and thews ;
E. is rather like Flaxman, lines strait and severe,
And a colorless outline, but full, round, and clear ;—
To the men he thinks worthy he frankly accords
The design of a white marble statue in words.
C. labors to get at the centre, and then
Take a reckoning from there of his actions and men ;
E. calmly assumes the said centre as granted,
And, given himself, has whatever is wanted.

  " He has imitators in scores, who omit
No part of the man but his wisdom and wit,—
Who go carefully o'er the sky-blue of his brain,
And when he has skimmed it once, skim it again ;
If at all they resemble him, you may be sure it is
Because their shoals mirror his mists and obscurities,
As a mud-puddle seems deep as heaven for a minute,
While a cloud that floats o'er is reflected within it.

  " There comes ——, for instance ; to see him 's rare
    sport,
Tread in Emerson's tracks with legs painfully short ;
How he jumps, how he strains, and gets red in the
    face,
To keep step with the mystagogue's natural pace !

He follows as close as a stick to a rocket,
His fingers exploring the prophet's each pocket.
Fie, for shame, brother bard ; with good fruit of your
    own
Can't you let neighbor Emerson's orchards alone ?
Besides, 't is no use, you 'll not find e'en a core,—
—— has picked up all the windfalls before.
They might strip every tree, and E. never would catch
    'em,
His Hesperides have no rude dragon to watch 'em ;
When they send him a dishfull, and ask him to try 'em,
He never suspects how the sly rogues came by 'em ;
He wonders why 't is there are none such his trees on,
And thinks 'em the best he has tasted this season.

" Yonder, calm as a cloud, Alcott stalks in a dream,
And fancies himself in thy groves, Academe,
With the Parthenon nigh, and the olive-trees o'er him,
And never a fact to perplex him or bore him,
With a snug room at Plato's, when night comes, to
    walk to,
And people from morning till midnight to talk to,
And from midnight till morning, nor snore in their
    listening ;—
So he muses, his face with the joy of it glistening,
For his highest conceit of a happiest state is
Where they 'd live upon acorns, and hear him talk
    gratis ;
And indeed, I believe, no man ever talked better—
Each sentence hangs perfectly poised to a letter ;
He seems piling words, but there 's royal dust hid
In the heart of each sky-piercing pyramid.
While he talks he is great, but goes out like a taper,

If you shut him up closely with pen, ink, and paper ;
Yet his fingers itch for 'em from morning till night,
And he thinks he does wrong if he don't always write ;
In this, as in all things, a lamb among men,
He goes to sure death when he goes to his pen.

" Close behind him is Brownson, his mouth very full
With attempting to gulp a Gregorian bull ;
Who contrives, spite of that, to pour out as he goes
A stream of transparent and forcible prose ;
He shifts quite about, then proceeds to expound
That 't is merely the earth, not himself, that turns
    round,
And wishes it clearly impressed on your mind,
That the weather-cock rules and not follows the wind ;
Proving first, then as deftly confuting each side,
With no doctrine pleased that 's not somewhere denied,
He lays the denier away on the shelf,
And then—down beside him lies gravely himself.
He 's the Salt River boatman, who always stands will-
    ing
To convey friend or foe without charging a shilling,
And so fond of a trip that, when leisure 's to spare,
He 'll row himself up, if he can't get a fare.
The worst of it is, that his logic 's so strong,
That of two sides he commonly chooses the wrong ;
If there *is* only one, why, he 'll split it in two,
And first pummel this half, then that, black and blue.
That white 's white needs no proof, but it takes a deep
    fellow
To prove it jet-black, and that jet-black is yellow.
He offers the true faith to drink in a sieve,—
When it reaches your lips there 's naught left to believe

But a few silly- (syllo-, 1 mean,) -gisms that squat 'em
Like tadpoles, o'erjoyed with the mud at the bottom.

  " There is Willis, so *natty* and jaunty and gay,
Who says his best things in so foppish a way,
With conceits and pet phrases so thickly o'erlaying 'em,
That one hardly knows whether to thank him for say-
        ing 'em ;
Over-ornament ruins both poem and prose,
Just conceive of a muse with a ring in her nose !
His prose had a natural grace of its own,
And enough of it, too, if he 'd let it alone ;
But he twitches and jerks so. one fairly gets tired,
And is forced to forgive where he might have admired ;
Yet whenever it slips away free and unlaced,
It runs like a stream with a musical waste,
And gurgles along with the liquidest sweep ;—
'T is not deep as a river, but who 'd have it deep ?
In a country where scarcely a village is found
That has not its author sublime and profound,
For some one to be slightly shoal is a duty,
And Willis's shallowness makes half his beauty.
His prose winds along with a blithe, gurgling error,
And reflects all of Heaven it can see in its mirror.
'T is a narrowish strip, but it is not an artifice,—
'T is the true out-of-doors with its genuine hearty phiz ;
It is Nature herself, and there 's something in that,
Since most brains reflect but the crown of a hat.
No volume I know to read under a tree,
More truly delicious than his A l'Abri,
With the shadows of leaves flowing over your book,
Like ripple-shades netting the bed of a brook ;
With June coming softly your shoulder to look over,

Breezes waiting to turn every leaf of your book over,
And Nature to criticise still as you read,—
The page that bears that is a rare one indeed.

" He's so innate a cockney, that had he been born
Where plain bare-skin 's the only full-dress that is
     worn,
He 'd have given his own such an air that you 'd say
'T had been made by a tailor to lounge in Broadway.
His nature 's a glass of champagne with the foam on 't,
As tender as Fletcher, as witty as Beaumont ;
So his best things are done in the flush of the moment,
If he wait, all is spoiled ; he may stir it and shake it,
But the fixed air once gone, he can never re-make it ;
He might be a marvel of easy delightfulness,
If he would not sometimes leave the *r* out of spright-
     fulness ;
And he ought to let Scripture alone—'t is self-slaughter,
For nobody likes inspiration and water.
He 'd have been just the fellow to sup at the Mermaid,
Cracking jokes at rare Ben, with an eye to the bar-
     maid,
His wit running up as Canary ran down,—
The topmost bright bubble on the wave of The Town.

" Here comes Parker, the Orson of parsons, a man
Whom the Church undertook to put under her ban,—
(The Church of Socinus, I mean)—his opinions
Being So- (ultra) -cinian, they shocked the Socinians ;
They believed—faith I 'm puzzled— I think I may call
Their belief a believing in nothing at all,
Or something of that sort ; I know they all went
For a general union of total dissent :

He went a step farther ; without cough or hem,
He frankly avowed he believed not in them ;
And, before he could be jumbled up or prevented,
From their orthodox kind of dissent he dissented.
There was heresy here, you perceive, for the right
Of privately judging means simply that light
Has been granted to *me*, for deciding on *you*,
And, in happier times, before Atheism grew,
The deed contained clauses for cooking you, too.
Now at Xerxes and Knut we all laugh, yet our foot
With the same wave is wet that mocked Xerxes and
  Knut ;
And we all entertain a sincere private notion,
That our *Thus far !* will have a great weight with the
  ocean.
'T was so with our liberal Christians : they bore
With sincerest conviction their chairs to the shore ;
They brandished their worn theological birches,
Bade natural progress keep out of the Churches,
And expected the lines they had drawn to prevail
With the fast-rising tide to keep out of their pale ;
They had formerly dammed the Pontifical See.
And the same thing, they thought, would do nicely
  for P. ;
But he turned up his nose at their murmuring and
  shamming,
And cared (shall I say ?) not a d— for their dam-
  ming ;
So they first read him out of their Church, and next
  minute
Turned round and declared he had never been in it.
But the ban was too small or the man was too big,
For he recks not their bells, books, and candles a fig ;

(He don't look like a man who would *stay* treated
    shabbily,
Sophroniscus' son's head o'er the features of Rab-
    elais ;)—
He bangs and bethwacks them,—their backs he salutes
With the whole tree of knowledge torn up by the roots ;
His sermons with satire are plenteously verjuiced,
And he talks in one breath of Confutzee, Cass, Zer-
    duscht
Jack Robinson, Peter the Hermit, Strap, Dathan,
Cush, Pitt (not the bottomless, *that* he 's no faith in),
Pan, Pillicock, Shakspeare, Paul, Toots, Monsieur
    Tonson,
Aldebaran, Alcander, Ben Khorat, Ben Jonson,
Thoth, Richter, Joe Smith, Father Paul, Judah Monis,
Musæus, Muretus,— μ Scorpionis,
Maccabee, Maccaboy, Mac—Mac—ah ! Machiavelli,
Condorcet, Count d'Orsay, Conder, Say, Ganganelli,
Orion, O'Connell, the Chevalier D'O,
(Whom the great Sully speaks of,) τo $\pi a \nu$, the great
    toe
Of the statue of Jupiter, now made to pass
For that of Jew Peter by good Romish brass,—
(You may add for yourselves, for I find it a bore,
All the names you have ever, or not, heard before,
And when you 've done that—why, invent a few more.)
His hearers can't tell you on Sunday beforehand,
If in that day's discourse they ' ll be Bibled or Koraned,
For he 's seized the idea (by his martyrdom fired,)
That all men (not orthodox) *may be* inspired ;
Yet, though wisdom profane with his creed he may
    weave in.
He makes it quite clear what he *does n't* believe in,

While some, who decry him, think all Kingdom Come
Is a sort of a, kind of a, species of Hum,
Of which, as it were, so to speak, not a crumb
Would be left, if we did n't keep carefully mum,
And. to make a clean breast, that 't is perfectly plain
That *all* kinds of wisdom are somewhat profane ;
Now P.'s creed than this may be lighter or darker,
But in one thing, 't is clear, he has faith, namely—
    Parker ;
And this is what makes him the crowd-drawing preacher,
There 's a back-ground of god to each hard-working
    feature,
Every word that he speaks has been fierily furnaced
In the blast of a life that has struggled in earnest :
There he stands, looking more like a ploughman than
    priest,
If not dreadfully awkward, not graceful at least,
His gestures all downright and same, if you will,
As of brown-fisted Hobnail in hoeing a drill,
But his periods fall on you, stroke after stroke,
Like the blows of a lumberer felling an oak,
You forget the man wholly, you 're thankful to meet
With a preacher who smacks of the field and the street,
And to hear, you 're not over-particular whence,
Almost Taylor's profusion, quite Latimer's sense.

"There is Bryant, as quiet, as cool, and as digni-
    fied,
As a smooth, silent iceberg, that never is ignified,
Save when by reflection 't is kindled o' nights
With a semblance of flame by the chill Northern
    Lights.

He may rank (Griswold says so) first bard of your
 nation,
(There's no doubt that he stands in supreme iceola-
 tion,)
Your topmost Parnassus he may set his heel on,
But no warm applauses come, peal following peal on,—
He 's too smooth and too polished to hang any zeal on :
Unqualified merits, I 'll grant, if you choose, he has
 'em,
But he lacks the one merit of kindling enthusiasm ;
If he stir you at all, it is just, on my soul,
Like being stirred up with the very North Pole.

 " He is very nice reading in summer, but *inter
Nos*, we don't want *extra* freezing in winter ;
Take him up in the depth of July, my advice is,
When you feel an Egyptian devotion to ices.
But, deduct all you can, there 's enough that 's right
 good in him,
He has a true soul for field, river, and wood in him ;
And his heart, in the midst of brick walls, or where'er
 it is,
Glows, softens, and thrills with the tenderest chari-
 ties,—
To you mortals that delve in this trade-ridden planet ?
No, to old Berkshire's hills, with their limestone and
 granite.
If you 're one who *in loco* (add *foco* here) *desipis*,
You will get of his outermost heart (as I guess) a piece ;
But you 'd get deeper down if you came as a precipice,
And would break the last seal of its inwardest foun-
 tain,
If you only could palm yourself off for a mountain.

Mr. Quivis, or somebody quite as discerning,
Some scholar who 's hourly expecting his learning,
Calls B. the American Wordsworth ; but Wordsworth
Is worth near as much as your whole tuneful herd's
      worth.
No, don't be absurd, he 's an excellent Bryant ;
But, my friends, you'll endanger the life of your client,
By attempting to stretch him up into a giant :
If you choose to compare him, I think there are two
      per-
-sons fit for a parallel—Thomson and Cowper ;[1]
I don't mean exactly,—there's something of each,
There 's T.'s love of nature, C.'s penchant to preach ;
Just mix up their minds so that C.'s spice of craziness
Shall balance and neutralize T.'s turn for laziness,
And it gives you a brain cool, quite frictionless, quiet,
Whose internal police nips the buds of all riot,—
A brain like a permanent strait-jacket put on
The heart which strives vainly to burst off a button,—
A brain which, without being slow or mechanic,
Does more than a larger less drilled, more volcanic ;
He 's a Cowper condensed, with no craziness bitten,
And the advantage that Wordsworth before him has
      written.

   " But, my dear little bardlings, don't prick up your
      ears,
Nor suppose I would rank you and Bryant as peers :
If I call him an iceberg, I don't mean to say

[1] To demonstrate quickly and easily how per-
   versely absurd 't is to sound this name *Cowper*,
   As people in general call him named *super*,
   I just add that he rhymes it himself with horse-trooper.

There is nothing in that which is grand, in its way ;
He is almost the one of your poets that knows
How much grace, strength, and dignity lie in Re-
    pose ;
If he sometimes fall short, he is too wise to mar
His thought's modest fulness by going too far ;
'T would be well if your authors should all make a
    trial
Of what virtue there is in severe self-denial,
And measure their writings by Hesiod's staff,
Which teaches that all has less value than half.

    " There is Whittier, whose swelling and vehement
    heart
Strains the strait-breasted drab of the Quaker apart,
And reveals the live Man, still supreme and erect
Underneath the bemummying wrappers of sect ;
There was ne'er a man born who had more of the
    swing
Of the true lyric bard and all that kind of thing ;
And his failures arise, (though perhaps he don't know
    it,)
From the very same cause that has made him a
    poet,—
A fervor of mind which knows no separation
'Twixt simple excitement and pure inspiration,
As my Pythoness erst sometimes erred from not know-
    ing
If 't were I or mere wind through her tripod was blow-
    ing ;
Let his mind once get head in its favorite direction
And the torrent of verse bursts the dams of reflec-
    tion,

While, borne with the rush of the meter along,
The poet may chance to go right or go wrong,
Content with the whirl and delirium of song ;
Then his grammar 's not always correct, nor his rhymes,
And he 's prone to repeat his own lyrics sometimes,
Not his best, though, for those are struck off at white-
      heats
When the heart in his breast like a trip-hammer
      beats,
And can ne'er be repeated again any more
Than they could have been carefully plotted before :
Like old what 's-his-name there at the battle of Hast-
      ings,
(Who, however, gave more than mere rhythmical bast-
      ings,)
Our Quaker leads off metaphorical fights
For reform and whatever they call human rights,
Both singing and striking in front of the war
And hitting his foes with the mallet of Thor ;
Anne haec, one exclaims, on beholding his knocks,
Vestis filii tui, O, leather-clad Fox ?
Can that be thy son, in the battle's mid din,
Preaching brotherly love and then driving it in
To the brain of the tough old Goliath of sin,
With the smoothest of pebbles from Castaly's spring
Impressed on his hard moral sense with a sling ?

  " All honor and praise to the right-hearted bard
Who was true to The Voice when such service was
      hard,
Who himself was so free he dared sing for the slave
When to look but a protest in silence was brave ;
All honor and praise to the women and men

Who spoke out for the dumb and the down-trodden
    then !
I need not to name them, already for each
I see History preparing the statue and niche ;
They were harsh, but shall *you* be so shocked at hard
    words
Who have beaten your pruning hooks up into swords,
Whose rewards and hurrahs men are surer to gain
By the reaping of men and of women than grain ?
Why should *you* stand aghast at their fierce wordy war,
    if
You scalp one another for Bank or for Tariff ?
Your calling them cut-throats and knaves all day
    long
Don't prove that the use of hard language is wrong ;
While the World's heart beats quicker to think of such
    men
As signed Tyranny's doom with a bloody steel-pen,
While on Fourth-of-Julys beardless orators fright one
With hints at Harmodius and Aristogeiton,
You need not look shy at your sisters and brothers
Who stab with sharp words for the freedom of
    others :—
No, a wreath, twine a wreath for the loyal and true
Who, for sake of the many, dared stand with the few,
Not of blood-spattered laurel for enemies braved,
But of broad, peaceful oak-leaves for citizens saved !

" Here comes Dana, abstractedly loitering along,
Involved in a paulo-post-future of song,
Who 'll be going to write what 'll never be written
Till the Muse. ere he thinks of it, gives him the
    mitten,—

Who is so well aware of how things should be done,
That his own works displease him before they're
    begun,—
Who so well all that makes up good poetry knows,
That the best of his poems is written in prose ;
All saddled and bridled stood Pegasus waiting,
He was booted and spurred, but he loitered debating,
In a very grave question his soul was immersed,—
Which foot in the stirrup he ought to put first ;
And, while this point and that he judicially dwelt on,
He, somehow or other, had written Paul Felton,
Whose beauties or faults, whichsoever you see there,
You 'll allow only genius could hit upon either.
That he once was the Idle Man none will deplore,
But I fear he will never be any thing more ;
The ocean of song heaves and glitters before him,
The depth and the vastness and longing sweep o'er
    him,
He knows every breaker and shoal on the chart,
He has the Coast Pilot and so on by heart,
Yet he spends his whole life, like the man in the
    fable,
In learning to swim on his library-table.

    " There swaggers John Neal, who has wasted in
        Maine
The sinews and chords of his pugilist brain,
Who might have been poet, but that, in its stead,
    he
Preferred to believe that he was so already ;
Too hasty to wait till Art's ripe fruit should drop,
He must pelt down an unripe and colicky crop ;
Who took to the law, and had this sterling plea for it,

It required him to quarrel, and paid him a fee for it ;
A man who 's made less than he might have, because
He always has thought himself more than he was,—
Who, with very good natural gifts as a bard,
Broke the strings of his lyre out by striking too hard,
And cracked half the notes of a truly fine voice,
Because song drew less instant attention than noise.
Ah, men do not know how much strength is in poise,
That he goes the farthest who goes far enough,
And that all beyond that is just bother and stuff.
No vain man matures, he makes too much new wood ;
His blooms are too thick for the fruit to be good ;
'T is the modest man ripens, 't is he that achieves,
Just what 's needed of sunshine and shade he receives ;
Grapes, to mellow, require the cool dark of their
      leaves ;
Neal wants balance ; he throws his mind always too
      far,
And whisks out flocks of comets, but never a star ;
He has so much muscle, and loves so to show it,
That he strips himself naked to prove he 's a poet,
And, to show he could leap Art's wide ditch, if he
      tried,
Jumps clean o'er it, and into the hedge t' other side.
He has strength, but there 's nothing about him in
      keeping ;
One gets surelier onward by walking than leaping ;
He has used his own sinews himself to distress,
And had done vastly more had he done vastly less ;
In letters, too soon is as bad as too late,
Could he only have waited he might have been great,
But he plumped into Helicon up to the waist,
And muddied the stream ere he took his first taste.

" There is Hawthorne, with genius so shrinking and
　　rare
That you hardly at first see the strength that is there;
A frame so robust, with a nature so sweet,
So earnest, so graceful, so solid, so fleet,
Is worth a descent from Olympus to meet;
'T is as if a rough oak that for ages had stood,
With his gnarled bony branches like ribs of the wood,
Should bloom, after cycles of struggle and scathe,
With a single anemone trembly and rathe;
His strength is so tender, his wildness so meek,
That a suitable parallel sets one to seek,—
He 's a John Bunyan Fouqué, a Puritan Tieck;
When Nature was shaping him, clay was not granted
For making so full-sized a man as she wanted,
So, to fill out her model, a little she spared
From some finer-grained stuff for a woman prepared,
And she could not have hit a more excellent plan
For making him fully and perfectly man.
The success of her scheme gave her so much delight,
That she tried it again, shortly after, in Dwight;
Only, while she was kneading and shaping the clay,
She sang to her work in her sweet childish way,
And found, when she 'd put the last touch to his soul,
That the music had somehow got mixed with the whole.

" Here 's Cooper, who 's written six volumes to show
He 's as good as a lord : well, let 's grant that he 's so;
If a person prefer that description of praise,
Why, a coronet 's certainly cheaper than bays;
But he need take no pains to convince us he' s not
(As his enemies say) the American Scott.
Choose any twelve men, and let C. read aloud

That one of his novels of which he 's most proud,
And I 'd lay any bet that, without ever quitting
Their box, they 'd be all, to a man, for acquitting.
He has drawn you one character, though, that is new,
One wildflower he 's plucked that is wet with the dew
Of this fresh Western world, and, the thing not to
     mince,
He has done naught but copy it ill ever since;
His Indians, with proper respect be it said,
Are just Natty Bumpo daubed over with red,
And his very Long Toms are the same useful Nat,
Rigged up in duck pants and a sou'-wester hat,
(Though, once in a Coffin, a good chance was found
To have slipt the old fellow away underground.)
All his other men-figures are clothes upon sticks,
The *dernier chemise* of a man in a fix,
(As a captain besieged, when his garrison 's small,
Sets up caps upon poles to be seen o 'er the wall;)
And the women he draws from one model don't vary,
All sappy as maples and flat as a prairie.
When a character 's wanted, he goes to the task
As a cooper would do in composing a cask;
He picks out the staves, of their qualities heedful,
Just hoops them together as tight as is needful,
And, if the best fortune should crown the attempt, he
Has made at the most something wooden and empty.

" Don't suppose I would underrate Cooper's abilities,
If I thought you 'd do that, I should feel very ill at ease;
The men who have given to *one* character life
And objective existence, are not very rife,
You may number them all, both prose-writers and
     singers,

Without overrunning the bounds of your fingers,
And Natty won't go to oblivion quicker
Than Adams the parson or Primrose the vicar.

"There is one thing in Cooper I like, too, and that
  is
That on manners he lectures his countrymen gratis ;
Not precisely so either, because, for a rarity,
He is paid for his tickets in unpopularity.
Now he may overcharge his American pictures,
But you 'll grant there 's a good deal of truth in his
  strictures ;
And I honor the man who is willing to sink
Half his present repute for the freedom to think,
And, when he has thought, be his cause strong or
  weak,
Will risk t' other half for the freedom to speak,
Caring naught for what vengeance the mob has in
  store,
Let that mob be the upper ten thousand or lower.

"There are truths you Americans need to be told,
And it never 'll refute them to swagger and scold ;
John Bull, looking o'er the Atlantic, in choler
At your aptness for trade, says you worship the dollar ;
But to scorn such i-dollar-try 's what very few do,
And John goes to that church as often as you do.
No matter what John says, don't try to outcrow him,
'T is enough to go quietly on and outgrow him ;
Like most fathers, Bull hates to see Number One
Displacing himself in the mind of his son,
And detests the same faults in himself he 'd neglected
When he sees them again in his child's glass reflected ;

To love one another you 're too likely by half,
If he is a bull, you 're a pretty stout calf,
And tear your own pasture for naught but to show
What a nice pair of horns you 're beginning to grow.

    " There are one or two things I should just like to
        hint,
For you don't often get the truth told you in print;
The most of you (this is what strikes all beholders)
Have a mental and physical stoop in the shoulders;
Though you ought to be free as the winds and the
        waves,
You 've the gait and the manners of runaway slaves;
Tho' you brag of your New World, you don't half
        believe in it,
And as much of the Old as is possible weave in it;
Your goddess of freedom, a tight, buxom girl,
With lips like a cherry and teeth like a pearl,
With eyes bold as Herè's, and hair floating free,
And full of the sun as the spray of the sea,
Who can sing at a husking or romp at a shearing,
Who can trip through the forests alone without fearing,
Who can drive home the cows with a song through the
        grass,
Keeps glancing aside into Europe's cracked glass,
Hides her red hands in gloves, pinches up her lithe
        waist,
And makes herself wretched with transmarine taste;
She loses her fresh country charm when she takes
Any mirror except her own rivers and lakes.

    " You steal Englishmen's books and think English
        men's thought,
With their salt on her tail your wild eagle is caught;

Your literature suits its each whisper and motion
To what will be thought of it over the ocean ;
The cast clothes of Europe your statesmanship tries
And mumbles again the old blarneys and lies ;—
Forget Europe wholly, your veins throb with blood
To which the dull current in hers is but mud ;
Let her sneer, let her say your experiment fails,
In her voice there 's a tremble e'en now while she rails,
And your shore will soon be in the nature of things
Covered thick with gilt driftwood of runaway kings,
Where alone, as it were in a Longfellow's Waif,
Her fugitive pieces will find themselves safe.
O, my friends, thank your God, if you have one, that he
'Twixt the Old World and you set the gulf of a sea ;
Be strong-backed, brown-handed, upright as your pines,
By the scale of a hemisphere shape your designs,
Be true to yourselves and this new nineteenth age,
As a statue by Powers, or a picture by Page,
Plough, dig, sail, forge, build, carve, paint, make all
       things new,
To your own New-World instincts contrive to be true,
Keep your ears open wide to the Future's first call,
Be whatever you will, but yourselves first of all,
Stand fronting the dawn on Toil's heaven-scaling peaks,
And become my new race of more practical Greeks.—
Hem ! your likeness at present, I shudder to tell o' 't,
Is that you have your slaves, and the Greek had his
       helot."

   Here a gentleman present, who had in his attic
More pepper than brains, shrieked—" The man 's a
       fanatic,
I 'm a capital tailor with warm tar and feathers,

And will make him a suit that 'll serve in all weathers ;
But we 'll argue the point first, I 'm willing to
    reason 't,
Palaver before condemnation 's but decent,
So, through my humble person, Humanity begs
Of the friends of true freedom a loan of bad eggs."
But Apollo let one such a look of his show forth
As when ἥιε νύκτι ἐοικώς, and so forth,
And the gentleman somehow slunk out of the way,
But, as he was going, gained courage to say,—
" At slavery in the abstract my whole soul rebels,
I am as strongly opposed to 't as any one else."
" Ay, no doubt, but whenever I 've happened to meet
With a wrong or a crime, it is always concrete,"
Answered Phœbus severely ; then turning to us,
" The mistakes of such fellows as just made the fuss
Is only in taking a great busy nation
For a part of their pitiful cotton-plantation.—
But there comes Miranda. Zeus ! where shall I flee to ?
She has such a penchant for bothering me too !
She always keeps asking if I don't observe a
Particular likeness 'twixt her and Minerva :
She tells me my efforts in verse are quite clever ;—
She 's been travelling now, and will be worse than ever ;
One would think, though, a sharp-sighted noter she 'd
    be
Of all that 's worth mentioning over the sea,
For a woman must surely see well, if she try,
The whole of whose being 's a capital I :
She will take an old notion and make it her own
By saying it o'er in her Sybilline tone,
Or persuade you 't is something tremendously deep,
By repeating it so as to put you to sleep ;

And she well may defy any mortal to see through it,
When once she has mixed up her infinite *me* through
　　it.
There is one thing she owns in her own single right,
It is native and genuine—namely, her spite :
Though, when acting as censor, she privately blows
A censor of vanity 'neath her own nose."

　　Here Miranda came up. and said, " Phœbus ! you
　　　know
That the infinite Soul has its infinite woe,
As I ought to know, having lived cheek by jowl,
Since the day I was born, with the Infinite Soul ;
I myself introduced, I myself, I alone,
To my Land's better life authors solely my own,
Who the sad heart of earth on their shoulders have
　　　taken,
Whose works sound a depth by Life's quiet unshaken,
Such as Shakspeare, for instance, the Bible, and
　　　Bacon,
Not to mention my own works ; Time's nadir is fleet,
And, as for myself, I 'm quite out of conceit,"—

　　" Quite out of conceit ! I 'm enchanted to hear it."
Cried Apollo aside, " Who 'd have thought she was
　　　near it ?
To be sure one is apt to exhaust those commodities
He uses too fast, yet in this case as odd it is
As if Neptune should say to his turbots and whitings,
' I 'm as much out of salt as Miranda's own writings,'
(Which, as she in her own happy manner has said,
Sound a depth, for 't is one of the functions of lead.)
She often has asked me if I could not find

A place somewhere near me that suited her mind ;
I know but a single one vacant, which she,
With her rare talent that way, would fit to a **T**.
And it would not imply any pause of cessation
In the work she esteems her peculiar vocation,—
She may enter on duty to-day, if she chooses,
And remain Tiring-woman for life to the Muses."

(Miranda meanwhile has succeeded in driving
Up into a corner, in spite of their striving,
A small flock of terrified victims, and there,
With an I-turn-the-crank-of-the-Universe air
And a tone which, at least to *my* fancy, appears
Not so much to be entering as boxing your ears,
Is unfolding a tale (of herself, I surmise,
For 't is dotted as thick as a peacock's with I's.)
Apropos of Miranda, I 'll rest on my oars
And drift through a trifling digression on bores,
For, though not wearing ear-rings *in more majorum,*
Our ears are kept bored just as if we still wore 'em.
There was one feudal custom worth keeping, at least,
Roasted bores made a part of each well-ordered feast,
And of all quiet pleasures the very *ne plus*
Was in hunting wild bores as the tame ones hunt us.
Archæologians, I know, who have personal fears
Of this wise application of hounds and of spears,
Have tried to make out, with a zeal more than
    wonted,
'T was a kind of wild swine that our ancestors hunted ;
But I 'll never believe that the age which has strewn
Europe o'er with cathedrals, and otherwise shown
That it knew what was what, could by chance not
    have known.

(Spending, too, its chief time with its buff on, no
    doubt,)
Which beast 't would improve the world most to thin out,
I divide bores myself, in the manner of rifles,
Into two great divisions, regardless of trifles ;—
There 's your smooth-bore and screw-bore, who do not
    much vary
In the weight of cold lead they respectively carry.
The smooth-bore is one in whose essence the mind
Not a corner nor cranny to cling by can find ;
You feel as in nightmares sometimes, when you slip
Down a steep slated roof where there 's nothing to grip,
You slide and you slide, the blank horror increases,
You had rather by far be at once smashed to pieces,
You fancy a whirlpool below white and frothing,
And finally drop off and light upon—nothing.
The screw-bore has twists in him, faint predilections
For going just wrong in the tritest directions ;
When he 's wrong he is flat, when he 's right he can't
    show it,
He 'll tell you what Snooks said about the new poet,[1]
Or how Fogrum was outraged by Tennyson's Princess ;
He has spent all his spare time and intellect since his
Birth in perusing, on each art and science,
Just the books in which no one puts any reliance,
And though *nemo*, we 're told, *horis omnibus sapit*,
The rule will not fit him, however you shape it,
For he has a perennial foison of sappiness ;
He has just enough force to spoil half your day's hap-
    piness,

----

[1] If you call Snooks an owl, he will show by his looks
That he 's morally certain you 're jealous of Snooks.)

And to make him a sort of mosquito to be with,
But just not enough to dispute or agree with.

These sketches I made (not to be too explicit)
From two honest fellows who made me a visit,
And broke, like the tale of the Bear and the Fiddle,
My reflections on Halleck short off by the middle;
I shall not now go into the subject more deeply,
For I notice that some of my readers look sleep'ly,
I will barely remark that, 'mongst civilized nations,
There 's none that displays more exemplary patience
Under all sorts of boring, at all sorts of hours,
From all sorts of desperate persons, than ours.
Not to speak of our papers, our state legislatures,
And other such trials for sensitive natures,
Just look for a moment at Congress,—appalled,
My fancy shrinks back from the phantom it called;
Why, there 's scarcely a member unworthy to frown
'Neath what Fourier nicknames the Boreal crown;
Only think what that infinite bore-pow'r could do
If applied with a utilitarian view ;
Suppose, for example, we shipped it with care
To Sahara's great desert and let it bore there.
If they held one short session and did nothing else,
They 'd fill the whole waste with Artesian wells.
But 't is time now with pen phonographic to follow
Through some more of his sketches our laughing
        Apollo :—

"There comes Harry Franco, and, as he draws near,
You find that 's a smile which you took for a sneer;
One half of him contradicts t' other, his wont
Is to say very sharp things and do very blunt;

His manner 's as hard as his feelings are tender,
And a *sortie* he 'll make when he means to surrender ;
He 's in joke half the time when he seems to be
    sternest,
When he seems to be joking, be sure he 's in earnest ;
He has common sense in a way that 's uncommon,
Hates humbug and cant, loves his friends like a
    woman,   ·
Builds his dislikes of cards and his friendships of oak,
Loves a prejudice better than aught but a joke,
Is half upright Quaker, half downright Come-outer,
Loves freedom too well to go stark mad about her,
Quite artless himself is a lover of Art,
Shuts you out of his secrets and into his heart,
And though not a poet, yet all must admire
In his letters of Pinto his skill on the liar.

   "There comes Poe with his raven, like Barnaby
    Rudge,
Three-fifths of him genius and two-fifths sheer fudge,
Who talks like a book of iambs and pentameters,
In a way to make people of common-sense damn metres,
Who has written some things quite the best of their
    kind
But the heart somehow seems all squeezed out by the
    mind,
Who—but hey-day ! What 's this ? Messieurs Mat-
    thews and Poe,
You must n't fling mud-balls at Longfellow so,
Does it make a man worse that his character 's such
As to make his friends love him (as you think) too
    much ?
Why, there is not a bard at this moment alive

More willing than he that his fellows should thrive;
While you are abusing him thus, even now
He would help either one of you out of a slough;
You may say that he 's smooth and all that till you 're
    hoarse,
But remember that elegance also is force;
After polishing granite as much as you will,
The heart keeps its tough old persistency still;
Deduct all you can that still keeps you at bay,—
Why, he 'll live till men weary of Collins and Gray;
I 'm not over-fond of Greek metres in English,
To me rhyme 's a gain, so it be not too jinglish,
And your modern hexameter verses are no more
Like Greek ones than sleek Mr. Pope is like Homer;
As the roar of the sea to the coo of a pigeon is,
So, compared to your moderns, sounds old Melesigenes;
I may be too partial, the reason, perhaps, o' 't is
That I 've heard the old blind man recite his own
    rhapsodies,
And my ear with that music impregnate may be,
Like the poor exiled shell with the soul of the sea,
Or as one can't bear Strauss when his nature is cloven
To its deeps within deeps by the stroke of Beethoven;
But, set that aside, and 't is truth that I speak,
Had Theocritus written in English, not Greek,
I believe that his exquisite sense would scarce change
    a line
In that rare, tender, virgin-like pastoral Evangeline.
That 's not ancient nor modern, its place is apart
Where time has no sway, in the realm of pure Art,
'T is a shrine of retreat from Earth's hubbub and
    strife
As quiet and chaste as the author's own life.

" There comes Philothea, her face all aglow,
She has just been dividing some poor creature's woe,
And can't tell which pleases her most, to relieve
His want, or his story to hear and believe ;
No doubt against many deep griefs she prevails,
For her ear is the refuge of destitute tales ;
She knows well that silence is sorrow's best food,
And that talking draws off from the heart its black
      blood,
So she 'll listen with patience and let you unfold
Your bundle of rags as 't were pure cloth of gold,
Which, indeed, it all turns to as soon as she's touched it,
And, (to borrow a phrase from the nursery,) *muched* it,
She has such a musical taste, she will go
Any distance to hear one who draws a long bow ;
She will swallow a wonder by mere might and main
And thinks it geometry's fault if she's fain
To consider things flat, inasmuch as they 're plain ;
Facts with her are accomplished, as Frenchmen would
      say,
They will prove all she wishes them to—either way,
And, as fact lies on this side or that, we must try,
If we're seeking the truth, to find where it don't lie ;
I was telling her once of a marvellous aloe
That for thousands of years had looked spindling and
      sallow,
And, though nursed by the fruitfullest powers of mud,
Had never vouchsafed e'en so much as a bud,
Till its owner remarked as a sailor, you know,
Often will in a calm, that it never would blow,
For he wished to exhibit the plant, and designed
That its blowing should help him in raising the wind ;
At last it was told him that if he should water

Its roots with the blood of his unmarried daughter,
(Who was born, as her mother, a Calvinist said,
With a Baxter's effectual call on her head,)
It would blow as the obstinate breeze did when by a
Like decree of her father died Iphigenia ;
At first he declared he himself would be blowed
Ere his conscience with such a foul crime he would load
But the thought, coming oft, grew less dark than
  before,
And he mused, as each creditor knocked at his door,
If *this* were but done they would dun me no more ;
I told Philothea his struggles and doubts,
And how he considered the ins and the outs
Of the visions he had, and the dreadful dyspepsy,
How he went to the seer that lives at Po'keepsie,
How the seer advised him to sleep on it first
And to read his big volume in case of the worst,
And further advised he should pay him five dollars
For writing 𝕳𝕦𝕞, 𝕳𝕦𝕞, on his wristbands and collars ;
Three years and ten days these dark words he had studied
When the daughter was missed, and the aloe had budded ;
I told how he watched it grow large and more large,
And wondered how much for the show he should charge,
She had listened with utter indifference to this, till
I told how it bloomed, and discharging its pistil
With an aim the Eumenides dictated, shot
The botanical filicide dead on the spot ;
It had blown, but he reaped not his horrible gains,
For it blew with such force as to blow out his brains,
And the crime was blown also, because on the wad.
Which was paper, was writ 'Visitation of God,'
As well as a thrilling account of the deed
Which the coroner kindly allowed me to read.

" Well, my friend took this story up just, to be sure,
As one might a poor foundling that 's laid at one's door
She combed it and washed it and clothed it and fed it,
And as if 't were her own child most tenderly bred it,
Laid the scene (of the legend, I mean,) far away a-
-mong the green vales underneath Himalaya.
And by artist-like touches, laid on here and there,
Made the whole thing so touching, I frankly declare
I have read it all thrice, and, perhaps I am weak,
But I found every time there were tears on my cheek.

" The pole, science tells us, the magnet controls,
But she is a magnet to emigrant Poles,
And folks with a mission that nobody knows,
Throng thickly about her as bees round a rose ;
She can fill up the *carets* in such, make their scope
Converge to some focus of rational hope,
And, with sympathies fresh as the morning, their
        gall
Can transmute into honey,—but this is not all ;
Not only for those she has solace, oh, say,
Vice's desperate nursling adrift in Broadway,
Who clingest, with all that is left of thee human,
To the last slender spar from the wreck of the woman,
Hast thou not found one shore where those tired droop-
        ing feet
Could reach firm mother-earth, one full heart on whose
        beat
The soothed head in silence reposing could hear
The chimes of far childhood throb thick on the ear ?
Ah, there 's many a beam from the fountain of day
That to reach us unclouded, must pass, on its way,
Through the soul of a woman, and hers is wide ope

To the influence of Heaven as the blue eyes of Hope ;
Yes, a great soul is hers, one that dares to go in
To the prison, the slave-hut, the alleys of sin,
And to bring into each, or to find there, some line
Of the never completely out-trampled divine ;
If her heart at high floods swamps her brain now and
  then,
'T is but richer for that when the tide ebbs agen,
As, after old Nile has subsided, his plain
Overflows with a second broad deluge of grain !
What a wealth would it bring to the narrow and sour
Could they be as a Child but for one little hour !

 "What ! Irving ? thrice welcome, warm heart and
  fine brain,
You bring back the happiest spirit from Spain,
And the gravest sweet humor, that ever were there
Since Cervantes met death in his gentle despair ;
Nay, don't be embarrassed, nor look so beseeching,—
I sha'n't run directly against my own preaching,
And, having just laughed at their Raphaels and
  Dantes,
Go to setting you up beside matchless Cervantes ;
But allow me to speak what I honestly feel,—
To a true poet-heart add the fun of Dick Steele,
Throw in all of Addison, *minus* the chill,
With the whole of that partnership's stock and good
  will,
Mix well, and while stirring, hum o'er, as a spell,
The fine *old* English Gentleman, simmer it well,
Sweeten just to your own private liking, then strain,
That only the finest and clearest remain,
Let it stand out of doors till a soul it receives

From the warm lazy sun loitering down through green
    leaves,
And you 'll find a choice nature, not wholly deserv-
    ing
A name either English or Yankee,—just Irving.

"There goes,—but *stet nominis umbra*,—his name
You 'll be glad enough, some day or other, to claim,
And will all crowd about him and swear that you knew
    him
If some English hack-critic should chance to review
    him ;
The old *porcos ante ne projiciatis*
MARGARITAS, for him you have verified gratis ;
What matters his name ?   Why, it may be Sylvester,
Judd, Junior, or Junius, Ulysses, or Nestor,
For aught *I* know or care ; 't is enough that I look
On the author of ' Margaret,' the first Yankee book
With the *soul* of Down East in 't, and things farther
    East,
As far as the threshold of morning, at least,
Where awaits the fair dawn of the simple and true,
Of the day that comes slowly to make all things new.
'T has a smack of pine woods, of bare field and bleak
    hill
Such as only the breed of the Mayflower could till.
The Puritan 's shown in it, tough to the core,
Such as prayed, smiting Agag on red Marston moor ;
With an unwilling humor, half-choked by the drouth
In brown hollows about the inhospitable mouth ;
With a soul full of poetry, though it has qualms
About finding a happiness out of the Psalms ;
Full of tenderness, too, though it shrinks in the dark,

Hamadryad-like, under the coarse, shaggy bark ;
That sees visions, knows wrestlings of God with the
    Will,
And has its own Sinais and thunderings still."—

Here,—"Forgive me, Apollo," I cried, "while I
    pour
My heart out to my birth-place : O, loved more and
    more
Dear Baystate, from whose rocky bosom thy sons
Should suck milk, strong-will-giving, brave such as
    runs
In the veins of old Graylock,—who is it that dares
Call thee pedler, a soul wrapt in bank-books and shares ?
It is false ! She's a Poet ! I see, as I write,
Along the far railroad the steam-snake glide white,
The cataract-throb of her mill-hearts I hear,
The swift strokes of trip-hammers weary my ear,
Sledges ring upon anvils, through logs the saw screams,
Blocks swing up to their place, beetles drive home the
    beams :—
It is songs such as these that she croons to the din
Of her fast-flying shuttles, year out and year in,
While from earth's farthest corner there comes not a
    breeze
But wafts her the buzz of her gold-gleaning bees :
What though those horn hands have as yet found small
    time
For painting and sculpture and music and rhyme ?
These will come in due order, the need that pressed
    sorest
Was to vanquish the seasons, the ocean, the forest,
To bridle and harness the rivers, the steam,

Making that whirl her mill-wheels, this tug in her
    team,
To vassalize old tyrant Winter, and make
Him delve surlily for her on river and lake ;—
When this New World was parted, she strove not to
    shirk
Her lot in the heirdom, the tough, silent Work,
The hero-share ever, from Herakles down
To Odin, the Earth's iron sceptre and crown ;
Yes, thou dear, noble Mother ! if ever men's praise
Could be claimed for creating heroical lays,
Thou hast won it ; if ever the laurel divine
Crowned the Maker and Builder, that glory is thine !
Thy songs are right epic, they tell how this rude
Rock-rib of our earth here was tamed and subdued ;
Thou hast written them plain on the face of the
    planet
In brave, deathless letters of iron and granite ;
Thou hast printed them deep for all time ; they are
    set
From the same runic type-fount and alphabet
With thy stout Berkshire hills and the arms of thy
    Bay,—
They are staves from the burly old Mayflower lay.
If the drones of the Old World, in querulous ease,
Ask thy Art and thy Letters, point proudly to these,
Or, if they deny these are Letters and Art,
Toil on with the same old invincible heart ;
Thou art rearing the pedestal broad-based and grand
Whereon the fair shapes of the Artist shall stand,
And creating, through labors undaunted and long,
The true theme for all Sculpture and Painting and
    Song !

"But my good mother Baystate wants no praise of
     mine,
She learned from *her* mother a precept divine
About something that butters no parsnips, her *forte*
In another direction lies, work is her sport,
(Though she 'll curtsey and set her cap straight, that
     she will,
If you talk about Plymouth and one Bunker's hill.)
The dear, notable goodwife ! by this time of night,
Her hearth is swept clean, and her fire burning bright,
And she sits in a chair (of home plan and make) rock-
     ing,
Musing much, all the while, as she darns on a stock-
     ing,
Whether turkeys will come pretty high next Thanks-
     giving,
Whether flour 'll be so dear, for as sure as she 's
     living,
She will use rye-and-injun then, whether the pig
By this time ain't got pretty tolerable big,
And whether to sell it outright will be best.
Or to smoke hams and shoulders and salt down the
     rest,—
At this minute, she'd swop all my verses, ah, cruel !
For the last patent stove that is saving of fuel ;
So I'll just let Apollo go on, for his phiz
Shows I've kept him awaiting too long as it is."

  "If our friend, there, who seems a reporter, is
     through
With his burst of emotion, our theme we 'll pursue,"
Said Apollo : some smiled, and, indeed, I must own
There was something sarcastic, perhaps, in his tone ;—

"There 's Holmes, who is matchless among you for
    wit ;
A Leyden-jar always full-charged, from which flit
The electrical tingles of hit after hit ;
In long poems 't is painful sometimes and invites
A thought of the way the new Telegraph writes,
Which pricks down its little sharp sentences spitefully
As if you got more than you 'd title to rightfully,
And if it were hoping its wild father Lightning
Would flame in for a second and give you a fright'ning.
He has perfect sway of what *I* call a sham metre,
But many admire it, the English hexameter,
And Campbell, I think, wrote most commonly worse,
With less nerve, swing, and fire in the same kind of verse,
Nor e'er achieved aught in 't so worthy of praise
As the tribute of Holmes to the grand *Marseillaise.*
You went crazy last year over Bulwer's New Timon ;—
Why, if B., to the day of his dying, should rhyme on,
Heaping verses on verses and tomes upon tomes,
He could ne'er reach the best point and vigor of
    Holmes.
His are just the fine hands, too, to weave you a lyric
Full of fancy, fun, feeling, or spiced with satiric
In so kindly a measure, that nobody knows
What to do but e'en join in the laugh, friends and foes.

"There is Lowell, who 's striving Parnassus to climb
With a whole bale of *isms* tied together with rhyme,
He might get on alone, spite of brambles and boulders,
But he can't with that bundle he has on his shoulders,
The top of the hill he will ne'er come nigh reaching
Till he learns the distinction 'twixt singing and preach-
    ing ;

His lyre has some chords that would ring pretty well,
But he 'd rather by half make a drum of the shell,
And rattle away till he 's old as Methusalem,
At the head of a march to the last new Jerusalem.

"There goes Halleck whose Fanny 's a pseudo Don
Juan,
With the wickedness out that gave salt to the true one,
He 's a wit, though, I hear, of the very first order,
And once made a pun on the words soft Recorder;
More than this, he 's a very great poet, I 'm told,
And has had his works published in crimson and gold,
With something they call ' Illustrations.' to wit,
Like those with which Chapman obscured Holy Writ,[1]
Which are said to illustrate. because, as I view it,
Like *lucus a non*, they precisely don't do it;
Let a man who can write what himself understands
Keep clear, if he can, of designing men's hands,
Who bury the sense, if there 's any worth having,
And then very honestly call it engraving.
But, to quit *badinage*, which there is n't much wit in,
No doubt Halleck 's better than all he has written;
In his verse a clear glimpse you will frequently find,
If not of a great, of a fortunate mind,
Which contrives to be true to its natural loves
In a world of back-offices, ledgers and stoves.
When his heart breaks away from the brokers and banks,
And kneels in its own private shrine to give thanks,
There 's a genial manliness in him that earns
Our sincerest respect, (read, for instance, his " Burns ")
And we can't but regret (seek excuse where we may)
That so much of a man has been peddled away.

[1] (Cuts rightly called wooden, as all must admit.)

"But   what 's that ? a mass-meeting ?   No, there
        come in lots
The American Disraelis, Bulwers, and Scotts,
And in short the American everything-elses,
Each charging the others with envies and jealousies ;—
By the way, 't is a fact that displays what profusions
Of all kinds of greatness bless free institutions,
That while the Old World has produced barely eight
Of such poets as all men agree to call great,
And of other great characters hardly a score,
(One might safely say less than that rather than more,)
With you every year a whole crop is begotten,
They 're as much of a staple as corn, or as cotton ;
Why, there 's scarcely a huddle of log-huts and shanties
That has not brought forth its own Miltons and Dantes ;
I myself know ten Byrons, one Coleridge, three Shelleys,
Two Raphaels, six Titians, (I think) one Apelles,
Leonardos and Rubenses plenty as lichens,
One (but that one is plenty) American Dickens,
A whole flock of Lambs, any number of Tennysons,—
In short, if a man has the luck to have any sons,
He may feel pretty certain that one out of twain
Will be some very great person over again.
There is one inconvenience in all this which lies
In the fact that by contrast we estimate size,[1]
And, when there are none except Titans, great stature
Is only a simple proceeding of nature.
What puff the strained sails of your praise shall you
        furl at, if

[1] That is in most cases we do, but not all,
    Past a doubt, there are men who are innately small,
    Such as Blank, who, without being 'minished a tittle,
    Might stand for a type of the Absolute Little.

The calmest degree that you know is superlative?
At Rome, all whom Charon took into his wherry must,
As a matter of course, be well *issimus*ed and *errimus*ed,
A Greek, too, could feel, while in that famous boat he
    tost,
That his friends would take care he was ισrοςed and
    ωτατοςed,
And formerly we, as through grave-yards we past,
Thought the world went from bad to worse fearfully
    fast;
Let us glance for a moment, 't is well worth the
    pains,
And note what an average grave-yard contains;
There lie levellers levelled, duns done up themselves,
There are booksellers finally laid on their shelves,
Horizontally there lie upright politicians,
Dose-a-dose with their patients sleep faultless phy-
    sicians,
There are slave-drivers quietly whipt under-ground,
There book-binders, done up in boards, are fast
    bound,
There card-players wait till the last trump be played,
There all the choice spirits get finally laid,
There the babe that 's unborn is supplied with a
    berth,
There men without legs get their six feet of earth,
There lawyers repose, each wrapt up in his case,
There seekers of office are sure of a place,
There defendant and plaintiff get equally cast,
There shoemakers quietly stick to the last,
There brokers at length become silent as stocks,
There stage-drivers sleep without quitting their box,
And so forth and so forth and so forth and so on,

With this kind of stuff one might endlessly go on ;
To come to the point, I may safely assert you
Will find in each yard every cardinal virtue ;[1]
Each has six truest patriots : four discoverers of
　　ether,
Who never had thought on 't nor mentioned it
　　either :
Ten poets, the greatest who ever wrote rhyme :
Two hundred and forty first men of their time :
One person whose portrait just gave the least hint
Its original had a most horrible squint :
One critic, most (what do they call it ?) reflective,
Who never had used the phrase ob- or subjective :
Forty fathers of Freedom, of whom twenty bred
Their sons for the rice-swamps, at so much a head,
And their daughters for—faugh ! thirty mothers of
　　Gracchi :
Non-resistants who gave many a spiritual black-eye :
Eight true friends of their kind, one of whom was a
　　jailor :
Four captains almost as astounding as Taylor :
Two dozen of Italy's exiles who shoot us his
Kaisership daily, stern pen-and-ink Brutuses,
Who, in Yankee back-parlors, with crucified smile,[2]
Mount serenely their country's funereal pile :
Ninety-nine Irish heroes, ferocious rebellers
'Gainst the Saxon in cis-marine garrets and cellars,
Who shake their dread fists o'er the sea and all
　　that,—

[1] (And at this just conclusion will surely arrive,
　　That the goodness of earth is more dead than alive.)

[2] Not forgetting their tea and their toast, though, the
　while.

As long as a copper drops into the hat :
Nine hundred Teutonic republicans stark
From Vaterland's battles just won—in the Park,
Who the happy profession of martyrdom take
Whenever it gives them a chance at a steak :
Sixty-two second Washingtons : two or three Jacksons :
And so many everythings else that it racks one's
Poor memory too much to continue the list,
Especially now they no longer exist ;—
I would merely observe that you 've taken to giving
The puffs that belong to the dead to the living,
And that somehow your trump-of-contemporary-doom's
        tones
Is tuned after old dedications and tombstones."

   Here the critic came in and a thistle presented [1]—
From a frown to a smile the god's features relented,
As he stared at his envoy, who, swelling with pride,
To the god's asking look, nothing daunted, replied,
"You 're surprised, I suppose, I was absent so long,
But your godship respecting the lilies was wrong ;
I hunted the garden from one end to t' other,
And got no reward but vexation and bother,
Till, tossed out with weeds in a corner to wither,
This one lily I found and made haste to bring hither."

   " Did he think I had given him a book to review ?
I ought to have known what the fellow would do,"
Muttered Phœbus aside, " for a thistle will pass
Beyond doubt for the queen of all flowers with an ass ;
He has chosen in just the same way as he 'd choose

   [1] Turn back now to page—goodness only knows what,
   And take a fresh hold on the thread of my plot.

His specimens out of the books he reviews ;
And now, as this offers an excellent text,
I 'll give 'em some brief hints on criticism next."
So, musing a moment, he turned to the crowd,
And, clearing his voice, spoke as follows aloud,—

" My friends, in the happier days of the muse,
We were luckily free from such things as reviews ;
Then naught came between with its fog to make clearer
The heart of the poet to that of his hearer ;
Then the poet brought heaven to the people, and they
Felt that they, too, were poets in hearing his lay ;
Then the poet was prophet, the past in his soul
Pre-created the future, both parts of one whole ;
Then for him there was nothing too great or too small,
For one natural deity sanctified all ;
Then the bard owned no clipper and meter of moods
Save the spirit of silence that hovers and broods
O'er the seas and the mountains, the rivers and woods ;
He asked not earth's verdict, forgetting the clods,
His soul soared and sang to an audience of gods ;
'T was for them that he measured the thought and the
        line,
And shaped for their vision the perfect design,
With as glorious a foresight, a balance as true,
As swung out the worlds in the infinite blue ;
Then a glory and greatness invested man's heart,
The universal, which now stands estranged and apart,
In the free individual moulded, was Art ;
Then the forms of the Artist seemed thrilled with de-
        sire
For something, as yet unattained, fuller, higher,
As once with her lips, lifted hands, and eyes listening,

And her whole upward soul in her countenance glisten-
    ing,
Eurydice stood—like a beacon unfired,
Which, once touched with flame, will leap heav'nward
    inspired—
And waited with answering kindle to mark
The first gleam of Orpheus that pained the red Dark;
Then painting, song, sculpture, did more than relieve
The need that men feel to create and believe,
And as, in all beauty, who listens with love,
Hears these words oft repeated—' beyond and above,'
So these seemed to be but the visible sign
Of the grasp of the soul after things more divine;
They were ladders the Artist erected to climb
O'er the narrow horizon of space and of time,
And we see there the footsteps by which men had
    gained
To the one rapturous glimpse of the never-attained,
As shepherds could erst sometimes trace in the sod
The last spurning print of a sky-cleaving god.

  " But now, on the poet's dis-privacied moods
With *do this* and *do that* the pert critic intrudes;
While he thinks he 's been barely fulfilling his duty
To interpret 'twixt men and their own sense of beauty,
And has striven, while others sought honor or pelf,
To make his kind happy as he was himself,
He finds he 's been guilty of horrid offences
In all kinds of moods, numbers, genders, and tenses;
He 's been *ob* and *sub*jective, what Kettle calls Pot.
Precisely, at all events, what he ought not,
You have done this, says one judge; *done that,* says
    another;

You should have done this, grumbles one ; *that,* says
    t' other ;
Never mind what he touches, one shrieks out *Taboo!*
And while he is wondering what he shall do,
Since each suggests opposite topics for song,
They all shout together *you're right!* or *you're wrong!*

  " Nature fits all her children with something to do,
He who would write and can't write, can surely review,
Can set up a small booth as critic and sell us his
Petty conceit and his pettier jealousies ;
Thus a lawyer's apprentice, just out of his teens,
Will do for the Jeffrey of six magazines ;
Having read Johnson's lives of the poets half through,
There's nothing on earth he's not competent to ;
He reviews with as much nonchalance as he whistles,—
He goes through a book and just picks out the thistles,
It matters not whether he blame or commend,
If he's bad as a foe, he's far worse as a friend ;
Let an author but write what's above his poor scope,
And he'll go to work gravely and twist up a rope,
And, inviting the world to see punishment done,
Hang himself up to bleach in the wind and the sun ;
'T is delightful to see, when a man comes along
Who has any thing in him peculiar and strong,
Every cockboat that swims clear its fierce (pop-) gun-
    deck at him
And make as he passes its ludicrous Peck at him,"—

  Here Miranda came up and began, " As to that,"—
Apollo at once seized his gloves, cane, and hat,
And seeing the place getting rapidly cleared,
I, too, snatched my notes and forthwith disappeared.

THE VISION OF SIR LAUNFAL.

PRELUDE TO PART FIRST.

OVER his keys the musing organist,
   Beginning doubtfully and far away,
First lets his fingers wander as they list,
   And builds a bridge from Dreamland for his lay;
Then, as the touch of his loved instrument
   Gives hope and fervor, nearer draws his theme,
First guessed by faint auroral flushes sent
   Along the wavering vista of his dream.

   Not only around our infancy
   Doth heaven with all its splendors lie;
   Daily, with souls that cringe and blot,
   We Sinais climb and know it not;

Over our manhood bend the skies;
   Against our fallen and traitor lives
The great winds utter prophecies;
   With our faint hearts the mountain strives;
Its arms outstretched, the druid wood
   Waits with its benedicite;
And to our age's drowsy blood
   Still shouts the inspiring sea.
Earth gets its price for what Earth gives us;
   The beggar is taxed for a corner to die in,

The priest hath his fee who comes and shrives us,
  We bargain for the graves we lie in ;
At the Devil's booth are all things sold,
Each ounce of dross costs its ounce of gold ;
  For a cap and bells our lives we pay,
Bubbles we earn with a whole soul's tasking ;
  'T is heaven alone that is given away,
'T is only God may be had for the asking ;
There is no price set on the lavish summer ;
And June may be had by the poorest comer.

And what is so rare as a day in June ?
  Then, if ever, come perfect days ;
Then Heaven tries the earth if it be in tune,
  And over it softly her warm ear lays :
Whether we look, or whether we listen,
We hear life murmur, or see it glisten ;
Every clod feels a stir of might,
  An instinct within it that reaches and towers,
And, grasping blindly above it for light,
  Climbs to a soul in grass and flowers ;
The flush of life may well be seen
  Thrilling back over hills and valleys ;
The cowslip startles in meadows green,
  The buttercup catches the sun in its chalice,
And there 's never a leaf or a blade too mean
  To be some happy creature's palace ;
The little bird sits at his door in the sun,
  Atilt like a blossom among the leaves,
And lets his illumined being o'errun
  With the deluge of summer it receives ;
His mate feels the eggs beneath her wings,
And the heart in her dumb breast flutters and sings ;

He sings to the wide world, and she to her nest,—
In the nice ear of Nature which song is the best ?

Now is the high-tide of the year,
 And whatever of life hath ebbed away
Comes flooding back, with a ripply cheer,
 Into every bare inlet and creek and bay ;
Now the heart is so full that a drop overfills it,
We are happy now because God so wills it ;
No matter how barren the past may have been,
'T is enough for us now that the leaves are green ;
We sit in the warm shade and feel right well
How the sap creeps up and the blossoms swell ;
We may shut our eyes, but we cannot help knowing
That skies are clear and grass is growing ;
The breeze comes whispering in our ear,
That dandelions are blossoming near,
 That maize has sprouted, that streams are flowing,
That the river is bluer than the sky,
That the robin is plastering his house hard by ;
And if the breeze kept the good news back,
For other couriers we should not lack ;
 We could guess it all by yon heifer's lowing,—
And hark ! how clear bold chanticleer,
Warmed with the new wine of the year,
 Tells all in his lusty crowing !

Joy comes, grief goes, we know not how ;
Everything is happy now,
 Everything is upward striving ;
'T is easy now for the heart to be true
As for grass to be green or skies to be blue,—
 'T is the natural way of living :

Who knows whither the clouds have fled ?
  In the unscarred heaven they leave no wake ;
And the eyes forget the tears they have shed,
  The heart forgets its sorrow and ache ;
The soul partakes the season's youth,
  And the sulphurous rifts of passion and woe
Lie deep 'neath a silence pure and smooth,
  Like burnt-out craters healed with snow.
What wonder if Sir Launfal now
Remembered the keeping of his vow ?

PART FIRST.

I.

" MY golden spurs now bring to me,
  And bring to me my richest mail,
For to-morrow I go over land and sea
  In search of the Holy Grail ;
Shall never a bed for me be spread,
Nor shall a pillow be under my head,
Till I begin my vow to keep ;
Here on the rushes will I sleep,
And perchance there may come a vision true
Ere day create the world anew."
  Slowly Sir Launfal's eyes grew dim,
  Slumber fell like a cloud on him,
And into his soul the vision flew.

II.

The crows flapped over by twos and threes,
In the pool drowsed the cattle up to their knees,
  The little birds sang as if it were
  The one day of summer in all the year,

And the very leaves seemed to sing on the trees :
The castle alone in the landscape lay
Like an outpost of winter, dull and gray ;
'T was the proudest hall in the North Countree,
And never its gates might opened be,
Save to lord or lady of high degree ;
Summer besieged it on every side,
But the churlish stone her assaults defied ;
She could not scale the chilly wall,
Though around it for leagues her pavilions tall
Stretched left and right,
Over the hills and out of sight ;
   Green and broad was every tent,
   And out of each a murmur went
Till the breeze fell off at night.

III.

The drawbridge dropped with a surly clang,
And through the dark arch a charger sprang,
Bearing Sir Launfal, the maiden knight,
In his gilded mail, that flamed so bright
It seemed the dark castle had gathered all
Those shafts the fierce sun had shot over its wall
   In his siege of three hundred summers long,
And, binding them all in one blazing sheaf,
   Had cast them forth : so, young and strong,
And lightsome as a locust-leaf,
Sir Launfal flashed forth in his unscarred mail,
To seek in all climes for the Holy Grail.

IV.

It was morning on hill and stream and tree,
   And morning in the young knight's heart ;

Only the castle moodily
Rebuffed the gifts of the sunshine free,
  And gloomed by itself apart ;
The season brimmed all other things up
Full as the rain fills the pitcher-plant's cup.

v.

As Sir Launfal made morn through the darksome gate,
  He was ware of a leper, crouched by the same,
Who begged with his hand and moaned as he sate ;
  And a loathing over Sir Launfal came ;
The sunshine went out of his soul with a thrill,
  The flesh 'neath his armor did shrink and crawl,
And midway its leap his heart stood still
  Like a frozen waterfall ;
For this man, so foul and bent of stature,
Rasped harshly against his dainty nature,
And seemed the one blot on the summer morn,—
So he tossed him a piece of gold in scorn.

VI.

The leper raised not the gold from the dust :
" Better to me the poor man's crust.
Better the blessing of the poor,
Though 1 turn me empty from his door ;
That is no true alms which the hand can hold ;
He gives nothing but worthless gold
  Who gives from a sense of duty ;
But he who gives but a slender mite,
And gives to that which is out of sight,
  That thread of the all-sustaining Beauty
Which runs through all and doth all unite,—

The hand cannot clasp the whole of his alms,
The heart outstretches its eager palms,
For a god goes with it and makes it store
To the soul that was starving in darkness before."

PRELUDE TO PART SECOND.

Down swept the chill wind from the mountain peak,
  From the snow five thousand summers old ;
On open wold and hill-top bleak
  It had gathered all the cold,
And whirled it like sleet on the wanderer's cheek
It carried a shiver everywhere
From the unleafed boughs and pastures bare ;
The little brook heard it and built a roof
'Neath which he could house him, winter-proof ;
All night by the white stars' frosty gleams
He groined his arches and matched his beams ;
Slender and clear were his crystal spars
As the lashes of light that trim the stars :
He sculptured every summer delight
In his halls and chambers out of sight ;
Sometimes his tinkling waters slipt
Down through a frost-leaved forest-crypt,
Long, sparkling aisles of steel-stemmed trees
Bending to counterfeit a breeze ;
Sometimes the roof no fretwork knew
But silvery mosses that downward grew ;
Sometimes it was carved in sharp relief
With quaint arabesques of ice-fern leaf ;
Sometimes it was simply smooth and clear
For the gladness of heaven to shine through, and here
He had caught the nodding bulrush-tops
And hung them thickly with diamond drops,

That crystalled the beams of moon and sun,
And made a star of every one :
No mortal builder's most rare device
Could match this winter-palace of ice ;
'T was as if every image that mirrored lay
In his depths serene through the summer day,
Each fleeting shadow of earth and sky,
  Lest the happy model should be lost,
Had been mimicked in fairy masonry
  By the elfin builders of the frost.

Within the hall are song and laughter,
  The cheeks of Christmas grow red and jolly,
And sprouting is every corbel and rafter
  With lightsome green of ivy and holly ;
Through the deep gulf of the chimney wide
Wallows the Yule-log's roaring tide ;
The broad flame-pennons droop and flap
  And belly and tug as a flag in the wind ;
Like a locust shrills the imprisoned sap,
  Hunted to death in its galleries blind ;
And swift little troops of silent sparks,
  Now pausing, now scattering away as in fear,
Go threading the soot-forest's tangled darks
  Like herds of startled deer.

But the wind without was eager and sharp,
Of Sir Launfal's gray hair it makes a harp,
    And rattles and wrings
    The icy strings,
  Singing, in dreary monotone,
  A Christmas carol of its own,
  Whose burden still, as he might guess,

Was—" Shelterless, shelterless, shelterless ! "
The voice of the seneschal flared like a torch
As he shouted the wanderer away from the porch,
And he sat in the gateway and saw all night
 The great hall-fire, so cheery and bold,
 Through the window-slits of the castle old,
Build out its piers of ruddy light
Against the drift of the cold.

PART SECOND.

I.

THERE was never a leaf on a bush or tree,
The bare boughs rattled shudderingly ;
The river was dumb and could not speak,
 For the frost's swift shuttles its shroud had spun :
A single crow on the tree-top bleak
 From his shining feathers shed off the cold sun ;
Again it was morning, but shrunk and cold,
As if her veins were sapless and old,
And she rose up decrepitly
For a last dim look at earth and sea.

II.

Sir Launfal turned from his own hard gate,
For another heir in his earldom sate ;
An old, bent man, worn out and frail,
He came back from seeking the Holy Grail ;
Little he recked of his earldom's loss,
No more on his surcoat was blazoned the cross,
But deep in his soul the sign he wore,
The badge of the suffering and the poor.

III.

Sir Launfal's raiment thin and spare
Was idle mail 'gainst the barbèd air,
For it was just at the Christmas time ;
So he mused, as he sat, of a sunnier clime,
And sought for a shelter from cold and snow
In the light and warmth of long ago ;
He sees the snake-like caravan crawl
O'er the edge of the desert, black and small,
Then nearer and nearer, till, one by one,
He can count the camels in the sun,
As over the red-hot sands they pass
To where, in its slender necklace of grass,
The little spring laughed and leapt in the shade,
And with its own self like an infant played,
And waved its signal of palms.

IV.

" For Christ's sweet sake, I beg an alms ; "—
The happy camels may reach the spring,
But Sir Launfal sees naught save the grewsome thing,
The leper, lank as the rain-blanched bone,
That cowers beside him, a thing as lone
And white as the ice-isles of Northern seas
In the desolate horror of his disease.

V.

And Sir Launfal said,—" I behold in thee
An image of Him who died on the tree ;
Thou also hast had thy crown of thorns,—
Thou also hast had the world's buffets and scorns,—
And to thy life were not denied

The wounds in the hands and feet and side :
Mild Mary's Son, acknowledge me ;
Behold, through him, I give to thee !"

VI.

Then the soul of the leper stood up in his eyes
   And looked at Sir Launfal, and straightway he
Remembered in what a haughtier guise
   He had flung an alms to leprosie,
When he caged his young life up in gilded mail
And set forth in search of the Holy Grail.
The heart within him was ashes and dust ;
He parted in twain his single crust,
He broke the ice on the streamlet's brink,
And gave the leper to eat and drink,
'T was a mouldy crust of coarse brown bread,
   'T was water out of a wooden bowl,—
Yet with fine wheaten bread was the leper fed,
   And 't was red wine he drank with his thirsty soul.

VII.

As Sir Launfal mused with a downcast face,
A light shone round about the place ;
The leper no longer crouched at his side,
But stood before him glorified,
Shining and tall and fair and straight
As the pillar that stood by the Beautiful Gate,—
Himself the Gate whereby men can
Enter the temple of God in Man.

VIII.

His words were shed softer than leaves from the pine,
And they fell on Sir Launfal as snows on the brine,

That mingle their softness and quiet in one
With the shaggy unrest they float down upon;
And the voice that was calmer than silence said,
" Lo it is I, be not afraid !
In many climes, without avail,
Thou hast spent thy life for the Holy Grail;
Behold, it is here,—this cup which thou
Didst fill at the streamlet for me but now;
This crust is my body broken for thee,
This water His blood that died on the tree;
The Holy Supper is kept, indeed,
In whatso we share with another's need;
Not what we give, but what we share,—
For the gift without the giver is bare;
Who gives himself with his alms feeds three,—
Himself, his hungering neighbor, and me."

IX.

Sir Launfal awoke as from a swound :—
"The Grail in my castle here is found !
Hang my idle armor up on the wall,
Let it be the spider's banquet-hall;
He must be fenced with stronger mail
Who would seek and find the Holy Grail."

X.

The castle gate stands open now,
    And the wanderer is welcome to the hall
As the hangbird is to the elm-tree bough;
    No longer scowl the turrets tall,
The Summer's long siege at last is o'er;
When the first poor outcast went in at the door,
She entered with him in disguise,

And mastered the fortress by surprise ;
There is no spot she loves so well on ground,
She lingers and smiles there the whole year round ;
The meanest serf on Sir Launfal's land
Has hall and bower at his command ;
And there 's no poor man in the North Countree
But is lord of the earldom as much as he.

NOTE.—According to the mythology of the Romancers, the San Greal, or Holy Grail, was the cup out of which Jesus partook of the last supper with his disciples. It was brought into England by Joseph of Arimathea, and remained there, an object of pilgrimage and adoration, for many years in the keeping of his lineal descendants. It was incumbent upon those who had charge of it to be chaste in thought, word and deed ; but one of the keepers having broken this condition, the Holy Grail disappeared. From that time it was a favorite enterprise of the knights of Arthur's court to go in search of it. Sir Galahad was at last successful in finding it, as may be read in the seventeenth book of the Romance of King Arthur. Tennyson has made Sir Galahad the subject of one of the most exquisite of his poems.

The plot (if I may give that name to anything so slight) of the foregoing poem is my own, and, to serve its purposes, I have enlarged the circle of competition in search of the miraculous cup in such a manner as to include, not only other persons than the heroes of the Round Table, but also a period of time subsequent to the date of King Arthur's reign.

Printed in the United States
127111LV00005B/11/A